BETWEEN HIERARCHIES AND MARKETS

BETWEEN HIERARCHIES AND MARKETS

The Logic and Limits of Network Forms of Organization

Grahame F. Thompson

OXFORD
UNIVERSITY PRESS

OXFORD
UNIVERSITY PRESS

Great Clarendon Street, Oxford OX2 6DP

Oxford University Press is a department of the University of Oxford.
It furthers the University's objective of excellence in research, scholarship,
and education by publishing worldwide in

Oxford New York

Auckland Bangkok Buenos Aires Cape Town Chennai
Dar es Salaam Delhi Hong Kong Istanbul Karachi Kolkata
Kuala Lumpur Madrid Melbourne Mexico City Mumbai Nairobi
São Paulo Shanghai Taipei Tokyo Toronto

Oxford is a registered trade mark of Oxford University Press
in the UK and in certain other countries

Published in the United States
by Oxford University Press Inc., New York

© Grahame F. Thompson, 2003

British Library Cataloguing in Publication Data

Data available

Library of Congress Cataloging in Publication Data

Thompson, Grahame.
    Between markets and hierarchy : the logic and limits of network forms of
    organization / Grahame F. Thompson.
        p. cm.
    Includes bibliographical references.
        1. Organizational behavior.   2. Business networks.   3. Social networks.   I. Title.

HD58.7 .T4786 2003   302.3′5–dc21   2002038190

ISBN 0-19-877526-1 (hbk.)
ISBN 0-19-877527-X (pbk.)

1 3 5 7 9 10 8 6 4 2

Typeset by Newgen Imaging Systems (P) Ltd. Chennai, India
Printed in Great Britain
on acid-free paper by
Biddles Ltd., www.biddles.co.uk

Contents

Preface

For many years I have had an interest in the nature of networks. This began in the late 1980s when I was working on the Open University course *Running the Country*. This used what at the time was the rather innovative approach of contrasting three 'modes of coordination' to explore the characteristics of the United Kingdom's political economy. The three modes used there were neatly summed up in the title of the specially developed Reader for that course that I helped edit: *Markets, Hierarchies, and Networks: The Coordination of Social Life* (Thompson *et al.* 1991). Subsequently, the bulk of the content of that course was redrafted and published in a separate book: *Managing the United Kingdom: An Introduction to its Political Economy and Public Policy* (Sage 1993) which I edited with Richard Maidment and for which I prepared the chapter on 'Network Coordination' (Maidment and Thompson 1993). Apart from a number of conference papers, my work on networks languished during the mid-1990s but it was during this period that I approached Oxford University Press to see if it might be interested in publishing a wide ranging book that confronted the contemporary significance of networks head on. David Musson from OUP expressed an interest. In the meantime, in the late 1990s I returned to the teaching of networks in the context of another Open University course that I was preparing: *Governing Europe*. In the part of this course dealing with the governance of the European economy I returned to the issue of 'self-organizing networks' as a governance mechanism, this time set alongside the notion of 'regulation' and the 'market' as contrasting governance mechanisms. The outcome of this was published as the volume I edited under the title *Governing the European Economy* (Thompson 2001).

Preface

The present book is in part the result of these teaching initiatives. But it is also much more than this. It is not a simple extension and rounding out of the arguments contained in these previously published teaching pieces, but a fully explored analysis of the nature and forms of network organization, both in theory and in practice. The debate about networks had moved on since the 1980s and there is now a much richer set of theoretical and practical raw materials to draw on. But it also became clear to me that the object of my analysis required some fresh and imaginative thinking in its own right, which I hope I have gone some way in providing with this wide-ranging and interdisciplinary approach to the subject.

Of course there is also the contemporary political background that informs an interest in networks. Foremost amongst these is a growing dissatisfaction with the way that market-led solutions originally offered by the New Right had actually worked out in practice, and second, how the immediate Social Democratic response to this, what became known as the 'Third Way', was also in danger of collapsing. Clearly, there is great disillusionment as all the fine talk about these solutions leading to a new dawn for growth and prosperity comes unstuck and the promised policy benefits unravel before our eyes. On the other hand, nobody can seriously argue for the reinstallation of the old hierarchical forms of governance and regulation to entirely replace the current emphasis on the market. The issue thus becomes one of finding the terms of another way, one formally independent of either market or hierarchy, but one that does not have the grand illusions of a totalizing 'Third Way' or anything else. This is where the notion of networks arises, since in this book it will be argued that, taken in their widest sense, networks offer the prospect of viable and feasible alternative mechanisms of social coordination and effective governance. The advantage of networks (in the sense interpreted here) is that they are already widely active in the social body, and they do not so much completely displace markets and hierarchical modes of governance as complement and support them in different ways. But they complement and support in a manner that often 're-moulds' the operation of markets and hierarchies to such an extent that these themselves become 'something different' with enhanced performative effectiveness.

This, anyway, is the burden of part of the argument to be found in this book.

Whilst the notion of networks has become a fashionable one there is no single text devoted exclusively to all the major facets of their operation. The aim of this book is to fill that gap. The book is both a 'monograph' and a 'text'. It is well suited for undergraduates studying on a wide range of courses particularly in the social sciences, geography, organizational studies, and business management. Although the main emphasis for the approach is the organizational economy and economic relations, political, social, and cultural networks are also extensively explored.

Thus, the book offers an overview of arguments and theories about networks from different perspectives in a range of overlapping fields. But at the same time as it is offered as a synthesizing text it also contains a definite thesis and argument of its own. It pulls together a range of disparate analyses into an argument with a strong and imaginative critical focus. A key aspect to the book is the way networks, understood as theoretical and analytical devices, are related to networks operating as definite practices of social organization and coordination. These twin senses of networks are played together and juxtaposed to bring out differences, lacunae, and problems.

A number of friends and colleagues have contributed to this enterprise in its long gestation period. In particular I would like to thank David Musson from OUP for his most helpful discussions and support of the project, but above all for his unending patience as one deadline after another for the delivery of the manuscript passed. My fellow colleagues at the Open University contributed a great deal in the context of the early teaching background that informs much of the book. Richard Maidment (now with the United States Open University in Denver), Christopher Pollit (now at Erasmus University in Rotterdam) and Tom Ling (now at Anglia Polytechnic University, Cambridge) were instrumental in originally stimulating my interest in networks as a teaching device. They were key members of the original *Running the Country* course team. Subsequently Simon Bromley and Montserrat Guibernau at the OU contributed to the revival of my teaching interest as we embarked on the collective endeavour of producing the *Governing Europe* course. More recently

Preface

my colleagues John Allen and Doreen Massey have read, commented upon and discussed parts of the book with me. Beyond the Open University, Garry Wickham from Murdoch University in Australia has taken a keen interest in many of the matters explored in the book. And finally, I must mention my writing colleague for many years and good friend Paul Hirst whose terrific conversations have been a constant source of stimulation for me as I was musing over this book. Paul has his own take on some of the issues discussed in this book, which he has written about under the title of 'Associationalism', and I will have the opportunity to comment on this in the text that follows. But I thank all of these people for their interest and help.

In a sense, then, the argument of this book is for a certain 'pluralism' in discussions of the different responses to the demise of hierarchical regulation on the one hand and neoliberal market decentralization on the other. If the notion of a single 'Third Way' is too overarching and grandiose in its own terms for this response, then what is needed is a plurality of claims to say how alternative forms of social organization might be conceived and organized. It is in such a spirit of pluralism that the following analysis is offered.

Chapter 1

Considering Networks: A Methodological Introduction

1.1. Introduction

'Not another book about networks!' At one level this would be a legitimate response to the arrival of this book. Networks seem to be everywhere. Written about at length and discussed interminably. For instance, as this book was being prepared during the later part of 2001 and the first half of 2002, two new academic journals appeared on my desk: *Global Networks* (first issue, January 2001) and *Policy Network* (first issue, Summer 2001). Both of these journals use the term networks liberally, and they join many others with similar titles and an equally extensive range of interests (e.g. *Social Networks, Connections, Communications, Network Magazine*). In the newspapers at the time was another—though much more sinister—example of the way networks were being introduced into contemporary discussion. Al-Qaeda ('The Base'), the organization headed by Osama bin Laden, was being described as a 'loose international terrorist network'—a many headed hydra—hunted by the Americans and their allies, but one that was proving elusive to pin down. And almost in the same breath, the style of the US military response to the atrocities in New York and Washington in early September 2001 was itself being described in network terms; as 'network-centric warfare' (*Financial Times*, 26 September 2001, ' . . . new methods of synthesizing data obtained from multiple sources, and transmitting details to commanders who can quickly order a strike . . . The combination of sensors, detection, communications, information management and computer power . . . ').[1] Many other examples of this multiple and often incompatible usage could easily be given.

So, at times I too become tired and annoyed of this widespread and loose usage of the term network. But such disquiet is in large part the reason for embarking on writing this book. The intention is to bring some analytical precision to the discussion of networks. Networks have become a ubiquitous metaphor to describe too many aspects of contemporary life. And in so doing, the category has lost much of its analytical precision. It has become a term with many uses but one that has lost any clear conceptual underpinnings—it has become a 'word' rather than a 'concept'. As has been argued many times before, something that claims to explain everything ends up by explaining nothing, and this is a clear danger in the case of networks.

One of the objectives of this book is to bring some clarity to the discussion of networks. It tests the case as to whether it is possible to construct a clearly demarcated idea of a 'network' as a separable form of socio-economic coordination and governance mechanism with its own distinctive logic. In doing this, the primary contrast is to markets and hierarchies as alternative and already well-understood forms of such socio-economic coordination each with its own particular logic. Thus, the focus here is upon the domain of the socio-economic (which includes political aspects of networks), and it is about the organizational domain of the socio-economic. By and

[1] For the academic/military debate about 'network-centric warfare', see Alberts *et al.* (1999), Alberts and Cerwinski (1997), Cerwinski (1998), Bender (1998), and Cebrowski and Gartska (1998).

large, the book does not deal with 'technological' or 'biological' networks, other than in passing as they impinge upon the way networks have been discussed within the socio-organizational domain. Anyone with even a fleeting familiarity with the contemporary way socio-economic networks are being framed will recognize that there are considerable intellectual borrowings from the disciplines of physics, biology, and mathematics to illuminate the nature of socio–economic networks.[2] So, some discussion of this connection cannot be avoided (see Chapter 5 in particular). But I claim no particular expertise in these fields.

As soon as one confronts the literature on socio-economic networks (which from now are referred to just as networks unless dealing explicitly with the other forms just mentioned), it is clear that there are many different ways that networks have been written about. For the purposes of this book, the writing about networks is considered as a way in which they are 'enacted'. Hence, in part the book is interested in the way networks are assembled, conducted, and performed. This is to say the way they are constructed; 'socially constructed' if you will (though, along with Ian Hacking (1999), I remain suspicious of the oversimplified and overgeneralized way that 'social construction' is often used in methodological discussions) see below.

But here we encounter the first of a number of unavoidable fine lines that have to be negotiated when dealing with networks in the context of this book. In asking about the 'conduct of networks', how they are 'enacted', and by what mechanisms, one is looking towards a particular position with respect to the intellectual discussion of networks. Although it is difficult to succinctly sum-up this position, it might be characterized as a 'neo-Foucauldian/post Actor-Network Theory (ANT)' approach.[3]

---

[2] One instance is Cohen 2002. He takes the example of 'scale free' networks as a general case of how *all* networks are supposed to operate (' . . . scale free networks are everywhere', p. 13). We are all living in the 'small worlds' of these mathematically specifiable 'ecological' networks. This illustrates a danger of simply transferring ideas from one intellectual discipline directly into another.

[3] I hesitate to gather all this under a single heading. But at the risk of oversimplification (and a potentially wrong attribution), I would cite the recent work of Michel Callon (1998) and the papers included therein, particularly that by Peter Miller (1998) (see also Miller 2001), Andrew Barry (2001), and the papers edited by Andrew Barry and Don Slater (2002) for the special issue of *Economy and Society*

Now, whilst I have some sympathy towards the aspects of this approach (if it can be characterized as such), I do not wish to adopt it completely. Here is the main point to emphasize. The objective of this book is not to 'adopt a firm position' and defend it at any cost. What it does is to conduct an *interrogation* into the ways the word network has been used and to see if there is a conceptual analytic behind these usages. As will become clear, there is a range of such usages, and I want to preserve their separate integrity as far as is possible. Thus, what happens here is that the book offers a *commentary* on, first, how the idea of network has been inserted into the literature on the contemporary forms of socio-economic organization (as with the idea of a 'network society' or a 'network state', for instance). Second, the discussion is set within the field of 'organizational studies' broadly conceived to include the political resonances of networks as well. And, finally, the discussion is directed towards the international expansion of economic and other activities (so called 'globalization'). These are the three main aspects that are concentrated on here: with respect to concrete socio-economic organizations, the literature of 'organizational studies', and the internationalization of networks. But in doing this, the emphasis is upon the *differences between* the way the idea of networks has been marshalled into these domains. It is not to investigate them in the light of a 'correct' characterization of a network logic that is set out at the beginning; to measure them all against the truth of this prior elucidation. In the case of what was rather clumsily termed above as a 'neo-Foucauldian/post-ANT' approach, for instance, the book runs as a critical *encounter* with this at various times, rather than as a full embrace.

Indeed, it also means that a critical engagement is conducted with all the other approaches discussed in the book. But these interrogations

---

on 'The Technological Economy' as examples of this emergent approach. I give this the prefixes *'neo*-Foucauldian' and *'post* Actor-Network Theory' since whilst it combines elements from each of these, it also represents a move along a rather different intellectual trajectory, one occupied more centrally by an 'economy of qualities' than has been present up to now in either of its progenitors. See Chapters 3, 5, and 8 where these issues are thoroughly discussed. There it will become clear what my serious reservations about this approach amount to.

are carried out in the light of two underlying programmatic issues that are indicated by the subtitle of the book. The first and most important of these is to respond to the question: 'Can there be a particular logic to the network form of organization?' This issue is kept in the forefront throughout the chapters as they engage with the various ways the idea of networks is used. But we may find that there are a *number of such logics* in operation as a result. I try to keep an open mind about this at the same time as I am sensitive to the idea that 'network coordination' in the singular might be characterized as something different to that performed by either hierarchical or market forms of organization. Perhaps, then, there are after all *several* clearly demarcated 'network forms of coordination' that are different to these other two (as, of course, there may be several of these as well). But, in order not to let the discussion get completely out of hand as the potential forms proliferate once again to encompass the interminable variety of the ways networks and networking are used in the literature, some sensible analytical compromises need to be made and sustained. In the end, it is for the reader to judge how successful this is. Thus, there is a tension running through the analysis that follows between, on the one hand, the need to limit the logics of networks so as to sharpen up their analytical focus and, on the other hand, the perfectly reasonable demand for a non-closure and non-preordained analytical schema that is imposed from the start.

But this warning should not lead one to expect *just* a critical commentary, whatever that may actually mean. As well as looking in detail at the conventional (and not so conventional) ways the idea of networks has been used in the literature, I also claim to offer a reconstruction and reformulation of my own. Thus, there are some exploratory attempts to provide a different, and perhaps more telling definition and use of networks as analytical devices, to overcome or get a round perceived problems identified with existing explanations, and to offer more appropriate descriptions of the actual working of the organizational economy involving networks. Thus, I also intend to advance the discussion of networks. But I do not claim any hard and fast superiority for these explorations, only that they may cast a more nuanced or subtle light on already existing analyses.

The second programmatic issue that runs throughout the book involves a linked concern to that of the logic of networks. This is to respond to the question: 'Are there any limits to networks?' From what has been said up to now, the quick and obvious answer would be 'yes'. But this is something that is equally subject to an interrogation and an analysis as the book proceeds. Clearly, the issue of the possible limits to networks is intimately connected to the issue of their logic. One enfolds the other. As will become apparent, an objective of the book is to make an argument that if networks are to mean *anything* then they must not mean *everything*, so this raises an obvious limit to their embrace. The questions thus become where and how one might draw these limits. And this immediately raises a further important linked issue.

1.2. Network as Conceptual Category and Network as Social Organization

Here we need to recognize the somewhat obvious point that networks are both a method of thinking through the contemporary nature of social existence and (potentially, at least) a concrete form of social organization. Networks are both a conceptual category or tool of analysis *and* an object of analysis in the form of an actual mode of coordination and governance. And this, of course, creates its own fascinating problems, though these are hardly unique or new. Quite how are these levels to be kept apart or, more importantly perhaps, what is the relationship between them? There are a number of ways of approaching this problem. The following remarks provide a short methodological introduction to how these issues could be tackled, not all of which I fully agree with.

1.2.1. The 'conduct' of networks

First, taking up again the issue of the conduct of networks, clearly there are a number of different 'conducts' that could be enumerated. And such multiple conducts imply multiple or plural approaches to an understanding of networks. Taking an analogy directly from Giles Deleuze, a horse moves in various ways: as a walk, a trot, a canter, a gallop, a jump, etc. As its different strides, these compose the manner of its 'conducts'. In this instance then, conducts are the way things are led, steered, or driven; a stride is a characteristic gait, pace, or motion (Deleuze in Alliez 1996). What, then, might be the conducts for networks? The suggestion is that these are embodied in the attributes, rules, conventions, habits, routines, standards, and 'qualities' of networks. As we will see in Chapter 5 in particular these features open up ways to consider both the institutional moment in the construction and functioning of networks and the dynamics of their evolutionary self-organization. And this is closely related to the 'work' of networks. A net captures some things but lets others through. How does it work to produce a particular insight or make a specific contribution? This, in particular, is where ANT and its related discourses provide a potentially telling approach to the analysis of networks, which are critically reviewed in Chapters 3 and 8 in particular, but also appear elsewhere.

1.2.2. Social construction and networks

Second, consider further the related issues of 'social construction' mentioned above. Following Hacking (1999), this involves the 'making up of networks'. Networks can be considered in terms of a way of 'world-making' or of 'kind-making', or perhaps more accurately, as a product of world-making and kind-making—a certain 'species of things' or 'interactive kinds'.[4] And this immediately raises a further set of issues. How are networks in particular 'made up'? Or equally importantly, how do they make themselves up? If they are assembled from parts, what are those parts? As a preliminary response, we can point to the nature of ideas or concepts, to people, to institutions, to social practices, to interactions, to bodies of knowledge, and to 'problems', as those constitutive elements that enter the configurative construction of a heterogeneous *matrix* that is the terrain of networks. The network is then seen as the *consequences* of the interactions between those elements, making up this matrix of

---

[4] Here Hacking is playing off a certain reading of Nelson Goodman's philosophical/aesthetic positions on 'social construction'. See Goodman (1951, 1978).

its powers. This would thus help in understanding networks as not so much a simple 'idea' but as a matrix embedded in a social milieu but not one totally beholden to that milieu (as in a crude 'social constructionist' approach). So it is not a simple 'social construction' that is being suggested here. This is because networks are typified by a 'feedback loop' mechanism. The intellectual formation and existence of networks itself 'guarantees' their reproduction and transformation in a particular manner dependent, in some large part at least, on the nature of that prior intellectual conceptualization. But this reproduction/transformation would be in no way pre-established by the elements from which it is wrought—rather it would be the contingent upshot of these specific intellectual raw materials combined with contingently specific historical events. The coordination of its attributes crafts or builds an outcome, just as it is crafted and built by them.

1.2.3. Networks as an assemblage

Third, this is in part to conceive of networks as akin to 'assemblages'. Network assemblages could be made up of diverse components—like persons, forms of knowledge, technical procedures, and modes of scrutiny, judgement and sanction, and rationalities—all these heterogeneous parts arriving from different sources producing odd couplings, possibly chance encounters, involving cogs and levers that pull together, but at the same time fail to quite fulfil their promise or the expectations invested in them (Rose 1996). So, there can be a potential built-in-failure in networks, something explored in greater detail in Chapters 3 and 8.[5] Thus, it might be informative to think of networks through the work of a limited kind of (social) *de*constructionism; through a kind of unmasking, an 'unsettling', and as a refutation of other coordinative devices. But this should not by any means be

---

[5] Such a built-in-'failure' is not, of course, confined just to networks. It is an endemic feature of all attempts at social coordination (Malpas and Wickham 1995). On the other hand, one might think of this slightly differently as a winding down and replacement process. Well before most things fail, their inadequacies and limitations are appreciated, and they are gradually wound-down and then replaced in an orderly fashion by an alternative. The idea of 'failure' is too abrupt and too mechanical. It is not so much radical failure but gradual replacement that best captures this process.

taken as a 'rage against reason'. As we will see, for instance, in the various discussions of trust in the chapters that follow, there can be *good reasons* for the failure of trust in network situations, which is an endemic problem for the reproduction of networks. It is in Chapter 4, in particular, where the boldest attempt is made to deploy this conceptual apparatus of assemblages—and the linked methodological issues discussed in this introduction—for an understanding of networks.

1.2.4. Discourses and networks

The fourth point in this methodological characterization would be to view networks very much through the lens of 'discourses'. Discourses involve a certain 'alignment' of events or assemblages of elements, scrutinies, narratives, practices, and mechanisms. In this way conventions, routines and standards, and the like, can be brought into a certain 'web of things and entities' that are 'stitched' and 'knotted' together to support and supplement the matrix. Often such 'discourse networks' (Kittler 1990) bring together quite disparate strands into a common register, bracketing them together in contingent but nevertheless quite robust and telling configurations. In Kittler's case, he constructs a rich depiction of the twentieth-century communicative cultural order as a complex combination of the technologies of the gramophone, the film, and the typewriter (Kittler 1990, 1999).[6]

These approaches to networks stress its role as a constituent moment in the buttressing and securing of social order. According to Michael Foucault, from whom they draw heavily, order can be considered in the context of:

. . . A 'system of elements'—a definition of the segments by which the resemblances and differences can be shown, the types of variation by which those segments can be affected, and lastly, the threshold above which there is a difference and below which there is a similitude—is indispensable for

---

[6] This is a way of 'reading science', I would suggest, somewhat different to the ANT approach considered most fully in Chapter 3, though there I do not go into the specific way ANT deals with science as such. In his books, Kittler combines themes from Foucault, Lacan, and Derrida. His are one of the most telling German deployments of these authors' works which, incidentally, amounts not to a simple appropriation or application of them but a transformative working use of them.

the establishment of even the simplest form of order. Order is, at one and the same time, that which is given in things as their inner law, the *hidden network* that determines the way they confront one another, and also that which has no existence except in the grid created by a glance, an examination, a language: and it is only in the blank spaces of this grid that order manifests itself in depth as though already there, waiting in silence for the moment of its expression.   (Foucault 1970, p. xx, emphasis added)

Discourses are seen here not as the confrontation between a reality and language or a thought, or between an experience and an intellect, or between something 'out-there' and its representation 'in-here', between things and words. Rather, it is seen as rules that define the ordering of objects, practices that systematically form objects of which they speak. This is something that is not *reducible* to a logic or a language (although it involves linguistic signs and logical statements). Rather, it is the groups of relationships between authorities of emergence, delimitation, and specification.[7]

1.2.5. Networks as a relation

Fifth, the way networks could be approached is to conceive of them as analogous to a 'relation', or rather as 'a relation' (Strathern 1995). This invokes once again the double edge of networks—as both a conceptual category and a means of organizational coordination. But, by concentrating on the relation here—the interactive kinds—it offers another register to consider the 'conducts' of networks; the 'kinds of connections' they set up and the work they do, which involves the routing of relations through networks. What sorts of relations are thereby invoked? The obvious candidates are intellectual, socio-economic, technological, symbolic (even fantastical) relations. And such perceptions of relations between relations involve systems of relations; their regularity, organization, and order. Networks both shape and regulate relations. With this expansive view of networks, they are conceived as both a description of relationships and as a means to their cohesion. This is not just a question of some pre-defined elements or entities, which 'exists'

---

[7] For an explicit treatment of networks in the manner described in these remarks, see Barry (2001).

and are known and understood, then related together (though they are also this in part). These entities are bought into existence by the relation and thus exist within it. So, in the analyses below, we concentrate on the relations, interactions, connections, etc., between things and actors, not so much on what the prior things so connected or related actually are. These are constructed, built, etc., by the relations between them. They are the outcome of the process of networking. We are dealing then with a relational view of socio-economic organization rather than a strictly resource view or transactions view.

Are network relations, then, holographic, in the sense of being examples of the phenomenon they construct? Do network relations model the phenomenon in such a way that it produces instances of itself? Clearly, this would be to model things from very much 'within' (see below), producing understandings that are the very activities of understanding. In making explicit a field of connections that already exists, knowledge of network relations is an open ended and complex process. It thereby repeats each time what is given and what is open to choice, thereby imparting an ambiguity to the very term 'network relation'. Such a relational approach would bring dissimilar orders or levels of knowledge together while conserving their differences. It, thus, slips across scales as well as keeping its distinctiveness.

Bringing 'complexity' and 'holography' together in this way opens up networks to be considered as self-organizing devices (considered in Chapters 2 and 5). This describes certain non-linear organizational effects, accounting for both the persistence of patterns and the capacity of systems (organic, social, economic, technological, intellectual) to take off into quite new paths. This concerns the irreversibility of outcomes of events and factors that could have taken many routes, potentially running simultaneously along several quite different temporal and spatial scales. The multistranded clumped networks that form a kind of non-linear (rhizome-like) organizational structure, containing different relational principles of connectivity and heterogeneity, are always 'pregnant' with the possibility of breakdown and breakup, leading to new trajectories and transformations in a self-organizing framework that overcomes the twin obstacles presented by 'necessary evolutionary advance' and 'path-dependency'. The creativity of these self-organizing networks is partly dependent upon the multiple complexity inherent in a combination of different types of knowledge; codified and tacit, embodied technological knowledges, differential capabilities, unsystematized information, etc. In principle, these would seem to be able to take any scale given advances in information and communication technologies (ICTs), or perhaps more accurately, to have advanced in scale with the evolution of ICTs. These claims are assessed at length in Chapters 4, 5, and 7.

1.2.6. Turning 'the Network' inside out

Sixth, a connected and radical way of explicitly dealing with the issue of networks as tools and networks as objects is offered by Annelise Riles (2001). She draws a distinction between something called 'the Network' and 'networks'. To deal with the latter first, 'networks' are the rather ordinary organizational entities with which we are all familiar from a day to day usage of the term network (in her case international networking activities associated with the UN women's conference held in Beijing in 1995). 'The Network' on the other hand, is defined to refer to ' . . . a set of institutions, knowledge practices, and artefacts thereof that *internally* generate the effects of their own reality by *reflecting* on themselves' (Riles 2001, p. 3, emphasis added). This definition is designed to cope with the absence of an analytical 'outside' of networks in her conception, so that the conduct of any investigation into networks is inevitably a highly reflexive operation. Riles assembles and engages with a range of ethnographic material in her investigations. But given this is dealt with reflexively as just suggested, it requires her to find a point of analytical access from *within* the material; hence to turn ' "the Network" inside out' (p. 6). This approach thereby denies the 'opposition-difference' (if it be such) between the two aspects referred to above: networks as tools and as objects. As the substantive modality of this operation Riles invokes a notion of the *aesthetics* of the network (after Bateson 1987)—the complex patterned quality of Network communications. Patterns, designs, gaps, absences, and figures appear here to both invoke the 'network' and 'the Network' in what is at one and the same time both an internal description and an enactment that has no outside. In particular, this aesthetics appears as a network of information (constantly flexible, constantly adjusting, constantly changing) pieced together from various parts of the globe and produced in a textual documented form, the prime mode of Network articulation in the case of the UN women's networks she is dealing with.

Now, whilst this 'ultra-constructivist' conception of networks has some merit, it is too incestuously self-reflexive to serve my purposes well. There is no desire in this book to reduce the conception of networks simply to a set of 'internal' aesthetic practices. Indeed, as will be argued in the chapters that follow, there is a need to provide an 'outside' to networks if they are not to fall prey to a range of methodological shortcomings, and in particular not to begin to become too all embracing in their conceptual claims. My preference, therefore, is to work with a more conventional conception than offered by many of the approaches discussed immediately above, one where there remains a tension between the inside and the outside of the network, between the idea of networks and their concrete reality, between tools and objects.

1.2.7. A more conventional frame

So, to return to a more conventional frame for a moment, such problems are endemic to all forms of analysis that uses concepts claiming this dual character—concepts and practical organization. And let us clear up another preliminary objection that could be seen as a way of avoiding, or bypassing, much of this difficulty.

Supposing it was argued that the three 'modes of coordination' focused upon in this book, namely the market, hierarchy, and network, should *not* be considered as both conceptual structures *and* organizational forms at one and the same time. Rather, we should consider a mapping that links these three terms with the categories of 'competition/price', 'command/authority', and 'cooperation/consensus/mutuality' in a contingent and non-attributable manner from the beginning.[8] This would then break with the seeming obviousness of a mapping that directly linked the market with

---

[8] This is similar to the way Paul Adler draws a distinction between three forms of organization: market, hierarchy, and community, and their concomitant mechanisms of coordination: price, authority, and trust (Adler 2001).

'competition/price', hierarchy with 'command/authority', and network with 'cooperation/consensus/mutuality'. Thus, the market, hierarchy, and network would occupy the position of 'concrete organizational forms', while a different set of categories—namely competition/price, command/authority, and cooperation/consensus/mutuality—would provide the purely intellectual or conceptual means to understand those concrete forms of organization, themselves conceived in a variable configuration. Aspects of each conceptual category could thus be used to highlight any of the organizational forms as seemed appropriate.

At one level this is another attractive suggestion, the merit of which is recognized and deployed in the analysis that follows in the book, at least to some extent (see Chapter 2 for instance). However, I do not wish to go completely down this particular path either. As should become clear, the association of markets with competition/price, hierarchies with command/authority, and networks with cooperation/consensus/mutuality, although perhaps a rather crude 'first cut', is a robust enough one to enable a demarcation in the different logics of the three as both distinct socio-economic modes of coordination and as concrete expressions of organizational difference. What I would defend, therefore, is a multiple attack. This is one that initially takes the conventional linkages rather for granted and then subsequently subjects them to a complication by introducing the above outlined differentiations. That at least is the strategy deployed in Chapters 3, 5, and 7 as far as is possible.

Despite all the qualifications announced above, however, it would be naïve to deny that there has to be at least some (perhaps low level) methodological protocols that orientate any analysis, so here I have come clean on these as far as is possible at this stage. They add further substance to the concerns of the book and serve to highlight the way in which the claims made in the rest of the analysis should be assessed. These methodological protocols reengage with the issue of how one manages the relationship between an inside and an outside in the analysis of networks. Although this sketches a broad canvas, what is offered in the substantive chapters of the book is not a comprehensive coverage of all these dimensions associated with networks. The book concentrates upon a limited set of issues, reconstructing the main line of arguments about the nature of networks and exploring some of the more interesting of their intricacies.

1.3. The Chapters to Come

The rest of the book is organized as follows. There are two parts. The first of these focuses on frameworking and theoretical issues whilst the second is given over to more illustrative material about real networks. There are three chapters in each of these parts. The first part treats networks more as analytical devices ('tools'), and the second part deals with them more as concrete organizational forms ('objects'). But in the light of what has been argued up to now in this introduction, neither of these two parts should be seen as thematically sealed. Rather, these two aspects to networks are treated very much together, so the differences between the two parts are one of orientation and emphasis, not of fundamental alternative focus or opposition.

Chapter 2 'Hierarchies, Markets, and Networks: A Preliminary Comparison' is used to set out the traditional analysis of network as a different organizational arrangement to either hierarchy or market. The contrast here is between these three as first coordinating devices and then as governance mechanisms. In this chapter, in the first instance these are set up as 'rivalrously complementary' ideal types of social organization to demarcate the different claims they make on how the organization of the social is to be understood. The object of this chapter is to lay out in a preliminary way, the basic claims made for networks in particular, as to how they are different from hierarchical and market forms of organization. In so doing, the chapter represents a first attempt to systematize what might be the logic of networks and the legitimate limits to their operation. The analysis of this chapter then becomes a base-point for demarcating networks, a point of reference for subsequent critical engagements with the traditional approach, and as the point of review and reconstruction for more radical alternatives.

In Chapter 3, 'Social Network Analysis, Transaction-Cost Analysis, Actor-Network Theory: Three Approaches to Networks', these three theoretically driven approaches to the analysis of networks are offered for comparison and critically commented upon. An interesting feature of these approaches is that in their own way they each make a claim to analysing hierarchy and market as well. Indeed, the suggestion pursued in the chapter is that these approaches try to do too much. They each want to account for *all* organizational situations and forms within a single analytical structure, and this founders on the difficulties highlighted with the discussion of the 'inside/outside' problem raised above. Indeed, this founders at two levels. One in respect to the theoretical claims the approaches make with respect to network considered as an analytical tool, and again in an organizational sense of wanting to extend the boundaries of networks to include everything organizational.

If networks do have a logic of their own, what is it? This is the issue tackled in Chapter 4 'Networks and the Issues of "Excess", the "Gift", "Non-exchange", and "Trust"'. Again, as its title suggests, this chapter looks at some radical and rather unusual categories that, it is argued, could provide the raw materials for the reconstruction of an analytical logic that is peculiar to networks. The chapter conducts an interrogation of these categories, juxtaposing and combining them together to investigate their analytical properties, and then 'applying' the results to a preliminary case where network structures are said to operate, namely ICT dot-com type relationships and their accounting practices. As is indicated in this chapter, the analysis remains a little ambivalent as to its success in providing such a logic, though the conclusion is that it is strong enough to warrant further exploration. And this is what is done in the second main part of the book.

Chapter 5 is the first of the three chapters that takes a more illustrative focus. In 'Industrial Organization as Networks', the most well rehearsed area for network studies provides the object of analysis, namely interorganizational networks. Since this has been dealt with at great length in the literature elsewhere, what is offered here does not go over this again in any detail. Rather, it concentrates upon some relatively neglected aspects of these relationships and pursues some of the more theoretical informed issues that they raise. This involves questions of the limits of an institutional analysis, the issue of knowledge with respect to these kinds of networks, the role of complexity and self-organization, evolutionary approaches to networks, and problems associated with embeddedness and variety production that they pose.

The organizational aspects to networks are not just confined to economic organization or social relations. They also pervade political relations. Chapter 6, 'Political Networks and the Politics of Network Governance', investigates these political manifestations of networks, particularly as they pertain to the governance of organizational and economic matters. The idea of 'policy networks' is concentrated on in the chapter, and this is used to open up a wide-ranging analysis of how these mechanisms operate. In particular, it looks at how the internal structure of decision-making is organized, much of which has a resonance outside of policy networks proper to address how networks more widely might operate, for example, in the case of game theoretic approaches which are reviewed here. This chapter also serves a major purpose in discussing the relationships between networks and other governance and coordination mechanisms. One of the main themes of this book is that networks are a limited governance/coordinating device, which have to be properly placed in a wider context of other socio-organizational mechanisms of management and regulation. This chapter lays out the principles and trends associated with this issue. Finally, the chapter opens up the issues of 'power' in networks, something that pervades these forms of organizational entity just as it does markets and hierarchies.

The final main chapter of the book extends the analysis of networks explicitly to the international sphere. Chapter 7, 'Networks and the International System', fulfils two main functions. First, it addresses the whole area of ICT and networks and particularly how they are argued to be radically transforming the nature of international relations (technological, economic, political, social, and personal), organized under the conceptual umbrella term of 'globalization'. Second, it looks at the internationalization of 'production networks' (conceived in various ways) and how these are also argued to be recasting the nature of global economic relationships. Both of these aspects to international networks are critically interrogated in the chapter. In addition, the relationships between national and international networking is reviewed and an issue posed in the previous chapter—the relationship between networks and other coordinating/governance devices—is taken up again, this time in an international context.

It should be emphasized here that the investigations undertaken in these latter three chapters are not meant to be direct explorations or applications of the 'logic of network' issues concentrated on in Chapter 4. What these chapters do is review the issues they address in light of the results of Chapter 4, which as suggested above is ambiguous in itself. So these three chapters are designed to add more weight to the specific thesis about a network logic as advanced in Chapter 4.

Finally, Chapter 8 concludes the book by returning to many of the issues set out in this introduction and those pursued throughout the main body of the text that follows, and which have just been outlined above. In particular, it sums up on the two subtitled themes that run throughout the book: what are the logic and limits of network forms of organization (and it might now be added, types of network analytical approaches as well)? In doing this, the chapter also re-reviews many of the controversial aspects of the analyses that are presented in the six substantive chapters to try to pin down the overall thesis of this book, one that makes it distinctive to other approaches.

Part I

Theoretical and Methodological Issues

Part I

Theoretical and
Methodological Issues

Chapter 2

Hierarchies, Markets, and Networks: A Preliminary Comparison

2.1. Introduction

As indicated in Chapter 1, networks have become increasingly popular as explanatory devices. The idea of networks has appeared as the driving motif for a great deal of intellectual work in the field of organization theory, in the structuring of social relations, understanding local and regional economies, learning and innovation strategies, in international relations and for analysing the social effects of information and communication technologies (ICTs). Although described in varying terms, that set of coordinative devices that cannot be easily reduced to hierarchically based ones on the one hand or equated with quintessentially market-based relationships on the other, has appeared as an attractive object of investigation by those attempting to come to terms with contemporary transformations in the structure of organizational arrangements and decision-making processes. The objective of this chapter is to provide a preliminary sketch of the differences between 'network coordination', conceived in rather general terms, and the other two better known and better explored coordination mechanisms of hierarchy and the market. This will also help to bring into focus exactly what is involved in those mechanisms that can be called 'network forms of coordination'. Thus, this chapter will begin exploring the question of whether there is a specific logic to networks that is distinct to the logic of either hierarchy or the market. The approach here is formal and abstract. It is deliberately designed to establish differences and incompatibilities. In subsequent chapters it will be shown how this approach can be criticized.

The chapter begins by sketching the nature of hierarchy and the market, and contrasting these to networks. A lot of this is well known, so it is done in outline only. As the analysis develops, however, a distinction is drawn between these three as *coordination* mechanisms and then as *governance* mechanisms, which, it is argued, are not quite the same thing. But initially hierarchy, market, and network are considered simply as coordinating devices and treated as such. This is followed by a more rigorous specification of the traditional approach to the analysis of networks, organized around the economic notions of transaction costs and embeddedness. Finally, the chapter returns to various ways of comparing the three coordinative/governance mechanisms.

2.2. Hierarchy

The key feature of hierarchy is that it requires some form of overt rule-driven design and direction. It requires explicit deliberative action with an objective or outcome in sight. Broadly speaking this can be called 'administration' or 'management'. Note that this could be an activity of both the private and the public sectors as usually understood. Private organizations, like firms, require administrative practices to coordinate their activity, and they rely on management to direct their operations. Similarly with public agencies like the UK National Health Service or the European Commission.

Clearly, however, there are major differences between private and public forms of hierarchical regulation or management. Most private sector economic organizations sell goods and services within a competitive market place, so their 'internal' managerial activity is geared up to, and constrained by, the need to perform effectively in that respect. If they fail they will eventually go out of business. Thus, their 'external' environment is quite different to most traditional public sector authorities. The latter do not have to meet the same 'commercial' criteria or constraints as private sector firms. They will not go out of business so readily if they fail in their organizational tasks. The 'external' relationships between private sector firms might thus be better broadly considered as 'governed' or coordinated by the market system as a consequence, as discussed in Section 2.3. In fact, as we shall see in the context of the subsequent discussion of the 'transaction cost' approach to coordination and governance, the boundary between the market and hierarchy is a flexible one, dictated by calculations of the benefits and costs of market versus hierarchical coordination. And in addition, there is a claim that networks also fulfil the function of coordinating the external relationships between firms. This is examined more in detail in the following chapters.

In the case of public sector activity, however, interorganizational 'external' relationships are relatively autonomous from the direct constraint of being coordinated by a market system and of being subject to market comparable 'commercial criteria' (though there have been obvious growing pressures for the public sector to actually behave in this way—to try to 'mirror' the way the private market sector conducts its business—and this is true of both 'internal' and 'external' public sector coordination and governance—see Chapter 6). But for our purposes at this stage hierarchy can be considered as coordination by *administrative means*. It requires 'political' decisions in the first instance, which are then followed up by directive action to implement those decisions. Often, this administrative action takes the form of rule-governed regulatory coordination and bureaucratic measures. Hierarchy is a structured mechanism of control, designed to run large and complex organizations. It usually involves a layered or tiered organizational structure, often called divisions or departments, which are ordered in a sequence of the superordination and subordination of authority or power. By such bureaucratic mechanisms as scrutiny, rule making and standard setting, the issuing of orders or directives, supervision, monitoring of activities and behaviours, auditing, and the like, the attempt is made to *control* the institution or organization so that all its parts act together for the collective purpose of producing the desired end result. The image here is one of a top-down command structure, where the flow of direction is 'downwards' from higher to lower tiers in a pyramid type matrix.

Clearly, as already mentioned, these hierarchical coordinative arrangements, can pertain to *intra*organization forms—that is, as between the 'internal' parts of a single organizational unit—or to the *inter*organizational level—that is, as an 'external' structure coordinating the activities between separate individual organizational units.

2.3. The Market

The key feature of a market is that it claims to be a mechanism that secures economic order and the coordination of economic activities without any conscious organizing centre that directs it. It is based upon 'decentralized' decision-making, involving a competitive process between dispersed economic agents who make their decisions according to the price mechanism and well demarcated contractual arrangements. So, it is an information gathering and dissemination process based upon prices, where no single agent controls things, but which arrives at an *ex post* optimum outcome that best satisfies social needs and maximizes social welfare. These, at least, are the strong *claims* made for this mechanism.

How exactly, then, does the price system work to provide the necessary information that leads to these virtuous outcomes? In fact there are two fairly well developed but distinct approaches to how this is argued to all operate. These are the 'neoclassical approach' and the 'Austrian approach'. Both of these claim a common lineage with Adam Smith's pioneering analysis of the market economy in his *An Inquiry into the Nature and Causes of the Wealth of Nations* (Smith, 1979, first published in 1776), but they derive somewhat different forms of analysis and conclusions from this heritage. Let us start with the neoclassical approach, which is the one that dominates contemporary economic analysis.

2.3.1. The neoclassicals

The pioneering theorists from within the neoclassical tradition are the English economists Alfred Marshal (1842–1924) and Arthur Pigou (1877–1959). They set about analysing what goes on in the act of exchange. They considered how a set of self-interested individuals, who were assumed to have a clearly defined set of *personal preferences*, would go about maximizing their own well-being. They put aside the rather bothersome question of how production might actually be organized to concentrate upon exchange. Given that each participant has a different bundle of consumption goods, how would these be distributed or allocated between them? Here the key move was to appeal to the notion of individual utility, and the rationality of the participants in assessing the gains they could make in satisfying their preferences and gaining the maximum utility by engaging in *mutual exchange*. They would *trade* between themselves, and such a trade would result in mutual gains to each party. Here, then, is the origin of a founding notion in economics, the mutual gains from trade.

As soon as we start to think about bundles of goods being exchanged and thereby reallocated or distributed around the system and between the parties involved in it, it is a short step to arrive at the notions of a supply and a demand for the different sets of goods. For the neoclassical economists this interaction between someone's willingness to supply goods and another's willingness to demand them constitutes the key moment in the construction of the notion of a *market*. A market, then, is somewhere where suppliers (and supplies) and demanders (and demands) are brought together. How does the interaction take place?

It does so through the medium of the *price* for the good or service in question. In fact, that market price is precisely established by the interaction of supply and demand in the market place. After a number of rounds of to-ing and fro-ing between suppliers and demanders, an *equilibrium price* will be established which will just clear the market. All demands will be satisfied, and all supplies will be taken up. The market will (temporarily) come to rest. It is in an (ordered) equilibrium.

And this story based upon a single transaction in a single market could easily be generalized. In practice there are assumed to be multiple buyers and sellers, no single one of which is able to exercise a control over the process. If there were such a single operator who could exercise control it would exercise a *monopoly position* in the market, and could potentially manipulate the market to its own advantage and against the interests of the majority. In addition, not only can we multiply the number of agents operating in a single market to make it more realistic, but we can also multiply the number of distinct markets themselves to create a *market system* of interacting individual markets. Finally, the way the market works in bringing supply and demand into an equilibrium not only sends the correct information to consumers about the state of the market, but it also sends this information to producers as well and therefore integrates them explicitly into the process. On the basis of the 'conditions of exchange', suppliers are provided with incentives to increase or decrease their own production, and to reduce their costs to a minimum consistent with them being able to stay in business. The lower their costs, the more likely they are to entice consumers to demand their particular goods as against their rivals because they can offer their goods at lower prices. Hence this generates *competition* between producers to supply the market. And such competition will drive costs down to make the system more efficient. Thus, producers are linked to consumer preferences; they are provided with an incentive to satisfy the consumer preferences as made manifest through the price consumers are willing to pay for their goods or services. In this way it is 'consumer preferences' that drive this system, and provide the links back to the producers.

Clearly, this is a rather simple and abstract presentation of the way the neoclassical system is argued to work, and it begs as many questions as it answers. For good or ill this is a very powerful and logical analytical approach, one that, as a result, attracts a strong and determined support. But it is not the only claim on how such a market system operates. We now turn to another leading contender.

2.3.2. The Austrians

This section considers the Austrian approach to the market, but in a little less detail since it shares some of the characteristics of the neo-classical model. Here the differences from the neoclassical model are stressed and the criticisms levelled at it from this alternative approach are highlighted. As its name implies, the Austrian approach is most closely associated with a group of Austrian economists including Friedrich von Hayek (1899–1992), Carl Menger (1840–1921), Ludwig von Mises (1881–1973), and Joseph Schumpeter (1883–1950). There are two key characteristics of the Austrian approach. The first is to stress the market as 'a process of creative destruction' and the second is to stress the signalling and information aspects of the market.[1]

The Austrians were concerned with *innovation and the creation of new products and processes*. Thus, they focused more on the *production side* of economic activity. Market competition works to promote the introduction of new products and new processes of production. Thus, the market is a constantly changing and adaptive system. New rivals continually challenge established producers. This sets up a process of *creative destruction*. Note how the emphasis here is upon the market as an *evolving process*. It is always in a state of dynamic flux and adaptation. So there is no 'static equilibrium' where prices act to coordinate supply and demand and establish a point of rest. The market is continually restless. It is in a constant state of *disequilibrium*. It is often argued that the neoclassical system has a difficulty in dealing with how new products and processes are introduced onto the market since it rather assumes this problem away.

If we think of the market in this way, as dynamically innovating, then those firms that fail to keep up with the competition will fall by the wayside and go out of business, *however large they are*. Thus, there is not such a concern with 'monopoly' and large-scale production amongst (some of) the Austrians. Indeed, monopoly is something to be expected, a reward for innovation, which will only confer

---

[1] As will be seen in subsequent chapters, both of these features are important for an understanding of what is also thought to go on in networks, conceived as parallel mechanisms to the market operating in the way understood by Austrian economists.

a temporary advantage since the 'gales of destruction' eliminate this in time. But there is a clear policy implication here. It is up to the public authorities to make sure that the possibility of entry into the market is not stifled.

The other feature of the Austrian approach is to stress the information generating and disseminating activity of the market. Again, the emphasis is on the market as a process, but a process of competitive price changes. Instead of concentrating on a process of adjustment involving price-taking behaviour that equilibrates existing supply and demand, the Austrians look to a process of adjustment where supply and demand are *continually out of equilibrium*. Here prices act as the incentive to guide the system forward and to innovate. The competitive market is thus akin to a 'machine' for sending out information to those who need it. Vital information about consumer tastes and production possibilities is continually transmitted by the market system, a lot of which will soon be redundant because it may be out of date by the time it can be used. So the issue is to remain nimble and fleet of foot in relation to such 'excesses of information' so as to gain an advantage over one's competitors. It is to seize and use the available information, to sort through it quickly, and to use it to your advantage precisely before it does go out of date.

Clearly, there are many points of similarity between these two images of the market. They are not totally opposed to one another, though they do emphasize different interpretations of its effectiveness. Despite their differences, these two approaches would both support the spontaneous and non-actively designed outcome emanating from the operation of the market system. Both the approaches support an ordered and coordinated outcome from the 'non-governance' offered by the market.

2.4. Networks

This section introduces networks as a third coordinating mechanism. As we will see later there can be two versions of this, namely an 'organized' variant and 'self-organizing' variant. The organized variant involves conscious directive action to establish and sustain the network while the self-organizing variant invokes interactions of a non-directive kind that continually reconfigure and evolve into an *ex post*-order. But so as not to overcomplicate things at this stage, and since this distinction is itself something that needs justifying and exploring, we leave it aside and concentrate just on the term 'network'. In fact, this distinction is analysed at length in Chapter 5.

Networks have proved a useful alternative conception in analysing how a range social activity is organized and governed at a number of levels.

First, this appears in the form of the conduct of social relations that organize and sustain the basic 'social structure' of any society. Social structure is here considered in the image of the direct and indirect interactions that typify interlinked chains of personalized friendships and acquaintances, families, work colleges, club members, etc., though this image can also take a non-personalized form to include the relationship between organizational entities as well. These aspects are considered at greater length in Chapter 3.

Second, networks are invoked to show how public policy is formulated with respect to economic decisions that affect the *de jure* governance of the economic system. It involves the way that 'policy networks' are formed and how political or economic elites generate relatively cohesive groups that set the agenda for policy discussions and guide decision-making processes within the institutional structures of domestic and international economic and political management. These policy networks form the main object for the analysis of Chapter 6, and are further considered in an international context in Chapter 7.

Third, it appears in the form of local networks of firms and public or semi-public organizations that have had an important impact on the innovation capacity of different economies. This thus affects the technological capability of the economy overall, raising issues of how this particular type of economic activity both is, and can be, fostered and governed. Chapters 5 and 7 deal with these issues.

Fourth, it appears as the social adjunct to how technical networks operate, as in the case of much discussion of ICT networks. The role of ICT networks forms a large part of the analysis of Chapter 7, particularly as they are argued to have radically recast the nature of international networking structures.

Networks operating in these areas are neither organized like a market, nor are they officially sanctioned in the form of a hierarchically regulated structure. They arise 'spontaneously', so to speak, or by deliberative design, but they are not coordinated solely by the price mechanism according to the dictates of purely competitive and commercial criteria, nor solely by a consciously designed administrative or management structure. They may involve these mechanisms in part, but they can be considered as distinctive enough in their own right to constitute a separate coordinative and governance system. These mechanisms are also important for understanding the 'bottom-up' type of organizational arrangement that characterizes much of civil society. They strongly connect to 'private interest governance' and the sphere of non-governmental organizations considered in detail in Chapter 6.

One problem with these mechanisms is that they are not so clearly definable as the other two we have been discussing up to now. As a consequence they are often considered to be nothing more than a variable and intermediate form, in many ways falling *between* hierarchy and the market. They are seen as involving and combining elements of these other two systems. But they are also often defined as much by what they are not as what they are, and by how they differ from either market or hierarchy. So in other ways they are conceived as a 'hybrid' organizational and governance form. But what have been put forward as their specific characteristics, in as much as these can be coherently isolated and elaborated?

Networks have often been considered as above all 'informal' practices of coordination. They rely upon direct personal contact. They tend to be localized as a result, or confined to a particular clearly defined group with similar concerns, interests, or aspirations. Such that they display a systematic orientation, these work through attributes like loyalty and trust rather than administrative orders or prices. Thus, these mechanisms have implications for how economic behaviour might be conceptualized. They provide a critique of market driven self-interested instrumental rationality on the one hand, and of the bureaucratic procedural rationality on the other.

The coordination of activities is achieved through the identity of a common purpose or interest, for which all will work for a collective result. These tend towards a 'flat' organizational structure, where at least there is a lot of formal equality between the participants (though there may actually be significant real differences of power and authority in practice—see Chapter 6).

2.5. A Formal Model of Networks

In this section, we generate a more formal economic model of networks to complement the discursive approach adopted so far.[2] A key way in which coordination and governance of economic matters is conceived is within terms of the transactions cost framework originally developed by Oliver Williamson (1996a). Indeed, one is tempted to say that this approach has become almost ubiquitous in the literature. This is particularly so with respect to Williamson's original dichotomy of 'market versus hierarchies', these being his central forms of economic coordination (Williamson 1975). But increasingly, as interest in a third and possibly distinct coordination or governance mechanism has emerged—that of networks—which are also being rendered within terms of the transaction cost approach (e.g. Jones et al. 1997). Thus the transactions cost approach has become a key theoretical technique for analysing all forms of economic coordination, whether this be with respect to markets, hierarchies, or networks.

The following chapters mount a criticism of this framework and develop alternative ways of considering the nature of economic coordination and governance, particularly in the case of networks. However, at this stage the concern is to elaborate the way the transaction cost approach might more coherently develop its analysis of networks. The analysis of markets and hierarchies within this approach is by now well advanced, and although the analysis of networks is often rendered into the same kind of a language or framework, that analysis still remains at a rather gestural and discursive level. The attempt

---

[2] This discussion was stimulated by Adams (1997), who uses a transactions cost framework to analyse the nature of the family firm as an economic institution.

here is to sharpen up the transactions cost approach to networks as a prelude to criticizing its terms more thoroughly in Chapter 3. For the moment we leave a fuller elaboration of what transaction costs actually mean and how they might be further implicated in the characterization of networks for Chapter 3. Here these are taken as understood and we elaborate a simple model based around the term.

The beginning of the basic model is illustrated by Fig. 2.1. This involves the relationship between two key terms associated with networks, namely 'trust' and 'embeddedness', and in turn their relationship to transaction costs. Again, for the moment I leave the precise definition of trust and embeddedness aside, which are the subject of a good deal of dispute and argument in the literature on networks as reviewed in subsequent chapters. For the purposes here, I take trust in its conventional sense in the economics literature, as a resource that is 'exchanged' between network parties as they 'transact' their business (Williamson 1993). Networks are established to precisely economize on transactions costs, via the deployment of trust.[3] For the purposes here, embeddedness refers to the degree of 'social location' of network participants—measured in terms of the 'depth' or 'degree of connectivity' associated with the established relationships amongst the network participants (Granovetter 1973, 1985—but see Chapter 5, Section 5.11, for a more nuanced analysis of embeddedness).

Part (a) of Fig. 2.1 expresses the relationship between trust (Tr) and embeddedness (Emb) in the form: $Tr = f(Emb)$. As the 'degree of embeddedness' rises, so the level of trust rises (embeddedness being measured along a scale from 0 to 1; from 'looser' to 'deeper' ties). In part (b) of the figure the relationship between trust and transaction costs is presented as an inverse one; the higher the level of trust the lower the transaction costs, and the lower the level of trust the higher the transaction costs ($Tc = f(Tr)$). These two sets of relationships are used to generate the 'partial network transaction cost function' (Tc_N') shown in part (d) of Fig. 2.1—$Tc_N' = f(Tr, Emb)$.

[3] One of the problems with this way of conceiving of trust is that it is a 'resource' that tends to *increase* with its use in networks, not decrease as the economizing tradition assumes. Further preliminary discussion of trust can be found in Section 2.6 below and in Chapters 4–6.

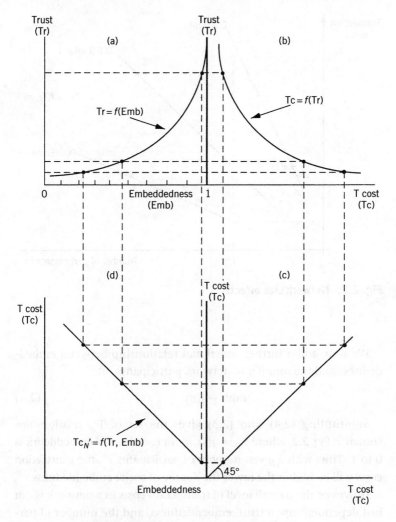

Fig. 2.1. Trust, embeddedness and transaction costs

Thus, from Fig. 2.1 we have a system as follows:

$$\text{Tr} = f(\text{Emb}). \tag{2.1}$$

$$\text{Tc} = f(\text{Tr}). \tag{2.2}$$

$$\text{Tc}_N' = f(\text{Tr, Emb}). \tag{2.3}$$

33

Theoretical and Methodological Issues

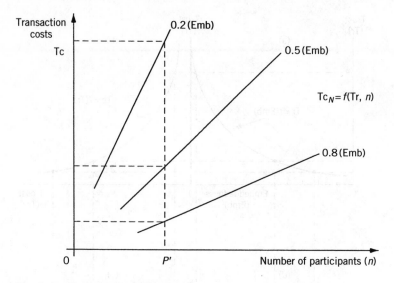

Fig. 2.2. Network size effects

We now add a further functional relationship between embeddedness and the number of network participants (n):

$$\text{Emb} = f(n). \tag{2.4}$$

Substituting (2.4) into (2.3) gives the set of Tc_n relationships shown in Fig. 2.2, where $\text{Tc}_N = f(\text{Tr}, n)$ for each level of embeddedness 0 to 1. Thus with a given number of participants P', the transaction costs will be higher the lower the degree of social embeddedness.

However, the overall level of transaction costs in a network is not just dependent upon trust, embeddedness, and the number of participants. There is also the crucial matter of *intensity* of the relationships between network members. This expresses the degree to which the members of any network are interconnected. I will call this variable the 'density' of the network (D). The relationship between D and Tc is as shown in Fig. 2.3 $(\text{Tc} = f(D))$, where Tc is a positive, but declining, function of density, so that 'economies of density scale' hold. The degree of density can also be measured on a scale of 0 to 1.

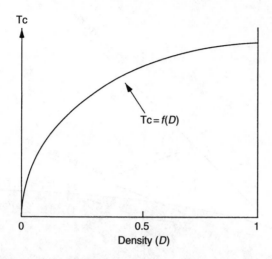

Fig. 2.3. Network density effects

Thus, the overall transaction cost function of a network takes the form:

$$Tc_N'' = f(\text{Tr, Emb, } D). \tag{2.5}$$

These relationships are sketched in the three dimensional Fig. 2.4. For any given degree of embeddedness (e.g. 0.6), level of trust, number of participant members (n_1), and density (d_1), a position like X can be established within the space of the diagram, which establishes a point on the network transaction cost function $Tc_N'' = f(\text{Tr, Emb, } D)$. The relationships between the number of network participants (n) and the density of the network (D) can, in turn, be designated as the 'complexity' of the network (Cp), so that point X in Fig. 2.4 marks out a point A on the 'complexity ray' 0Cp on the floor of the diagram.

Finally at this stage, the particular relationship between the levels of economic network complexity defined in this manner and transaction costs are shown in Fig. 2.5. Each of the Tc_N'' functions shown here corresponds to a particular embeddedness, trust, number of network members, and density level.

This model, then, formally establishes a number of characteristics of, and relationship between, variables that are traditionally argued

35

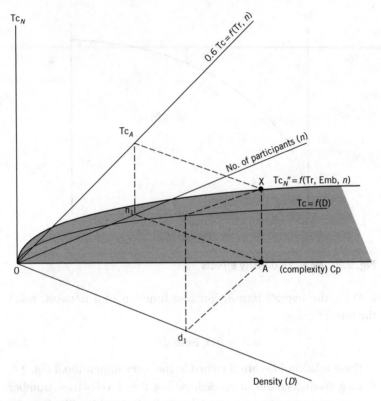

Fig. 2.4. Introducing complexity

to typify network forms of organization, all set within a transaction cost framework. For this analysis the transaction cost framework is the crucial feature, one which will be problematized in the next chapter.

2.6. A Hierarchical Order, a Market Order, and a Network Order

Having discussed the notion of hierarchy, the market, and network in highly abstract terms, we can now investigate how these translate into definite governance regimes. Here, then, we can begin to think more rigorously about the differences between these three mechanisms as

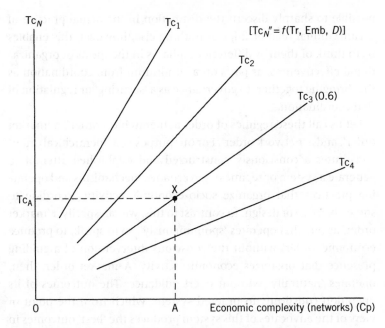

Fig. 2.5. **The overall network transaction cost function**

coordinating devices and their different role as *governance* mechanisms. By *coordination* we mean that the elements in the system are somehow brought into an alignment, considered and made to act together. By *governance* we mean the regulation of these elements; the effectiveness of their reproduction, of their alignment and coordination. Up to now these two have been rather run together, and to some extent they are on a continuum. At the 'coordination end', we have processes that simply bring together elements into an ordered pattern, but not necessarily by intent or design—'non-purposeful outcomes'. At the other 'governance end', we have mechanisms that overtly order and govern by direction and design—'purposeful outcomes'. Thus, governance is a 'stronger' category than coordination, though they may both end up with the same result; an ordered pattern of relationships. Throughout the rest of this book, this distinction should be borne in mind, and attention will be drawn to it where necessary, despite the fact that we will tend to continue to run them together for the most part. And this is because it is not always possible to sharply discern the distinction in the actual practice of organizational relationships. If nothing else, however, this enables us to think of them as different emphases in the forms of organizational effectiveness, as parts on a continuum from coordination as the 'bringing together' to governance as a 'securing' or regulation of that coordination.

Let us call these regimes of order a 'hierarchical order', a 'market order', and a 'network order'. For our purposes, a 'hierarchical order' constitutes a consciously constructed and established attempt to generate a system or regime of governance mechanisms and operating practices that organize socio-economic activity according to some objective or design. In contrast to this, we can specify a 'market order' as one that operates 'spontaneously', so to speak, to produce economic 'order' without the conscious intervention of a guiding presence that organizes economic activity. A market order, then, operates 'naturally' without overt guidance. The outcomes of its operation constitute an ordered system, which from the point of view of the advocates of this system produces the 'best' outcomes in terms of economic welfare, but without any obvious public presence to plan it. The classic example of such a market order would be the idea of the 'market system' of free competition, organized by the price mechanism, in which individual economic agents make their own decisions as to what to do based upon their preferences and constraints in an attempt to maximize their individual benefits. If this system works according to how it is supposed to, these initially *ex ante* uncoordinated individual activities will eventually produce the optimum outcomes of maximum welfare for the collectivity as a whole. The 'unseen-hand' or 'guiding-hand' of the market system leads to an *ex post* coordination or economic order that maximizes participants' satisfactions and welfare.

Clearly, what is being outlined here under the title of a 'market order' is something that does not conform to the idea of a consciously constructed governance system. Indeed, it is the very opposite of such a consciously guided governance system. Market order is a spontaneously generated one. So, it really represents the 'other' of a constructed, established and designed economic 'hierarchical order', the one promoted by official edict and planned organization.

For the purposes of this chapter, a hierarchical order and a market order are opposites. Or rather, they are perhaps better described as non-commensurable coordinating mechanisms since one is a genuine governance system (a hierarchical order) while the other rejects the idea that designed governance is needed to secure satisfactory economic outcomes (a market order). Both look towards 'order' as their desired *ex post* outcomes, but they see those orders as arising by way of quite different social and economic processes.

But why the emphasis on order? By order we mean an outcome that is not completely incoherent. It is a system that is genuinely coordinated, where the parts fit together in a reasonably consistent way. By contrast, a disordered system would be one in which complete fragmentation ruled, one which lacked coordinative governance and a systematic configuration of its parts. As we will see in subsequent chapters, however, it is often suggested that it is the tension between order and disorder encountered in networks that provides them with their peculiarly attractive dynamic properties. For the moment, however, we stick to order seen as a way of mobilizing coherence and systematicity.

2.6.1. Features of a network order

So what then would the notion of a network order offer and in what ways is it different to these other two? Here we approach this by specifying what might be termed the 'attributes' of networks. Any network involves a set of behavioural dispositions typifying the agents implicated in it and a certain structural arrangement that sustains those dispositions. Why should actors sustain a network (I leave out of account for now why they might *form* one in the first place)? At the moment it is sufficient to note the kinds of attributes that characterize a cohesive network. These attributes can be considered as the flow-forces that articulate a network. They are what constitute its 'order'. Conceptually they occupy the gaps and distances between network nodal points (recall the quotation from Foucault in Chapter 1).

When discussing networks, in the first instance at least, it is probably institutional arrangements like *informal* groups, *mutual-aid* organizations, *small-scale* and *local institutional* networks, *cooperative* forms of social existence, *self-help* groups, and so on that come immediately to mind. The words italicized indicate the key terms when discussing these types of social relations. Another way of describing these kinds of social arrangements is as 'flat' organizational forms. They seem to involve a kind of *equality of membership*, where *joint responsibility* holds. One further term sometimes used to describe these contexts is that of the 'collegiate' form. This is most often deployed where it is a set of *professional* people that form the network. Thus, it could be applied to the legal, medical, architectural or accounting professions, for instance, which tend to organize and regulate themselves in a close (and often closed) network context. Continuous coordination in these types of situations outside the market or hierarchy could be predicated upon a mixture of coexistent attributes such as sympathy, customary reciprocity, moral norms, common experience, trust, duty, obligation, and similar virtues. What is needed, therefore, is to prise open these notions to see what they involve and how they operate.

This section focuses on the terms *'solidarity'*, *'altruism'*, *'loyalty'*, *'reciprocity'*, and *'trust'* which, it is suggested, are the attributes that best summarize the reasons why networks exist and function.[4] It is these terms that best differentiate the specific features of a network model from either a hierarchical one or a market one. But it should also be emphasized that subsequent chapters will unpick these conventional notions themselves as more radical and less orthodox conceptions of networks are encountered and uncovered.

Solidarity. How is solidarity formed? To a large extent this can be attributed to the sharing of a common experience. Social classes, for instance, are often thought to form a solidaristic ethic because the people in them are 'objectively' placed in the same social or economic position and they therefore experience the same kinds of pressures, cultural stimuli, work regimes, income consequences, and so on. They 'stick together' as a result. Similarly, family groups, linguistic groups, ethnic groups, and the like, might also be thought to generate a solidaristic ethic for much the same reasons. The category *experience* is thus crucial to this type of explanation. It is peoples' common or shared experience that forges the solidarity between them.

---

[4] Some of these notions are nicely posed in Kaufman *et al.* (1986).

In the history of the concept of solidarity, a distinction is often drawn between 'mechanical solidarity', 'organic solidarity', and 'instrumental solidarity' (Durkheim 1933). Mechanical solidarity typifies a segmentary community, often small in scale, in which there are clearly separated roles between its members and clear standards by which their behaviour can be assessed. This produces collective conscience in a 'mechanical' way as the members of the community interact along these strictly demarcated lines. People 'know their place' and then act accordingly. Tribal life is often thought to demonstrate this kind of a solidarity.

Organic solidarity, on the other hand, refers to a functionally differentiated society of a more complex character. In this case, solidarity is more difficult to generate. The complexity of the functions in a differentiated society implies a greater variability of social relations, where the social roles members are called upon to play are less clear-cut (and often multiple) and the behavioural norms associated with those roles equally complex. This leads to a more serious problem in forging the organic solidarity required to establish a collective consciousness. In these types of societies, self-interest, alienation, and anomie can develop which hinder the formation of the necessary social consciousness (necessary for social order). The advanced industrial economies provide good examples of this form of organic solidarity.

Finally, we can point to what might be termed 'instrumental solidarity' as a specific response to the problem identified under the heading of organic solidarity just described. How can the pursuit of self-interest in a functionally differentiated society lead to solidarity between its members? The generation of this, it is suggested, involves a certain calculus of the benefits and losses by individuals to determine whether, and under what circumstances, they would stand to achieve an overall gain in their welfare by cooperating. In this case then, solidarity would be instrumental to the calculation of individual *net* benefits. This kind of a conception thus shares an intellectual affinity with the neoclassical economic approach to the market. It is the interaction between welfare maximizing individuals in the context of the price system that produced an efficient market solution to the coordination problem. We return to this below.

Each of these forms of solidarity may have its place in explaining the existence of networks as we shall see later. But what they demonstrate is that explaining network solidarity is a *problem* in modern complex societies. How can a system in which individual calculation of benefit is central, produce a network of solidaristic relationships? Is not this better understood as producing a market type set of relationships? This problem is explicitly taken up in Chapter 6 around the issues of generating cooperation in a game theoretic context. We now move on to see how the other concepts might provide some further insights into this problem.

Altruism. Why do some people go to the help of others without any expected gain to themselves, indeed, sometimes even to sacrifice themselves? This is the problem the category altruism addresses, and it is clearly linked to the issue of the generation of solidarity between people. Strictly speaking, altruism implies *selflessness*. Thus, in being altruistic we expect no self-gain to arise from our actions. We act solely in the interests of others. It certainly does not involve an instrumental act in the way the final form of solidarity was discussed above. Presumably, humans are understood to display a kind of 'generalized benevolence' towards others. This could be in accordance with an ethical principle—'love of humanity' or 'devotion to one's family' perhaps. Clearly, it could also constitute part of a feeling of solidarity in this sense.

Some have suggested that although altruism involves no calculation of a personal *material* gain, it might be compatible with a feeling of internal well-being on the part of the initiator of the selfless action. As a result of introspection, it induces a positive feeling—having done some good. If this is socially recognized in some way—through explicit approval by others—a kind of 'psychical pleasure' might arise and encourage greater altruism.

But altruism interpreted in the way just outlined goes against its most radical feature. It is better understood to be totally unselfish in character, even at the introspective level. One consequence of this is the need to recognize that although there may be individual acts of altruism in any society, to expect a society in general to run on altruistic lines is impossible. At a minimum, society must pay attention to the *rewards* (and penalties) for action. People will act on the basis of the incentives associated with rewards. Of course this does not imply simply material rewards. There may be a range of non-material rewards that will encourage individuals (or any social agent) to act—psychical pleasures, feelings of well-being, social recognition, etc. These issues are returned to in Chapter 4, where the notion of a non-reciprocal gift is discussed.

Loyalty. Once a network is intact, why should people remain committed to it, or how can 'repeated transactions' be guaranteed? To answer this, we need to examine loyalty. In his analysis of the way members of organizations react to disturbances in the operation of those organization, Albert Hirshman suggests they have three strategies open to them; 'exit', 'voice', and 'loyalty' (Hirshman 1970). To exit means that they simply decide to leave the organization to get on with its own problems rather than try to help sort these out; they may take their custom elsewhere, they may retreat to some quiet corner, they may seek another job, or whatever. Second, members may stay and exercise their voice. In this case, they actively try to change things for the better as they see it. They may organize, petition, demonstrate, campaign, and so on—that is, voice their opposition or support for some change or action. Finally, they have the option of simply remaining loyal to the organization. In this case, they would very much 'carry on as before', perhaps in a rather passive way, supporting the organization and its leadership. In a network context, ties of personal and professional loyalty can be very important in securing a stable, robust set of enduring relationships, ones that are quite resistant to the temptations of voice or exit. Of course, in any real situation, it is unlikely that network agents would only exercise one of these strategies exclusively. They are likely to be found in some combination, or in a sequence—voice *and* loyalty, voice *and* exit (but clearly not exit *and* loyalty!): or in the sequence *first* loyalty, *then* voice, and *then* exit.

To some extent it might seem loyalty is synonymous with a kind of indifference or acceptance. As long as things go reasonably well, why bother to voice (loudly) or exit? But it really needs to be buttressed by some more positive attributes like *faith* in the ability (and loyalty) of others, *affection* for them, norms of *trust*, *duty*, and *obligation*. Interestingly, these latter two 'norms'—duty and obligation—may not be secured just as 'social relations' but also as *'symbolic relations'*. Why are we prepared to do our duty and meet our obligations; to sacrifice our lives for the Queen and the country, say? The point here is that the Queen and the country have a symbolic significance— popularly represented by the crown and the flag. The emblematic character of rituals and the motifs of pomp and ceremony all serve to *symbolically* embed us in loyalty. They thereby effect a *legitimation* of those practices and mechanisms of symbolic recognition that are so powerful in shaping many of the contours of contemporary social and political life. In fact, this is the site of a very important critique of 'coordination through networks of solidarity', which is pursued in a later chapter. Where does loyalty end and the manipulation and corruption it might engender or tolerate begin? (See Chapter 6.)

Finally, in this subsection, we need to say a little more about the concept of voice. In its literal sense, 'voice' has to do with the power of language. Thus, one of the ways networks might be secured—one of the means by which they are organized—is through the activity of *argument, debate*, and *persuasion*. This activity of argument, debate, and persuasion is sometimes referred to as the 'art of rhetoric'. Networks can thus be articulated in a rhetorical or discursive fashion. In fact, this is an important way networks operate. Given that they are often informal, cooperative, local, small scale, and the like, they are amenable to these kinds of devices. Given that they rely upon the attributes of trust, affection, sympathy, and so on, consultation and negotiation are likely to be strongly present in the practices of networks. Consultation and negotiation are nothing but the exercise of language and rhetoric.

Reciprocity. One further way of stabilizing coordination in a network situation is through the symmetry between giving and receiving. This also involves the norm of obligation. When someone gives a gift, for instance, there is not only an expectation that something will be given in return, perhaps later, but also an obligation on the part of the receiver to reciprocate (Mauss 1990). A kind of moral sanction operates here, but this is not altruistically motivated. With altruistic behaviour, there is *no* obligation expected or received. You give something when you genuinely expect nothing in return.

Written somewhat larger than just gift exchanging, the 'give and take' of social interaction is an important contact building and sustaining mechanism. It implies the temporary foregoing of advantage by one party, knowing that it can (and will) 'collect' later. But gift exchanging is important in illustrating one feature that pervades these kinds of reciprocal relationships; their symbolic character. Just as in the case of loyalty, reciprocity is not simply a social relation but also a symbolic one. In the constant ritual of the exchange, deep obligations and duties are established, symbolic statuses confirmed, metaphorical social references invoked.

The success of generalizing the expectation of reciprocation depends on several factors: (a) it is easier in small collectivities; (b) it is easier when the 'social distance' between actors is short, and chains of action are not extended; (c) it is less difficult when the actors are homogeneous in outlook, style of life, material circumstances, customs of action, etc.; (d) in larger arenas, which are more heterogeneous with respect to actors and institutions, the generation of reciprocity is most successful when differentiated (multiple) standards are developed by which different kinds of reciprocal expectation can be specified. Clearly, many of these features required for reciprocity to work could also be duplicated for the effective operation of networks more generally.

As we will see later, however, in Chapter 4 there is a sustained discussion of the problem of reciprocity conceived as a key attribute in the construction of a specific logic for networks. This has to do with the attempt in that chapter to think of networks in a non-exchange based analytical framework. Further discussion is left for that chapter, which also deals with the following issues of trust at some length.

Trust. Finally, one other belief upon which cooperation is predicated is trust, as introduced in the model considered in Section 2.5. Cooperation is both a fragile and a vital relationship for networks, in which trust plays a central organizing role. Clearly, if everybody behaved absolutely honestly, there would be no need for trust. Trust appears as a category when there is an uncertainty about how people will behave—a risk is always involved in a relationship because of a potential for dishonesty, to which the notion of trust is the response. The more we trust people, the more honestly we expect them to behave, and vice versa.

Theoretical and Methodological Issues

Risk and uncertainty are endemic in a complex world. But the risks and uncertainties to which trust is the response are not those 'natural' risks and uncertainties imposed upon us by the vagaries of fortune. They are, rather, the result of a potential opportunistic behaviour on the part of cooperating agents when such 'natural' events strike, as they are always threatening to do. Trust in this sense is a behavioural response to these kinds of events—we can 'bet against them' by building up trust, and its allied concepts of *reputation* and *consistency*. *Cooperation* is more secure and robust when agents have a *trust* because of the *reputation* of themselves and other agents in the network for *honesty* and *consistency*. Thus, trust implies an expected action, to our benefit or not detrimental to it, which we cannot monitor in advance, or the circumstances associated with which we cannot directly control. It is a kind of device for coping with the freedoms of others. It minimizes the temptation to indulge in purely opportunistic behaviour (Gambetta 1988*a,b*). In this sense, it is closely linked to loyalty.

Two important points we will have to return to throughout this book concerning trust are posed by the above discussion. One is, what comes first, trust or cooperation? And the second related question is, how do trust and cooperation become established? Up to now we have rather presumed these to exist and gone about describing their characteristics. We return to these issues in a moment.

Clearly, the attributes of networks discussed in this section are not mutually exclusive. They overlap a good deal, complementing and reinforcing each other. Collectively they act to generate a *solidaristic–cooperative* behaviour between network agents. They do not guarantee it, of course—the social order marked out by networks may well break down and disintegrate; it may be replaced by hierarchy or the market. Solidaristic-cooperation can be interpreted very broadly to mean the set of rules or norms, agreed to between agents, that are then to be observed in the course of their interaction. These rules and norms constitute a kind of 'contract' between the agents (which could be individuals, firms, or governments). Such agreements need not be formal and legally binding contracts, however (though they might be of this kind in part); they can be informal ones that have arisen implicitly in the course of the interaction, that need not be written down but are established as a result of habit, prior successful experience, trial and error, and so on (see Chapter 5, where the nature of rules and norms are discussed at length).

A major problem with cooperation is how to organize long-term agreement between the members of any group or club. This can become particularly acute in collegiate forms, or where there is a formal equality amongst those involved. No one single member has the power or authority to impose his/her own will on others. One strategy under these circumstances is to enter a bargaining arrangement. Diplomacy around a *quid pro quo* stance might be effective. Under these circumstances, all the usual characteristics and caveats associated with bargaining become operative—careful deployment of arguments, persuasive skills, the revelation of only the most necessary information, deliberate concealment of objectives, even the possibility of minor infringements of honesty at times. Clearly, all the features of networks discussed in this section could be implicated here. But, *if* the network is going to actually work and survive, then a generalized trust, honesty, and solidarity must transcend any minor negotiating infringements of these, and a shared common overriding objective be in place. These help produce those credibility commitments so necessary for network configurations (Chapter 6).

One thing that some have found attractive about networks discussed in this manner is that they provide a set of *ethical virtues* at the same time as providing a realistic means to coordinate economic, political, and social life. If there is a sensitivity to the threat posed by the monopolization of moral discussion by 'top-down' religious and political discourses, then the trust, loyalty, and cooperation—which might be said to arise 'spontaneously' in the context of 'bottom-up' network governance—take on a renewed significance as a result.

2.6.2. A summary of three orders compared

A summary of the three main socio-economic orders considered in this section can be found in Table 2.1. Note that for the network order, two solutions are suggested depending upon whether this is considered an overtly organized or a self-organizing system.

Given that it is sensible to approach the analysis of network in a way that tries to establish its abstract identity separate from that of

Table 2.1. Types of socio-economic order

Basic attributes	Hierarchical order	Market order	Network order
Type of order envisaged	Designed and consciously organized outcomes	Spontaneously generated outcomes	Designed outcomes; or spontaneously generated outcomes
Behaviour of agents	Rule driven and active authoritative inputs	Private competitive decisions	Cooperation and consensus seeking
Mechanisms of operation	Hierarchically organized/bureaucratic administration/monitoring, scrutiny, interventions	Price mechanism, competition, self-interest, self-regulation	Loyalty, reciprocity, and trust
Type of overall coordination or governance offered	Overt, purposeful guidance and 'active-governance', *ex ante* coordination	Unseen 'guiding-hand', 'non-governance', *ex post* coordination	Formally organized coordination and governance; or 'self-organized' informal 'non-governance'

either hierarchy or market, the kind of results summarized in this table are at one level quite conventional. It mirrors the approach of Powell (1990) and Adler (2001), for instance, amongst others. Again, subsequent chapters will subject this approach to a thorough critical examination. For now, however, we are in a position to begin a relational comparison between these three models as they might contribute towards an overall explanation of the nature of social organization.

2.7. The Overall Relationship between Hierarchies, Markets, and Networks

In this section, we deal with two separate approaches to the comparison of the three modes of coordination/governance outlined in this chapter. The first, which compares markets with networks as definite organizational forms, builds on the model developed in Section 2.5. The second compares all three models, conceived as different conceptual approaches to the analysis of concrete organizational forms. Therefore, these comparisons mirror, the distinction between these two aspects of network conceptualization considered in Chapter 1.

2.7.1. Markets or networks?

First, let us go back to the economic model of networks set out in Section 2.5, which allows us to make a comparison between just the market and network forms of coordination.

A total network transactions cost function like $Tc_N'' = f(Tr, Emb, D)$ drawn from Figs 2.4 and 2.5 and converted into a long-run average cost version is shown in Fig. 2.6 (assuming a usual U-shaped form)—$LRATc_N''$. In addition, Fig. 2.6 shows what can be thought of as the equivalent market version of that transaction cost function ($LRATc_M$). This is drawn in such a way that it cuts the network average cost function at point Z.

If this were the case, the area to the left of Z would be one in which the network form of coordination and governance had a comparative advantage, while the area to the right of this point would be one

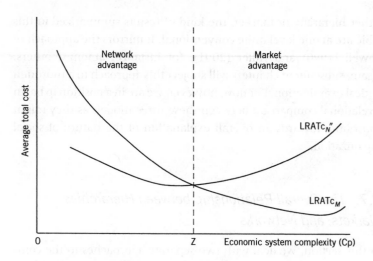

Fig. 2.6. Comparing market with network

where the market form assumes a comparative advantage over the network form. From the point of view of this analysis—and it is suggested, that of the transaction cost approach in general—it is the level of economic system complexity that is crucial for the comparative advantage of either of the forms of coordination/governance. Networks do better with lower levels of such complexity, while markets have the advantage as the level or degree of complexity increases.

2.7.2. Hierarchies, markets, or networks?

A somewhat different way of understanding the potential relationship between all three coordination/governance mechanisms is illustrated in Fig. 2.7. Supposing we thought of the three mechanisms as separate *analytical approaches* (rather than definite organizational forms) which each throw a different beam of light on any object of analysis (cf. Chapter 1). They could thus illuminate only part of that object, or all of it, depending on the appropriateness of that particular torch for the analysis being undertaken. In theory, then, it is possible that any single conceptual torch could illuminate or explain the whole of the issue or object under investigation by itself. But this is unlikely, since in the social sciences we are dealing with complex

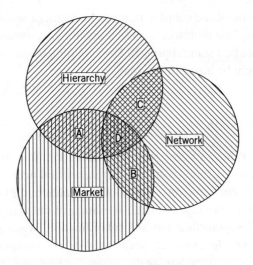

Fig. 2.7. Hierarchy, market, and network compared

objects of analysis, which do not lend themselves easily to a single conceptual schema. Rather, we are likely to find that there is a combination of conceptual torches that either illuminate different aspects of the overall organizational object of analysis or that highlight one part more strongly than another. This is illustrated in Fig. 2.7.

The three 'footprints' of the conceptual torches are partly separated but also partly overlapping. The appropriateness of each conceptual approach could be indicated by the size of the footprint of each, or alternatively, they could be judged of equal importance and appropriateness, in which case, they are all given the same sized footprint.

If it were more a combination of hierarchy and the market that better illustrates the problem under investigation, we are in zone A; if hierarchy and networks are the better guides, we are in zone C; and if networks and the market were the appropriate combination, we would be in zone B. On the other hand, if all three of our governance/coordination mechanisms in their own way, but operating in combination, offer greater illumination on the issue or problem, then we are in zone D. The task of any concrete investigation using the tools of market, hierarchy, and network would then be to precisely 'unpick' the objects of their investigation along these lines, to see which one of the coordination mechanisms, or what combination of them, best illuminates the activity under consideration. And this need not be a static approach. The evolution of the coordinative regimes might be historically variable.

2.8. Conclusion

This chapter has concentrated on elaborating the conventional features argued to typify hierarchical, market, and network forms of organization. For hierarchical forms of coordination, the key features for governance are rule-bounded bureaucracy, authority, administration, and superordination and subordination, while for market forms, the key features are price, self-interest, competition, and formal contracts. But what are the modes of governance that articulate network forms of coordination? This has occupied a large part of the discussion so as to outline the distinctive features of the object of this book. The chapter has presented a range of these features that begin the task of providing the characteristics of a distinctive logic for networks. The task for the rest of the book is to both criticize these and to explore more fully the nature of that logic for networks. And this takes the form of a genuine investigation. It does not presume that such a logic exists, only that it may be possible to establish and needs to be theoretically articulated.

Finally, we should be cautious about attributing too much to our three conceptual and organizational tools—the coordination/governance mechanisms. Like any analytical tool, they are not designed to illuminate everything about organizational relationships, nor could they do so even if they were designed for it. Actual socio-economic life is too complex for this to happen. Whilst they provide a comprehensive package of conceptual tools to begin an analysis of the organizational economic space, there will inevitably be areas of economic life that escape their analytical embrace. As we will see, there are aspects to economic life that are not captured by these three coordinative/governance mechanisms.

Chapter 3

Social Network Analysis, Transaction-Cost Analysis, and Actor-Network Theory: Three Approaches to Networks

3.1. Introduction

An issue acutely raised by the discussion in the previous chapter is whether it is appropriate to analyse networks as an exclusive 'ideal typical' arrangement. The Venn diagram illustrated by Fig. 2.7 sets up networks as strictly separable entities, different from either markets or hierarchies in their essential logic and character. Once separated in this manner the form of the analysis is to bring networks into a complex combination with the other two modes of coordination to highlight particular aspects of the overall structure of social organization. The 'ideal typical' market, hierarchy, or network modes of coordination are conceived to exist 'prior' to their concrete articulation in respect to any empirical object of analysis. They 'exist' abstractly and formally as closed 'systems', and then are brought to bear together in an investigative framework where there is an inevitable blurring of their respective illustrative boundaries.

The first problem with demarcating a specific boundary around the concept of networks in this way is that any general definition of a network is often so all embracing that it encompasses both markets and hierarchies within it. Suppose we provide a formal definition of a network as:

A specific set of relations making up an interconnected chain or system for a defined set of entities that forms a structure.

This is a loose definition, designating nothing more than a set of interlinked elements that form a coordinating structure. As such it could quite easily embrace both market and hierarchical forms of organization. Indeed, when the sociological approach of 'social network analysis' (SNA—see Knoke and Kuklinski 1982; Wasserman and Faust 1994) provides a definition of 'network analysis' along these lines it includes economic sales and purchases, and authority and power relations as types of networking relations. In addition, there is the so-called 'Swedish' approach to modelling industrial systems, associated with the contrast between a network analysis and the transactions-cost approach of Oliver Williamson, where each of these is making a claim to say how firms operate *within* market situations (Johanson and Mattsson 1987). So here again markets and networks are analysed as synonymous. What is more, some of the relationships describing networks in the Swedish model are also perfectly compatible with what are usually thought of as hierarchical forms of organization.

3.2. Social Network Analysis

Since SNA is such an important analytical approach in demarcating the nature of networks it is worth devoting space to its particular claims and forms of analysis. Indeed, SNA is one of those general analytical schemas that often challenge the ubiquity of transactions-cost analysis (TCA) for the claim to an overall explanation of all socio-economic organizational forms (we will deal with TCA in a moment).

This can be illustrated by looking at the fields in which the approach has been utilized. In the book on the techniques of SNA Wasserman and Faust (1994) list the following as examples of its application:

Occupational mobility; the impact of urbanization on individual well-being; the world political and economic system; community elite decision making; social support; community; group problem solving; diffusion and adoption of innovations; corporate interlocking; belief systems; cognition or social perception; markets; sociology of science; exchange and power; consensus and social influence; coalition formation.   (pp. 5–6)

A glance at this list indicates the range of areas in which SNA has been deployed, and markets are clearly stated as one of them. We come back to the way markets are treated in SNA in a moment but first we just deal with the approach in general. After all, this is mainly designed to analyse 'networks', but not much seems to be able to escape its embrace if this list is anything to go by (and the range of examples could be expanded—see Knoke 2001).

Social network analysis claims above all else to be concerned with *relationships* between interacting units or entities. Thus it meets one of the main methodological points outlined in the introductory chapter to this book. And relationships can be drawn widely. The units or entities could be individuals, separate organizations, parts of organizations, groups of various kinds, countries, cities, 'spheres' of influence or shared characteristics. Five distinctive features of the approach can be summed up along the following lines (developed from Wasserman and Faust, p. 4):

1. Actors and their actions are viewed as *interdependent* rather than independent, autonomous units.
2. The *relational ties* that networks set up are conceived as a '*structure*', so the analysis is an overtly structural one in the sense that the network system is given an epistemological precedence over the activities of actors involved in it.

3. Relational ties or linkages between agents are channels for the *transfer* or *flow of resources*, which can be material or non-material (symbolic).
4. Network models focusing on individuals view the network structural environment as providing *opportunities* for, or *constraints* on, individual action.
5. Socio-network structures establish *lasting patterns* of relationships amongst actors.

The establishment of the structural regularity of patterned associations within networks is operationalized through extensive data collection and sophisticated statistical techniques, which is the distinctive feature of SNA. Thus, SNA is broadly an empirically driven approach, which is often accused of being epistemologically empiricist as a result. It lets the 'data' determine the network structure (thus, it is methodologically inductive). But above all else it is a 'mapping' technique that uncovers patterned sets of relationships between interlinked participants. Thus, its particular notion of 'structure' is one that exists 'on the surface', so to speak. It is not a depth structural model; one where the analytical procedure is to move from the phenomena to penetrate the hidden depths of the social relationship that give rise to those phenomena.

A large number of 'network shapes' can in principle be generated by SNA. The simplest relational unit is the dyad; a link between just two entities. But extensive analytical techniques are applied to large actor sets to uncover a wide range of network forms. Amongst these are what are termed 'open' or 'closed' network systems; cohesive or fragmented 'group' arrangements; 'balanced' or 'imbalanced' affiliation and bridging interactions; 'cliques' and 'clusters' of varying homogeneity, intensity, and density; 'weakly' or 'strongly' articulated network arrangements; and many more besides. All these terms are given a precise definitional meaning within SNA.

3.3. Interlocking Directorates as an Example of the SNA Approach

One of the earliest and well researched examples of the SNA type approach concerns the relationships between firms and their owners and between these and the directors of companies. Although this has taken a number of forms in the literature (Stockman *et al.* 1985), here for the purposes of the exposition we concentrate upon questions of company control and particularly on interlocking directorates between various commercial organizations (Scott and Griff 1984). It also concentrates upon the historical example of the 1970s period to illustrate the general approach.

This particular approach revolves around the way directors of companies tend to 'interlock' between a number of different companies. Three main types of interlock were identified in a book analysing these relationships for the United Kingdom in 1976 (Scott and Griff 1984, pp. 25–6). These are illustrated in Fig. 3.1.

The first—a *primary interlock*—occurs when an inside, executive director of one company A, holds an outside, non-executive directorship in another company B. Second, an *induced interlock* occurs as a consequence of the prior existence of two primary interlocks carried by one director. If an executive of company A holds outside directorships of companies B and C, then the primary interlocks A–B and A–C induce a loose interlock between companies B and C. Finally, a *secondary interlock* is totally unconnected with primary interlocks and exists because a person with a base outside the companies being sampled (e.g. a politician or an eminent professional) sits on two or more boards as an outside director. Thus, in this case that director can indirectly create a loose link between A and C. Added together, these connections could make up a network of contacts with considerable potential influence over commercial decisions.

The results of analyses using this kind of a framework for large public companies in the United Kingdom and elsewhere have

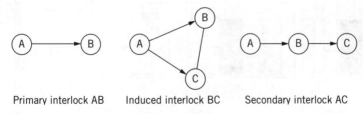

Primary interlock AB   Induced interlock BC   Secondary interlock AC

Fig. 3.1. Types of interlocking directorates

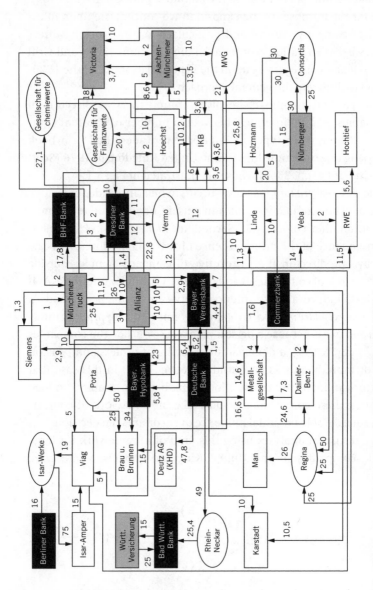

Fig. 3.2. German corporate cross-shareholding (mid-1990s)

Source: Jurgens *et al.* (2000, fig. 1, p. 61.)

shown that extensive networks of multiple directorates are a familiar feature of the British commercial environment, creating a network of contacts between 'the captains of industry'. In Chapter 6, we return to some of the implications of this type of analysis. For instance, the directors of companies may in turn be linked in a network including political leaders thus creating a 'ruling elite' or oligarchy.

A further example of the complexity of the networks that operate in this area of economic life is demonstrated by Fig. 3.2. This illustrates a slightly different way of representing the network of corporate interlocks. It shows the cross-shareholdings between West German financial institutions and other companies (the figures are percentage holdings between organizations). One of the distinctive features of the German economic structure has been the close links fostered between financial organizations, particularly banks, and industrial companies, which is amply illustrated by Fig. 3.2.

3.4. SNA and 'hierarchy'

To give an idea of how a 'hierarchical structure' can be developed within SNA we consider the case of 'clusters'. A cluster is a form of network that is not structurally balanced since it gathers together participants into subsets with similar characteristics or attributes in terms of connectedness. Formally, 'clustering techniques' group entities or actors into 'hierarchical' subsets, producing collections in which pairs are nearly structurally equivalent in some dimension x with value μ. As the value of μ varies 'chaining' allows the grouping of clusters along a more or less 'closeness hierarchy'. This can then be represented as a dendrogram illustrating a movement from direct to indirect linkages amongst the network set. Such a dendrogram is illustrated in Fig. 3.3 for wage variation between skilled and unskilled male workers (MS and MU, respectively) in US industrial sectors for the years 1921–37 (annual rates of wage change). It shows that variation in wage changes between skilled and unskilled workers appear closer together *within* industries as opposed to *between* industries. The measure of closeness being indicated by a

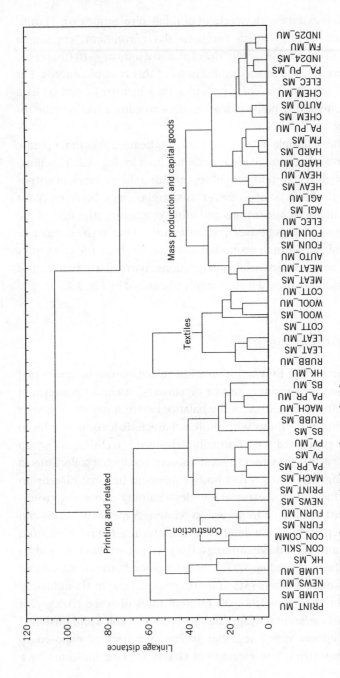

Fig. 3.3. Illustration of network clustering: a dendrogram

Source: Galbraith, J.K. and Berner, M. (eds) *Inequality and Industrial Change.* Cambridge: Cambridge University Press, 2001. Figure 3.2, p. 45.

'linkage distance' variable. Thus, wage changes *between* industries were almost always more important than changes between skilled and unskilled wages *within* industries in explaining the overall evolution of wage patterns during the period.

But hierarchy in this approach is really little more than a by-product of the form of network structure. It represents a way of clustering the intensity of connectedness in terms of the degrees of 'closeness' (which may be 'spatial' or 'social') that the entities exhibit. It does not have any operational significance in terms of the manner in which the coordination between entities is achieved. It is merely one of the devices that describe the pattern of interrelationships between them, rather than a specific analytical claim on the nature of social organization. (So, in the terms of Chapter 2, it is more a coordinative relationship rather than a governance one.) And this way of proceeding illustrates the larger picture of hierarchical networks as designated by SNA. This network approach has been applied to political elites and to policy makers (Chapter 6), and to interlocking directorates and the like (see above). But they are the ways of organizing actors into groups and subgroups that demonstrate different degrees of cohesiveness, gathered around particular functions or activities, which are then ranked 'hierarchically' one against another.

Another way of dealing with hierarchy in the framework of the SNA approach is to reconceptualize the market as a 'status order' (Podolny 1993). Status orders serve to raise quality and reduce costs by acting as a signalling mechanism on the cost and revenue profiles of potential competitor or partner companies. Transactions costs can be lowered and revenues increased for a company by it maintaining a high status profile in an industry or market segment. Status orders like this provide information and opportunities for companies to establish 'favoured' partners in a network, dependent upon the underlying value of their productive capacities. The position in a status hierarchy is dependent upon reputations built upon perceptions, expressed opinions, and actions of other agents (which are assessed in a multivariate context). This approach, thus, draws attention to the hierarchical pattern of market exchange set within a network of potential rivals and partners. It combines networks and markets, placing them in an overall hierarchical framework.

3.5. Markets as Networks

A more substantial example of the SNA approach that also challenges the separate identity of networks and markets is to consider markets as 'structural' phenomena as well. From this perspective, markets are not so much efficient information generating mechanisms as 'self-perpetuating systems of structural constraints' where 'the only tangible guidance available to the actor is that which can be inferred from the patterns of outcomes which emerge from the relations among actors' (Leifer and White 1987, pp. 85–6). Thus the maximization of advantage to produce the most efficient outcome is not the key to how a market works from this perspective. Maximization implies a calculativeness of opportunity where all possible alternatives are surveyed and assessed, and the least efficient eliminated. But the 'social structural' approach is concerned only with *existing outcomes* where individuals make their choices by observing the fate of others who have faced similar choices. They are guided to make new outcomes purely by the results of existing ones in a cycle of *'adaptive reproducibility'*, set within the context of the network of relationships that they inhabit. Competition and the price mechanism 'work' here as part of the observed outcomes from previous consumption or production periods, informing and encouraging the adaptation of activities to find new niche positions in the market (Burt 1992). Given that this cannot be calculated in advance, the following round of outcomes are as much a matter of fate as of astute or expert judgement. But the 'fate' involved here is one moulded within the structure of the network that is 'the market' and its competition.

So, from the point of view of SNA, market actors and potential entrants are usually known to one another, they monitor how each other act and take other past and present actions into account as they formulate their 'strategies', they share a good deal of information in the sense that this is observed within the social context in which they operate, and they observe how each other relate to customers and other suppliers (White 1988). Role behaviours are formulated within the network context, setting up expectations about each firm's distinct *market schedule*—which is made up of its costs, prices, output volumes, product characteristics, trading style, and marketing approach. 'Feedback loops', based upon encounters with customers, show up divergences, dispersions and deviations in outcomes from expectations, and provide the basis for new trade offs between the elements in the market schedule for the next round of encounters.

For Berkowitz (1988) SNA demonstrates how these types of relationships are sustained over time between establishments, firms, and enterprises within an industrial system by operationalizing complex and overlapping 'market-areas'. Such market-areas demarcate the relevant boundaries between these levels of entities as a consequence of the organizational networks within which they exist. It is 'structurally similar locations' in terms of the equivalent types of activities with which the establishments, firms, and enterprises are involved that demarcates the boundaries around the relevant market-areas. These clusters of segmented 'production chains' or 'interlocking market locations' are flexibly arranged and articulated by multiple bridging and interfacing relationships, which in turn establish the structure of the industrial system overall.

As far as the empirical demarcation of concrete forms of networked market structures conceived in this way is concerned White (1981) and Burt (1988) provide a range of examples. Based upon extensive data sets, typologies of markets and their vulnerabilities (White) or stabilities (Burt) have been established. Vulnerabilities refer to two things. First, the robustness of the network in sustaining itself when threatened by the removal of nodes and connections. Second, the way 'free-loading' by potential entrants to the market-areas and weak feedback loops enable potential entrants to 'lurk' and gather market schedule information while not revealing their own hand. Stabilities are the reverse, enabling the existing participants and the systems that they establish to survive and thrive as new nodes and connections are added, or despite inequalities between the members which threaten to undo the network.

Overall, these analyses report a perhaps surprising continuity and stability in the 'tangible cliques of producers' that made up the American market network system through the 1960s and 1970s. One suspects, however, that since then US domestic vulnerabilities have appeared more forcefully, particularly with the economic turmoil in the 1980s and 1990s and the rapid change in industrial structure being wrought by the advent of ICTs. In fact, the SNA approach to industrial structure has moved on to embrace a more international focus. It has been widely used to examine the 'world-systems' approach to the structural location of national trading patterns as part of the trend towards globalization, and as a way of testing the emergence of the 'world cities' thesis in this context. Both of these developments are examined in Chapter 7 later on, but in these areas, once again, it is the 'stabilities' that have been stressed over 'vulnerabilities'.

3.6. Evaluating SNA

What are we to make of this SNA approach to networks as considered in this book? Clearly, as far as it goes, it often provides an interesting 'thick description' of the inter-linkages between the production entities that make up parts of a complex industrial sector. But the number and range of studies are small. Interestingly, there is little in this approach about the role of the consumer, and the 'networks of consumers' that might complement those of producers. It has been overtly 'productionist' in its orientation. This may be one of the reasons why it appeals so strongly to the 'world systems' analysts, who also demonstrate a similar productionist bias—see Chapter 7. And it has certainly failed to engage with conventional economics, which is resolutely committed to the intertwining of producers' and consumers' activities within a maximizing framework. In addition, there is a problem about theoretical explanation and causation. SNA seems thin in terms of explaining *why* the patterns observed are such that they are, other than because they were like that in the past. It remains rather 'one-dimensional' in largely explaining existing patterns in terms of past ones, somewhat resistant to opening up to a richer and more varied set of theoretical lines of reasoning and potential determinants.

Also, there is a related problem over the notion of 'governance', which this approach lacks. It is better at describing a certain manner of coordination between entities than accounting for their governance, where that coordination is itself rather 'passive' in character. Finally, of course, it in a sense claims too much. In offering a blanket technique for analysing all systems of connectedness and interlinking, and calling all these 'networks', the potential complexity of social coordination and the modality of different forms of governance mechanisms are lost.

However, one of the most influential SNA analysts, David Knoke (2001), has suggested that SNA does represent a distinctive *theory* of organizational analysis, encompassing political and economic organizations as well as social and personal ones. He argues that it can identify the overall structure of an organizational system and offer an opportunity for weaving together the various strands of organization studies: institutional theory, resource dependency approaches, transaction cost economics, and population ecology theory. But his is a theory of a particular and rather restrictive type. It resolutely sticks to the field of 'organizational studies' rather than embracing a wider arena of governance structures (states, associations, neocorporate structures—see Chapters 6–8). There is nothing wrong with this, of course. It can provide an opportunity to link organizational approaches together, but only in *ad hoc* and loose configurative arrangement. In part this is because the technique is in fact trying to do something else. Strictly speaking it is not overtly concerned with coordination or governance. A scrutiny of the subject index in Wasserman and Faust (1994) reveals no entry under either of these terms. Rather it is concerned with revealing the 'social structure of connectedness', and that is considered sufficient. Only in passing does this have some coordinative side effects, through the information contained in the market schedules.

It is, thus, difficult to know what the exact resources that flow through these market networks are, other than information contained in the market schedules. There is nothing in these networks as such that implies a *substantive vitality* about them in terms of governance capabilities; considerations of power and authority seem lacking. At best its networks are 'weakly coordinating' but not 'governing' ones. These issues will be revisited in Chapter 7 when the approach is reviewed in the international context of networks.

However, the social structural approach to networks has probably been more successful in its specific sociological context. The work of

Barry Wellman (1999) is useful in pointing to the growth of a different form of sociability around networks—which he terms 'network individualism'—and which he argues is threatening to displace more traditional forms of sociability associated with the notion of 'community' (Wellman 1979). As networks substitute for places as supports of sociability, interpersonal ties can lose their 'organic' connection to a particular locality, being replaced by a more strategic choice of contacts and ties selected according to interests and values. But the problem with this approach is that it also often claims too much, extending this to register a complete change in identities and patterns of social existence brought upon by the development of the Internet and other ICTs. A more developed critique of this is pursued in Chapter 7, which deals with the claims made about the advent of a 'global network society' (Castells 1996, 2001; Messner 1997). Castells, in particular, situates his description of the network society very much in terms of SNA.

3.7. Networks, Transaction Costs, and the New Institutional Economics

In this section, we look at another intellectual claim made to analyse all socio-networks, namely TCA. We have already encountered this in Chapter 2 where there was an attempt to sharpen up the way networks could be demarcated and analysed using this technique. In this chapter, we concentrate on a critical engagement with TCA.

To begin with, what are the arguments against the ubiquity of TCA for the analysis of socio-economic coordination and governance of this type? First, a question begged by the use of TCA is whether it can be transferred quite so easily from a domain dealing with *market failure* to situations where (a) hierarchies are concerned, and (b) then to environments where public policy and public action are involved, and (c) then to embrace networks as well. TCA is used to analyse both markets and hierarchies, and to say something about the nature of public policy and action, particularly as this pertains to the institutions that embody public policy and public action (e.g. Dixit 1995); and further to account for the operation of networks. In all these cases a logic initially developed to throw light on transactions under market conditions (Klaes 2000*a,b*) is broadened to deal with hierarchy, public policy, personal and social networks, and institutions more generally.

From a TCA perspective, hierarchy, for instance, is seen as nothing more than a consequence of a failure (of the market). In a sense there is nothing positive to be said about hierarchy other than that it arises when markets fail. Market exchanges are the 'norm'; their logic prevails over that of anything else that pretends to coordinate or govern ('. . . in the beginning there were markets', Williamson 1975, p. 20). Thus, a market 'transactions logic' is brought to bear on things that are not inherently or necessarily transactions based. But TCA makes a theoretical claim to say exactly how these other forms of organizational activity operate. How otherwise could a comprehensive cost–benefit calculation of their respective orders be organized?

Second, we should remember that although TCA as applied to the analysis of hierarchy was originally devised to account for the emergence of firms as hierarchical organizations, it has been extended to account for the hierarchical forms of interorganizational relationships as well (e.g. Stinchcombe 1985).

Let us remind ourselves why transaction costs emerge in Williamson's theory. Three key concepts operate in his approach: bounded rationality, asset specificity, and opportunism. *Bounded rationality* refers to the difficulty of making fully informed and totally encompassing decisions. Cognitive limitations—the inability to formulate and solve complex problems—leads to a limiting of choices and a non-comprehensive adaptation to contingencies. This is particularly so for Williamson in the case of contracting arrangements. All possible contingencies cannot be accounted for in advance. *Asset specificity* arises where exchanges require specific investments to make contracts effective or where idiosyncratic knowledge is acquired in the course of contractual enforcement. This implies an investment in the activity and asset rigidities, which cannot be flexibly redeployed at will.

Cognitive limitations and asset specificity then present scope for *opportunism*, since these always give rise to contingent uncertainties, which market actors can exploit as circumstances change. If there were no bounded rationality, asset specificity or opportunism ubi-quitous market contracting could continue and the standard competi-tive equilibrium model would hold. Otherwise, alternative means of coordination and governance need to be found, of which the firm and hierarchy are the two most obvious, but to which networks can be easily added. Thus, if any one of the three conditions—bounded rationality, asset specificity, and opportunism—did not exist then market contracts could still be relied upon to allocate resources properly. However, situations where all three remain significant are pervasive in economic organization. The key, then, to market failure and the call for a different means of coordination like hierarchy is the coincidental operation of all three conditions (Kay 1992).

However, Kay points to some decisive shortcomings of the transaction cost approach in dealing with anything other than the market form of coordination, notably in his case that of hierarchy. He accuses Williamson of constructing 'false' hierarchies though much of Kay's analysis on this score is challenged in Williamson (1992). False hierarchies arise for Kay because the contracting ana-logy is used to deal both with the internal organization of a hierarchy as well as the external organization of a market. Kay argues that this is illegitimate because hierarchy is not organized analogously to a contract rich market; rather it is organized administratively via a different logic of rules, edicts, orders and fiat, as sketched in the pre-vious chapter. The 'authority' that these bureaucratic procedures vest in a hierarchy represent a genuine alternative to the market. The logic of these two means of coordination is so different that a transaction cost does not arise in the case of hierarchy. Kay asks what is actually exchanged in the case of a hierarchy that is directly analogous to a market exchange?

In addition, does full opportunism operate under hierarchy? The propensity to behave opportunistically would seem to be under-mined in the case of the bureaucratic functionaries that run non-market but hierarchically organized entities. It is rather difficult to imagine, Kay suggests, how opportunism can arise in a world where obedience to administrative edict, rule driven decision-making, bureaucratic management, close scrutiny of behaviours, adherence to collective norms, etc., is the mode of operation demanded by the organization. This must at least severely circumscribe opportunistic behaviour in its individualistic sense as deployed in Williamson's analysis (we come back to this in a moment). In general, then, there is a large question mark hanging over whether individual opportunism works in a 'pure' hierarchy.

Finally, what about the third condition, that of asset specificity? Here we could point to those industrial organizational and coordination situations where it is precisely *because* of asset specificity that transaction cost problems *do not arise* or are avoided. Take the case of subcontracting in the context of specialized and flexible process technologies. A good deal of the 'quasi-vertical disintegration' first identified by Sable (1989) and others has been undertaken by firms to create asset specificities in the name of increased competitive efficiency and performance for themselves and the system as a whole. (These organizational arrangements are analysed at length in Chapters 5 and 7.) The creation of an interdependence between the elements in a 'value-adding chain' in this way, for instance, not only creates asset specificities but is also designed to avoid transaction costs through the operation of trust, loyalty, mutual dependency, etc. The reasonable claim could be made, therefore, that these types of coordination arrangements cannot strictly be analysed in terms of the transaction cost approach. Trust, loyalty, and mutual dependency involve no necessary transaction costs because they are argued to conform to a different logic of coordination. If this is the case, it is not a question of cutting down on transaction costs or of eliminating them by these arrangements because they just do not arise in terms of these concepts.

It is in respect to the idea of 'network governance' that the strongest claims for the deployment of TCA in network situations has been made (Jones *et al.* 1997). In fact Jones *et al.* want to combine TCA with SNA discussed above, and the 'structural embeddedness' approach first popularized by Granovetter (1973, 1982, 1985), and used in Chapter 2. The structural embeddedness approach fits neatly with SNA since Granovetter defines embeddedness as '. . . the fact that economic action and outcomes . . . are affected by actors' dyadic (pairwise) relations *and* by the structure of the overall network of relations' (Granovetter 1992, p. 33). Jones *et al.* add TCA to this combination in the form of the requirement of networks to safeguard exchanges more efficiently than other governance mechanisms, otherwise they will not survive in the long run. To highlight the specific network features of a TCA approach Jones *et al.* develop parallel concepts analogous to the TCA approach to markets and hierarchies. These features are: *demand uncertainty* and stable supply (implying exchange and contract uncertainty); customized exchanges high in human *asset specificity* (the asset specificity condition); *complex tasks performance* under time pressure (implying bounded rationality); and *frequent exchanges* amongst parties comprising the network (implying reciprocity) (pp. 918–24). All these embedded features of networks help sustain them as a governance structure: through the minimization of transactions costs, safeguarding coordination, and enhancing reputations to secure a robust 'macroculture' of network social interaction.

Thus the general point to be concluded from these remarks is to question whether the utilization of a transaction cost framework can work when we are dealing with activity of a hierarchical nature or in the case of networks. The transaction cost approach may be acceptable for some situations and types of organizational coordination but not for others. At a minimum, confining it to situations where 'exchanges' of some form operate would seem appropriate. Indeed, as will be developed in the following chapter, this is exactly the radical position taken by an approach which argues that networks involve no 'exchange' or 'reciprocity' of any kind.

Another criticism of TCA is in respect to its almost exclusive concentration on opportunistic relationships to the exclusion of cooperative ones, something that is important for networks. This is a criticism made by Ghoshal and Moran (1996) in their defence of a 'logic of organizational advantage' as a distinct logic to that of TCA. As against Kay, however, they argue that the conception of hierarchy developed by Williamson is precisely designed to *avoid* the opportunism of the market, but that in fact is the kind of hierarchical control envisaged by TCA, which would actually *encourage* it within hierarchical types of organizational structure.

Ghoshal and Moran are particularly concerned to dispute the dual character of opportunism that they find in Williamson's work—as a 'universal' attitude inherent in all human nature and as a behavioural manifestation determined by a particular mode of coordination, namely the market. They want to treat opportunism as a 'variable', a variable that depends upon concrete settings of organizational control. In particular, hierarchy does not involve a logic that necessarily denies or eliminates opportunism, they argue. On the contrary, it can foster opportunism and encourage it precisely because hierarchy relies upon authoritarian rules, fiat, coercive control, distrust of employees, rationalistic surveillance, etc. These kinds of procedures set up an environment of deteriorating social control, eroding trust and cooperation, which exactly leads to a disposition towards opportunistic behaviour within (and between) organizations. A 'self-fulfilling prophecy' ensues in which the assumption of opportunism as an attitude and a behavioural outcome is precisely guaranteed by the measures used to combat it within hierarchical modes of organization. As these organizational forms then become progressively more uncompetitive and inefficient, they will be replaced by markets. In the end there will be just markets and, of course, no firms.

As against this scenario Ghoshal and Moran point to the existence of efficient, energetic, well functioning, and successful organizations and firms. To account for this, they see the need to develop a different style of reasoning, their 'logic of organizational advantage', where purposive adaptation (Barnard 1962) involving innovation enhancing activity and the development of shared norms and values, are afforded their true worth. The ability to adapt in the absence of prices and markets, to choose a flexible mix of autonomy and coordination in pursuing dynamic efficiency and creative innovation cannot, in their view, be fostered by substituting the directive and bureaucratic coordinative behavioural aspects of hierarchical organization. It requires, instead, the development and nurturing of 'a social context that shapes the values, goals, and expectations of members and alters their perceptions of the balance between "inducements" and "contributions" ' (p. 37). The development of such a 'collective energy' depends on fostering many of the range of network attributes discussed in the previous chapter; trust, loyalty, cooperation, social solidarity, etc. This is the only way to defeat 'rampant opportunism' (though they recognize that all organizational forms display some scope for opportunism).[1]

What these two critical approaches to the claims made by TCA to explain all coordination and governance forms provide is both a strong rebuke to that claim and hints about the nature of an alternative logic that might be developed to comprehensively sustain a different network logic. The aim of much of the rest of this book is to exploit these hints and ground such a logic. But before that we can deal with another rather general claim made to invoke networks as coordinative devices. This is another essentially sociological approach, but one that takes an approach quite different from that of SNA.

3.8. Actor-Network Theory

Actor-network theory (ANT) is essentially the creation of two French social theorists, Bruno Latour and Michel Callon, though it has a strong British connection through the collaboration of these two authors with John Law. Although originally emerging as a way of analysing the social nature of scientific experimentation and technological knowledge, it quickly spread to encompass a wide range of areas as disparate as the nature of space, place and time; representational processes; the forms of market exchange; the forces and mechanisms of political power; management practices and strategies; and much more besides these.[2]

The distinctive approach of ANT to networks is to dissolve any dualistic distinctions between 'society' and 'nature' in the construction of networks, or between 'the social' and 'the technical', or between

[1] The debate about the meaning and significance of 'opportunism' for TCA, and the general significance of 'a logic of organizational advantage' is pursued in Williamson's response to Goshal and Moran's original article and Moran and Goshal's reply—Williamson (1996*b*) and Moran and Ghoshal (1996). See also Williamson (1993).

[2] The literature on ANT is vast. For representative texts that outline the basis of ANT and its subsequent expansion see: Callon (1986), Latour (1987), Callon and Law (1989), the chapters by Callon, Latour, and Law in Law and Hassard (1999), Callon (1998), Hassard *et al.* (1999).

what is considered 'human' and 'non-human', or (sometimes even) between the 'inside' and the 'outside' of the network. Rather what one has are heterogeneous combinations of 'material elements' forged into an ordered set of placings that encompass a 'collage of differences'. There is no separate 'agency' and 'structure', or 'actor' and 'network', but, rather, a combination of these as 'actor-networks' that are designed to dissolve these dualisms. This bricolage of material elements somewhat controversially imparts an agency capacity not only to people but also to various documents and mechanical devices as well. The actor-network is an assemblage of these materials operating through 'immutable mobiles' (Latour 1990) to form an ordered representation. Immutable mobiles could be entities like maps, photographs, paintings, textual descriptions, and images of all kinds, but also heterogeneous artefacts (devices) like ships, cloths, cannon balls, or scientific instruments. Whilst 'fixed' in one sense these are also made 'mobile' by being rearranged and reconfigured through the network of places and agencies to which they are attached or through which they operate; they have the combined properties of mobility, stability, and combinability. The work of reconfiguration and rearrangement in this theory is conducted by the term *translation*: 'We define translation as a process in which sets of relationships between projects, interests, goals, and naturally occurring entities—objects which might otherwise be quite separate from one another—are proposed and brought into being' (Callon and Law 1989, pp. 58–9). A translation brings previously unconnected elements into an alignment. Thus from this perspective, the 'social' is nothing other than patterned actor-networks which are made up of heterogeneous materials.

This is a heavily relational network, therefore, and one that imparts a certain dynamic to the networks it constructs. Nothing is quite fixed in this universe, it is never 'being there' rather it is always in the process of 'being placed there'. Identities of actors, such that they can be clearly established, are determined within this shifting network of enrolment, and only in relationship to one another. Network ordering is, thus, always a somewhat uncertain process of overcoming resistances. As a consequence, there is no such thing as 'the social', with a single centre or stable set of relations.

Rather, there are social orders in the plural, confronting resistances that are never quite overcome. Because power operates in this distributed manner the approach would also deny the idea of a 'network society' or an 'information society' (Castells 1996, 2001). Indeed, there is no fixed 'society' of any kind.

So this way of considering the 'shape' of the social includes the network patterning that generates institutional and organizational effects, which include power and hierarchy as well as forms of market exchange. Thus it is akin to the SNA discussed above in that it encompasses these other coordinating and governance mechanisms. But it also differs from SNA in a number of ways particularly in the case of the notion of 'agency'. For ANT, agents are created as effects of the network, and such actors are also networks in themselves: 'For instance, a *machine* is a heterogeneous network—a set of roles played by technical materials but also by such human components as operators, users, and repair persons. So, too, it is a text. All of these are networks which participate in the social' (Law 1992, p. 384). In addition, ANT avoids Granovetter's (1973, 1985) terminology of embeddedness. Within ANT, for instance, markets are not embedded in networks in the sense that the social network is brought in as an additional element in explaining the nature of markets (Callon 1998, p. 192). Rather, markets are networked from the start; they are entanglements in a web of always partially formed relations and connections, which provided both the incentives and capacities for strategy and calculation by agents. Embedded common cultures, conventions, shared rules, and the like, do not completely govern behaviours but only open up possibilities of interpretation, negotiation, and discussion in the interactions between material entities. Market agents are neither totally immersed in the network nor completely framed by it. Unlike for SNA, here the network is not a context for the market. Rather, networks and agents are two facets of the same phenomenon. The 'context' is borrowed, forged, or chosen rather than determining.

This introduction to the way ANT treats an aspect of market type social activity provides us with an opportunity to investigate more fully how this approach tackles the issues of market exchange.

3.9. The ANT Approach to the Market, Organization, and Management

The ANT approach to the market is to self-consciously get back to explaining how real and specific markets work in all their variation. It argues that '. . . economics, in the broad sense of the term, shapes and formats the economy, rather than observing how it functions.' (Callon 1998, p. 2). The failing of conventional economics, it is argued, is that this relies upon an abstract deployment of the laws of supply and demand to all market situations. Such a formalization misses the complexity of the relationships between the market and the market place, between economics and the economy, something that ANT claims to provide. From this perspective, production and exchange are not distinct realms but are instead intimately linked, indissociable consequences of a single performative network. They are part of the same movement as supply and demand are mutually built and evolve together in the mobilization and translation of actor-networks creating mutual relations of exchange. For Callon the notion of a market implies three things: (a) the existence of 'calculative agencies' that resolve the potential conflict between buyers and sellers by establishing prices; (b) an organized arena in which these calculations take place, which could be variably configured according to different calculative agencies and their distribution; (c) a stabilization of the potential conflict implicit in market exchange via price formation under the conditions of peaceful competition. (Thus ANT dissolves the distinction between market as a 'tool' and as an 'object'—cf. Chapter 1.)

The material reality of calculation relies not just on the actions of human agents but on a range of figures, written mediums and inscriptions that can also be considered as actors in the market network. In addition, the attitudes towards calculation by these agencies and the competencies they deploy are culturally framed and constructed, not something naturally given just to *homo sapiens* as a propensity to truck and barter on their part. In the search for the socio-cultural conditions of calculativeness a key obstacle is the radical uncertainty experienced in markets. Here, ANT stresses the relational formatting, connectiveness and framing involved in market exchange and the way these, along with uncertainty, open up the space for strategy, negotiation, and gaming. It is strategy, negotiation, and gaming that help deal with uncertainty (something, it might be added, that very much mirrors the conventional economic approach to these matters—see also Chapter 6).

As far as the institutional arena for market exchange is concerned, here ANT stresses the creation processes of formatting (which relate, connect, and associate) in the dynamics of establishing and regulating the relationship between calculative agencies. Here framing both establishes actors who are clearly distinct and separate from one another, but also brings them into an alignment around the operation of the network. The institution of the network mobilizes the resources for actors thereby enabling them to undertake their calculative activities. An important appropriation from conventional economics is invoked here, that of externalities. An externality is considered as a potential 'overflowing' from the network, but at the same time it is drawn back into it, included within it. However, since there are no ends to these externalities—one externality just begets another further externality since everything is in principle connected to everything else, however, remotely—such an overflowing demonstrates the impossibility of a total framing (Callon 1998). So here is a slight difference with the conventional analysis of markets, where (a) externalities are just that, something 'external' to the main business of *private* economic exchange and not part of an inclusive network, and (b) some limit is always recognized to the extent of externalities such that they can be included within a *social* assessment of benefits and costs. The twin concepts of frame and externality also serve to undermine the traditional structuralist distinction between that which is below and ultimately determining, and that which is above and determined. Instead ANT postulates a set of objects, ideas, and practices that are internal to the frame and those that are external to it (though this distinction is itself difficult to systematically sustain for ANT—see below).

The fact that ANT addresses the 'mechanics of organization' has led to its increasing embrace within the study of management, involving inquiries into such managerial strategies as enterprise, administration, vocation, vision, innovation, and so on. As Law states:

The argument is that an organization may be seen as such strategies which operate to generate complex configurations of network durability, spatial mobility, systems or representation, and calculability—configurations which have the effect of generating the centre/periphery asymmetries and hierarchies characteristic of most formal organizations. (Law 1992, pp. 368–9)

So here is another claim to say how hierarchies are organized. In a 1999 Special Issue of the journal *Organization* several authors took up this challenge (*Organization*, 6(3), 387–471; see also Hassard *et al.* 1999). Organizations are the site where the technical and the social are brought into an exemplary alignment of stronger and weaker ties, where relations of subordination and superordination abound and are continually breaking down or being reproduced. In part, this relies upon an argument about how *discretion* arises and operates in organizations. Arenas for managerial (and other) discretion are opened up so that discretion is both distributed and accumulated within organizations. In this way 'centres of discretion' are aligned alongside 'centres of calculation' for managerial strategy (Munro 1999). Within this complex, hierarchical powers are inscribed. Management is not just about surveillance and sanctioning.

In addition, there is the weaving of organizational practices in to and out of different actor-networks. ANT is relentless in its invocation to pursue and explore the connections between actuants (a mixture of human and technical actors), which means that what could otherwise be considered quite isolated figures and resources are brought within the frame of the network and found to be highly dependent upon it. For instance, if one takes the idea of 'competitiveness' as a problem for management, the task of arranging and tracking corporate performance relies upon the mobilization and establishment of intricate networks, which in turn branch into other equally complex networks (Hansen and Mouritsen 1999). This inevitably manifests itself in something of an ordered hierarchy. Performances need monitoring, remedial adjustments arranged, reconfigurations of the networks organized, all in a continual process of adjustment and reproduction. What better way to consider this than in the context of the calculations and decisions of an actor-network framework and its analytical paraphernalia as described in detail above?

Of course, there is another way in which 'hierarchy' can be understood within ANT. Take the concept of 'action at a distance' that ANT often focuses on. This is one of the modalities through which the actor-network appears and operates. Objects and relays of power circulate through this mechanism; the actor-network being governed from the places where reasonably secure calculations and decisions can be made. In addition, although actors do not so much 'hold' power here, the strength of associations between actors as manifest in the outcomes of the actor-network embody the ability of powerful actors to convince, enlist, and enrol others into the network, allowing them to control the means of representation of the actor-network and to speak in its name. Power is thereby seen as part of the *composition* of the network, in principle lying anywhere where resources of mobilization exist, available to any actor to translate into a bond or an association.

3.10. An Assessment of ANT[3]

An obvious problem with this approach is quite how *boundaries* around any particular actor-network can be established, and perhaps equally importantly, whether there is anything that one can reasonably call social or connected to the social that is not made up of actor-networks. Actor-networks seem to be the singular and utterly ubiquitous inhabitants (more accurately, 'constructuants') of the social field. Given that the approach centrally addresses the issues of place and space this perhaps should have occupied ANT more than it has. A key injunction of ANT is to relentlessly 'follow the actor/agent' so as to search out and establish the 'limits' of network action (whether operating 'closely' or 'at a distance'), but this itself avoids the question because it is very difficult to see where these limits could lie. And this problem is confounded when one takes

---

[3] Murdoch (1995, 1997) provides perceptive commentary and critical reflections on ANT (amongst other things).

seriously the argument that ANT is *not* a systems theory (Latour 1993, 1999). The idea of a system would be too deterministic. Because any framing and (dis)entangling of a network is also redolent with the possibility of an overflowing, a leakage and its undoing, there remains a radical indeterminacy of the actor and the network. Of course, this emphasis on 'following-the-actor' and the 'avoidance-of-system-thinking' is in part supported by the way the term system is defined. For ANT this relies very much on the idea of systems as necessarily *semi-permanent* constructions involving embedded *structural* connections.

Now, whilst the idea of what might be called the 'open network' approach of ANT is attractive in one sense, it is also a difficult one to handle and to sustain. It is attractive because it seems to prevent ossification of thought and practice and an unimaginative, non-innovative analytical approach. But as Lee and Brown (1994) were the first to point out, it means that ANT lacks some conception of the 'other' which is its radical outside or its beyond. Early versions of ANT in particular failed to recognize that something that seemingly tries to explain everything about the social ends up explaining nothing about it (as pointed out in the Introductory chapter to this book). If 'the social' is just made up of a series of actor-networks, then perhaps these networks try to explain too much. An advantage of those approaches to networks that try to demarcate a more limited domain for their operation, and to contrast these with other coordinating or governance mechanisms, is that there is a ready-made boundary between these, with no ontological obstacle to the recognition of the 'beyond'.[4]

[4] For Lee and Brown (1994), this burden of the 'beyond' (which is a preferred term to that of the 'other') originally revolved around the resolute denial of any difference between the social and the natural, and the other dualisms mentioned above. Subsequently ANT seems to have reacted to this critique with a 'cool embrace' of the point (e.g. Lee and Hassard 1999, where ANT is argued to now be able to continually 'overcome' its boundaries, and this new found flexibility is to be welcomed and encouraged). But it subsequently reappeared in a different guise, in the form of the 'other/beyond' of ethical and the moral considerations as against just social or natural ones (Lee and Stenner 1999). Again ANT's seeming early indifference to these 'aspects of the social' is denied, but there still lingers a difficulty in imagining how the strident materiality of ANT can sit comfortably with ethical and moral dimensions to actor-networks. Indeed, in an attempt to open this issue up for investigation for ANT Hull (1999) interestingly resorts to a different

Theoretical and Methodological Issues

The problem with this open-network approach or, indeed, of 'open-systems' in general (to which I would argue ANT is conceptually linked at this level, despite its own protest to the contrary) is that such open networks inevitably display a high degree of redundancy. As they are expansive and always threatening to collapse (because of the continual threat of leakages, overflowings, and undoings) it becomes difficult to stabilize the network. Where and when does the 'following of the actors' stop and a relatively fixed network emerge? Or in the slightly different parlance of ANT, where does the 'performance' of the network end and a relatively stable 'representation' of its characteristics solidify? Yet another network could always be potentially attachable to the existing configuration, so that there is a never ending cascading of opportunities to disrupt and to reconfigure. This sets up high levels of redundancy as the 'system' must overcompensate for the inevitable experimental 'failures' that are written into its evolutionary dynamic.

But high redundancy comes at a cost (see also Chapter 5). Such 'systems' are expensive to run (intellectually and practically) and therefore relatively inefficient. Continual intellectual or social experimentation implies substantial waste as failure has to be paid for. The advantage of a differentiated and more limited intellectual and organizational horizon is that this offers the opportunity to compartmentalize the 'organization of the social' and, to some degree at least, to stabilize it. It means actors can find out where they are and what they are doing. An intellectual and organizational constancy is installed—at least for a reasonable period of time. This is useful in that it means experiences and reflections can be assessed, knowledge consolidated and reproduced, successful models copied and compared. Not everything is under a continual scrutiny and in a continual state of flux.

The retort to this criticism in the case of ANT's analysis of the market would be that it is the notion of 'framing' that allows a demarcation

perspective to explore it (Gillian Rose's philosophy of 'diremption'—or forced splitting). The use of the notion of the 'beyond' in the main text here does not restrict this just to moral or ethical issues, however. It should also be emphasized that this issue of the 'beyond' is not to be confused with the issue of the limit to a *specific* network. Specific actor-networks are undermined when the network 'fails'—see the main text.

between what ANT can analyse and what it cannot deal with. If we take ANT as celebrating the modalities of calculativeness involved in market exchange, for instance, then that which cannot be within the frame cannot be calculated and is therefore beyond explanation by ANT (Callon 1998, pp. 14–15). The network traces the boundary between the events and relationship that are included within the decision and those that are excluded from it. The latter embodies a 'disinterestedness' on the part of ANT. In addition, at its limit the *boundary between particular* networks can be found when and where the actor-network 'fails' (though the criteria for assessing a failure are not easy to discern in ANT—see also Chapter 1, footnote 5).

And in a rather interesting turn, Callon argues that this distinction between inclusion and exclusion is an expression of the relation of calculativeness to the gift. What is included (in the actor-network) implies a return of the gift (reciprocal relationships), whilst what is excluded implies a non-return of the gift and an asymmetrical attitude towards the gift.

Such an attitude towards the centrality of calculativeness for the ANT approach to analysing market networks, and the emphasis on the non-reciprocity of gift giving for demarcating between the legitimate domain of the economic and that in which it is 'disinterested', also reminds one of Williamson's similar analysis of the market, calculativness, and gift giving (Williamson 1993). Since this is discussed at length in Chapter 4, I leave the full critical reflections that could be brought to bear on the ANT appropriation of this to that chapter. At this stage it is suffice to say that an alternative conception would be to stress the boundary between different calculative modalities where incompatibilities and incommensurabilities arise. Economic calculation, to have any effectivity, makes commensurable what was previously incommensurable. It is difficult to conceive of a realm of the economic simply divided into a calculable domain and a non-calculable one around the gift giving/acceptance/reciprocity issue, rather than one divided into different modalities of the calculable. Can one escape calculation—and if so how—once the calculative domain is opened up? As we will see in Chapter 4 a more radical conception of the two realms is required to sustain a conceptual distinction between a calculable space for economic exchange and a radically non-calculable one for the operation of a different form of economic logic altogether. Indeed, whilst to some extent this formulation connects to the analysis conducted in Chapter 4, there it is almost the exact opposite that is argued. The distinguishing logic of a network, it is argued, is precisely the absence of a reciprocal (calculative) relationship to the gift, so that the absolute non-reciprocated gift marks out the logic of a network.

To sum up this discussion, the broad approach of ANT towards the economic can be illustrated in the form of Fig. 3.4. The 'raw-materials' for the analysis are to be found at the bottom of the figure, comprising the material elements that feed into a joint process of social exchange. Two routes out of this are made available. On the right-hand side the operation of disentanglement leads to the formation of a range of limited actor-networks of different organizational forms, which in turn gives rise to the calculative agencies that make clear cut and operational decisions. This is the route to the 'open-economic network' conception mentioned above. On the other hand, towards the left-hand side, the joint process remains entangled, so no clear-cut actor-networks emerge. Rather, a web-like randomness prevails between actors, which results in non-calculating agencies. This is the route to non-(economic) networks. Indeed, it might be seen as a route to non-networks of any kind, though this is left rather vague in the analysis. Quite what is occupied by this domain of non-calculating agencies is unclear. It is a kind of 'empty failure'—the unrecognized of a fully filled actor-networked 'social' domain. Given the way ANT insists that the social is made up of a myriad of different and ever expanding actor-networks, this could only be a terrain of other non-economic networks distinguished by their lack of calculativeness (if it is to remain part of the social). It could hardly be the 'beyond' of a radically different form of analysis/organizational arrangement altogether, which is an unrecognizable within the theory.

Of course, these two routes cannot be entirely or easily separated. The division between them is an indistinct one since the inevitable fluidity written into ANT's approach to the formation of the actor and the network; the non-completeness of ordering, its continual flux, its radical openness, etc., precludes a fixity of arrangements.

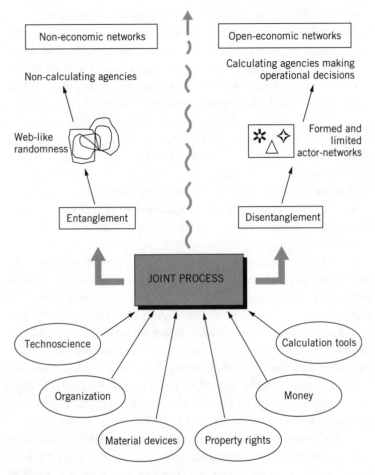

Fig. 3.4. Actor network analysis and the economic

The 'boundary', such that it is, is always threatening to collapse as the left-hand side is continually encroaching on the right-hand side, and vice versa. Again, this 'slipperiness' of ANT could be celebrated as a way it ensures an 'ontological flexibility' in engaging with new organizational forms (Lee and Hassard 1999). But it is not clear what these new organizational forms could be for ANT since the grid of the actor-network is thrown over these, whatever form they might take.

Theoretical and Methodological Issues

A final critical reflection on ANT rests upon its resolute refusal to *evaluate* different calculative agencies/modalities. Which translations, which framings, which formattings, which tools, and which calculative practices are worthwhile and pertinent and which are not? Which should be encouraged and for what purposes? Which yield adequate and worthwhile results and which lead to inefficiencies, costly mistakes, and failures? ANT remains largely silent on these issues, something that limits its analytical reach. The approach celebrates the *experimental* nature of the 'laboratory' as against what it would call the *legislative or interpretative* nature of 'philosophical speculation'. It lacks any systematic appeal to evaluative evidence, remaining neutral as to the appropriateness or otherwise of the different forms of market exchange and, in its wider context, the open actor-networks it uncovers/constructs.

A very final point to note about ANT is appropriate here. This theory has been evolving for nearly three decades, driven by its three main expositors, Callon, Latour, and Law, who have been admirably open to critical reflection. As a consequence there have been a number of changes in analytical position and style within the theory. Modifications in its early basic formulations were first announced in the book *Actor Network Theory and After* (Law and Hassard 1999). This introduced an emphasis on framing and overflowing externalities. Along with this, further reformulations were announced in *The Laws of the Market* (Callon 1998), where an obvious turn towards analysis of the relationship between economics and the economy was indicated. Subsequently, this turn has been consolidated with the move towards an 'economy of qualities' approach (Barry and Slater 2002).[5] But these changes mean that it is difficult to get a precise handle on a consistent and stable argument about actor-networks.

---

[5] An economy of qualities refers to the way commodities and services, and networks of these entities, are being reconfigured—qualified and re-qualified— as they pass along extended production chains. They are involved in a sequence of transformations—design, production, distribution, and consumption—where the qualities/characteristics of these goods and services are simultaneously made similar and different, compatible and incompatible, as they disengage and recombine in actor-networks (Callon *et al.* 2002). The connection of this to the commodity/value chain analysis conducted in Chapter 7 might be noted here.

Indeed, a more sustained reflection on ANT's development would allow some analysis of the differences between its three main protagonists. For instance, in a rather interesting but neglected piece by Callon that tackles the issue of technological diffusion in networks not all of the formal terminological architecture of the actor-network approach is resolutely adhered to (Callon 1993). Indeed, the explicit idea of an actor-network hardly appears, and actors, technical processes, and network configurations are treated very much as separate entities until aggregated into the dynamics of adoption and recruitment processes implicated in path-dependent technical change. This also adopts a rather neat use of the SNA technique of 'structural equivalence' analysis, stressing that it is not so much the *degree of connectivity* in a network that establishes adoption of common technical standards and processes as being in an equivalent 'social' position in the network.[6] Similar structural positions encourage adoption and adaptation, not any 'natural aggregation of preferences' or 'crude numbers (swaming)' of participant populations in the network (p. 247). Probably at the other end of the spectrum to this particular Callon is the John Law of *Organizing Modernity* (Law 1994). Here he makes a rather large claim for a strict ANT approach, and in doing so contrasts ANT with the other approaches to networks discussed in this chapter, but seen very much as competing general explanations for something called 'modernity'.

But despite these differences between its leading theorists and the problem of changes in the intellectual trajectory of ANT, what has been attempted above is to provide a reasonable account of the basic underlying framework of the approach combined with a sensitivity to its evolving dynamic. I leave a more thorough treatment of a very recent turn in the intellectual landscape associated with ANT to the final chapter. This concerns the attempt to respecify it in terms of a 'performance' or 'games' methodology (Hetherington and Law 2000; Hinchcliffe 2000; Thrift 2000). If nothing else, this discourse of 'after actor-networks' indicates to the essential dynamics of the ANT framework.

---

[6] And this terminology of 'equivalencies' should serve to remind us that it is the way ANT meets the criticism that it over-anthropomorphosizes the artefacts in its conception of actor-networks—treating them just like other social actors. For ANT these artefacts are *equivalent to* other actors but not the *same as* them (see Chapter 8).

3.11. Conclusions

This chapter has brought together three of the main analytical techniques that have been used to discuss the nature of 'networks', summed up in terms of their acronyms SNA, TCA, and ANT. In part, all three of these both make a theoretical claim on how to analyse networks as well as to say what networks actually are. In their analytical guises the approaches are also making a claim to say how markets and hierarchies operate from within their intellectual schemas. And in saying what networks actually are they construct rather different accounts. The chapter has brought these accounts, contrasts and comparisons together.

In this respect, it is important to recognize that a 'network' in the ANT approach is not an intermediate form of organization between hierarchy and market but a set of relations between actors and techniques (Callon 1993). And indeed a similar comment could be made about SNA. Both of these posit networks as an analytical tool that encompasses and explains both markets and hierarchies as *variations* of network structures. Only TCA offers an explicit defence of networks being intrinsically different from markets or hierarchies—in the way they coordinate and govern—but these differences can be conceptualized using a single analytical technique and transaction costs.

So underlying the analysis in the chapter has been an issue as to whether networks are radically different to either markets or hierarchies. And bearing in mind the comments just made, all three of the analytical techniques concentrated upon, in their own different ways, would deny this. A serious problem identified in the chapter is that all three make too great a claim because in the end they want to provide a general mechanism that tells us how *all* social relations could be organized. The burden of the various critical remarks made in respect to these claims has been to argue that there needs to be serious consideration given to the possibility of a different logic operating for each of the three coordinating mechanisms. The main burden of the following chapter is to further explore this possibility for the case of networks.

Chapter 4

Networks and the Issues of 'Excess', the 'Gift', 'Non-exchange', and 'Trust'[1]

4.1. Introduction

This chapter examines a series of radical and unorthodox ways of conceiving the logic of networks. Four interrelated issues are focused upon which can be summed up under the terms 'excess', 'the gift', 'non-exchange', and 'trust'. Of these, the notions of 'the gift' and 'trust' are the most widely discussed in the context of networks in their role as coordinating and governance devices. Trust has already been signalled as a key category for the analysis of networks in the previous chapters. Later in this chapter we return to

[1] This chapter is based upon a heavily reworked version of a paper originally prepared for the EAEPE Conference, Technical University of Lisbon, Portugal, 5–8 November 1998 under the title 'Networks and Trust'.

the literature on 'trust and networks' to explore some of its features anew. But the distinctive outcome of that discussion is to question whether the category of trust need be quite so central to the analysis of networks as is often claimed.

The other well recognized category in this list of issues is that of 'the gift'. Often 'the gift' is thought as a central alternative category to that of market based exchange for articulating the nature of the economic mechanism overall. But as will be argued in a moment, this alternative 'gifting economy' tends to be reappropriated back into the conventional logic of exchange by relying upon the further notion of 'reciprocity' as a key complement to the gift. The act of extending a gift implies a logic of return with the expectation that something will be reciprocally offered in exchange, either now or later.

Of course, as we will see, this particular notion of reciprocity relies upon a restricted calculation of 'mutual advantage'—a tendency to discharge an obligatory debt to another by an answer in kind; what Martin Hollis has called a 'bilateral backscratching' (Hollis 1998, p. 144). This is the reciprocity of rational calculation for self-interested material rewards, a kind of 'negative reciprocity'. The critical responses to this from within the conventional cannon is twofold. The first is to pitch a conception of 'positive reciprocity' against this predominant negative one. If negative reciprocity ultimately relies upon personal guile, suspicion, self-interest and a material gain, positive reciprocity relies—not necessarily on altruism as a kind of unconditional kindness—but upon the normative power of fairness and friendliness (e.g. Sugden 1984; Fehr and Gächter 2000). It is social norms rather than explicit contracts that prescribe this positive behavioural reciprocity (or what Sugden (1984) terms 'the principle of unconditional commitment'). Fehr and Gächter argue that experimental and observational evidence demonstrates that increased effort and efficiency results as a kind of 'excess gift' benefit arising from the implicit reciprocal contracts embodied in these norms (see below).

The second response is a connected philosophical one. It is to argue that reciprocity should not be taken in its individual self-interested sense but more as a consequence of a generalized obligation for the operation of a well-ordered, just, and fair society. In this case reciprocity and the trust it engenders are the result of 'good reasons' but not necessarily of 'good calculations' (Hollis 1998, pp. 143–54; see also Bachmann 2001, pp. 352–62). Recognizing obligations to others is the result of a reasoned deliberation on the longer term potential benefits that might arise, not just in case a debt be called (the Rawlsian gamble), but predicated in the first instance on social approval, public spiritedness, worthiness, and membership inclusiveness. However, note that both of these responses still cannot quite escape the basic architecture of a rationalistic reciprocal exchange, even as they desperately try to move away from a crude economistic interpretation of it and distance themselves from the negative versions of the conventional wisdom.

The issue of the return of the gift is examined again in a moment to try to establish a logic that does not require any form of reciprocal relationship between parties in the gift giving act: to disengage the logic of networks from an orthodox notion of exchange and reposition it within a context of 'non-exchange'. However, this will also argue that, such an alternative logic along these lines can actually be constructed (and this is not altogether clear), it should apply only to the arena of networks as coordinating and governance devices, and not be applied to the economic mechanism as a whole.

And here is where the analysis conducted in this chapter parts company with much of the traditional discussion of the so-called 'gift economy'.[2] The gift economy literature arises from a general critique of neoclassical economic analysis, with its rationalistic market exchange based style of reasoning. The debate involving this literature revolves around whether it is possible to construct an alternative total conception of the modern economic mechanism organized around gift exchanging, in many ways seen as a return to a more fundamental (and therefore more 'real') form of economic reasoning and activity. However, in this chapter we are not dealing with two alternative and competing 'total' explanations for all

---

[2] For representative examples of this literature and the debate between its main protagonists, see Arrow (1971), Hyde (1979), Gregory (1981, 1982), Cheal (1988), Mirowski (2001), Gudeman (2001), Davis (2001), Danby (2001). All these authors pay homage to Marcel Mauss's seminal text *The Gift* (Mauss 1990 [1923]) about which there will be much to say in the analysis that follows in the main text.

economic relationships—the market and exchange versus the gift and non-exchange. As will become clear these are seen more as complementary and limited logics, rather than as competing and totalizing ones. The logic of the gift, as nuanced in this chapter, would pertain to network forms of organization only—or, rather, informs part of the way a network might be conceived—and is not seen as an alternative logic for economic relationships as a whole.

Furthermore, the framework for much of the investigation that follows can be found in a form of analysis of economic activity that self-consciously denies the pertinence of calculation or measurement for either its operation or its accountability. This refers to the literature that invokes an analysis of 'non-productive expenditures' set within a so-called 'economy of excess' (Bataille 1984, 1997). Exactly what these terms mean, as in distinction to the 'economy of productivity' with which it is contrasted and one that has informed the analysis up until now, is elaborated in a moment.

But in a similar way to the attitude towards the gifting economy just outlined the point of confronting the economy of excess literature is not to embrace it wholeheartedly as providing an understanding for a different form of economic organization altogether, as is the suggestion of those fully committed to an 'economy of excess' approach.[3] Whilst the analysis that follows utilizes some of the analytical techniques developed by this school, it in no way implies a wholehearted adoption of its overall position. Rather it pragmatically 'plunders' that literature for useful insights where these seem appropriate. It argues that this approach could provide *some* of the conceptual means to think about the role of network-based organizational forms in the contemporary economy from a critical perspective.

---

[3] The 'economy of excess' approach is associated with the school of French sociological analysis known as the 'Collège de sociologie' that thrived between 1930 and 1950 in France. The key figures in this school were Georges Bataille, Roger Callois, and Michel Leiris. For a general analysis of this school and its positions see the Special Issue of the journal *Economy and Society* devoted to the Collège, edited by Frank Pearce (2002). These Collège authors were also involved in a critical engagement with Mauss's *The Gift*.

4.2. From the 'Restricted Economy of Productivity' to a 'General Economy of Excess'

This section takes up the argument that networks can in part be productively reconceptualized in the context of what has been termed a 'general economy of excess'. In particular, this position uses the notion of the 'gift' to analyse how this different type of economic mechanism might operate (Pawlett 1997; Wilkinson 1997; Thompson 1997*a*). In addition, through a reflection on the notion of 'gift giving' the argument is that this can in turn give the concept of 'trust' a new analytical twist. As we have seen trust is an elusive concept which has been very important for the articulation of network forms of organization. In this chapter, we reformulate this, and place it in a more limited analytical context for the analysis of networks.

The 'restricted economy' is the economy of utility, the kind of economy that is concerned with welfare, with the good (and 'goods'), with happiness, productivity, profitability, and so on. Utility is not confined to its individualistic sense in this account, but is a general category describing anything that celebrates the positively productive. Thus, for instance, the work of both Marx and Weber, and all of conventional economics, could be included under this same title.

As opposed to this we can pitch the notion of a 'general economy of excess'. The term 'general economy' is used here to signal that it is concerned with the general uses of wealth, not just those associated with commercial values. This economy concerns itself with the tragic, with extravagance, and abandon, with the destruction of wealth, unproductive expenditure, profitless exchange, with ritualistic, sacred and symbolic activity. Whilst the restricted economy concentrates upon the price mechanism and market exchange, the general economy concentrates upon the gift and symbolic transactions. With the restricted economy, economic activity can be measured and is the subject of a calculation. It involves well worked out and specified contracts. The activity of the general economy of excess, by contrast, cannot be measured in this way or subject to a rationality of calculation. There are no contracts (or, at best, only loose implicit contracts) within this general economy. While the restrictive economy is driven by scarcity, the general economy is driven by sacrifice—a kind of aimless energy. The 'truth' of the restricted economy and its wealth is to be found in the abject poverty occasioned by the full operation of the general economy. From this perspective it is in respect to 'poverty' that we find out what 'wealth' actually means.[4]

4.3. What would be Involved in a 'Gifting' Order?

It is with the notion of 'the gift' that the concerns of the general economy most closely match those of conventional economics and the restricted economy. A central issue is whether the gift should be considered in terms of an exchange, or in terms of something else. Potentially at least, the issue of whether the gift is an exchange or not could provide a fruitful site for further exploration of the distinctive nature of networks.

The conventional manner of treating gifts is to render them as precisely another form of exchange (e.g. Lyons and Mehta 1997). However, there is a problem with the predominant way gifts and exchanges are run together in conventional economics. This has to do with why people continue to give gifts, and reciprocate, when gifts are economically 'inefficient'. The problem is that people receiving gifts value them at a significant discount relative to what they cost the giver to buy (Waldfogel 1993). So why do people continue to give gifts to each other if their utility is lower than if they did not receive and give gifts? In part, this can be solved by introducing the notion of disutility and the interactive 'game' played between participants once gift giving has been started. The social pressure to continue with gifts arises, within this perspective, from the extra disutility received by an individual who refuses to return the gift. Formally, the disutility or 'social embarrassment' of not returning the gift must be higher than the utility loss of paying the price of the gift in the first place, hence the social pressure to continue with gift

---

[4] For a general critique of Bataille's formulations in respect to the economy of excess see Herrnstein Smith (1988, ch. 3) and Pecora (1997, ch. 8).

giving (Shy 2001, pp. 242–8). But this still means that 'social welfare' as a whole is lower than it would be without gift giving, but it is not now individually rational to give it up.[5] But note how this does not so much solve the problem as merely displace it. Disutility is conjured from thin air—given the continued fact of gift giving, a disutility parameter must be (implicitly) present and this can be called 'social embarrassment'. So social embarrassment is left unexplained other than as something revealed in the (dis)utility function.

In fact, despite these problems, there has been a lively debate about the precise nature of 'gifting' in conventional economics. Kenneth Arrow, for instance, in his review of Richard Titmuss' book on blood donating (Titmuss 1971), provided what was probably the first account from a modern economist of the idea of a gift economy (Arrow 1971). Two strategies are apparent here.

The first is the attempt to render the gift economy into the language of an exchange relation via the usual utility framework of a Rawlsian theory of justice, as discussed briefly above (which ignores the problem involving disutility just mentioned). 'One might be thought of as giving blood in the vague expectation that one may need it later on. More generally, perhaps, one gives good things, such as blood, *in exchange for* a generalized obligation on the part of fellow men to help in other circumstances if needed' (Arrow 1971, p. 348—italics added).

The second is to render 'giving'—conceived as an alternative logic to that of exchange—as a 'rump' social or personal practice once all the possibilities of conventional exchanging and calculativeness have been exhausted. Thus, this strategy continually whittles away at the social domain with the exchange/calculative metaphor, until what is considered to be an economically inexplicable residual is left which is then allocated to the activity of personal gift giving. The gift economy ends up as that which is left as more and more of social activity is rendered into the image of a means-ends calculus based

---

[5] This is one of the conclusions that arises from the application of game theory methods to what are called 'network industry' situations; in this instance the case of gift giving is treated analogously to a network industry (Shy 2001). For further analysis of game theory and networks see Chapter 6.

upon individual rationality. Indeed, this is precisely the strategy adopted by Arrow's main successor in the conventional economic analysis of the gift, Oliver Williamson, though in Williamson's case the emphasis is on the related notion of trust (Williamson 1993). This is discussed in a moment.

4.4. Treating the Gift as an Exchange and as a Non-Exchange

In many ways the interpretation of the gift as an exchange is supported by the predominant way gift giving is discussed by Marcel Mauss in his seminal work *The Gift* (1990; first published in 1923). He considers that a gift renders an obligation on the receiving party. It sets up a system of debt and repayment. But there is a profound ambiguity in *The Gift*. There is also a sense that the gift is a form of radical 'expulsion', something that also 'destroys' wealth as it is given, and that does not necessarily render an exchange with an obligation.

In a certain number of cases, it is not even a question of giving and returning gifts, *but of destroying, so as not to give the slightest hint of desiring your gift to be reciprocated* (p. 37). The obligation to reciprocate constitutes the essence of the potlatch, *in so far as it does not consist of pure destruction* (p. 41). One loses face for ever if one does not reciprocate, *or if one does not carry out destruction of equivalent value.* (p. 42) (all from Mauss 1990, italics added)

Indeed, this is just the way of conducting the analysis of gift giving that is seized upon by the 'economy of excess' approach. In its exchange mode the gift immediately brings back restricted economy notions since it implies a calculation and reciprocity (see below).

A second way of treating the gift as an exchange is to see it as the 'excess' of an ordinary contractual exchange. If someone is contracted to render a task with an agreement to pay a set amount for that task, then if as that contracted party completes the task they do it slightly better than had been anticipated (and had been 'contracted' to do) then they are giving the contractor a gift in the form of the excess quality of the output they produce. This kind of an excess gift exchange can arise in the case of labour contracts (Akerlof 1982), amongst others.

A third way of treating the gift does not just involve an exchange. This is to recognize that a present also involves a *presence*. There is something not exchanged in a gift, which has to do with what it does for the involved parties in a 'psychical' sense (see below). It is part of the construction of the self; part of the formation of the subject and its identity.

The fourth, and perhaps most radical, way of treating the gift is to suggest that giving a genuine gift is in a sense an 'impossible act' precisely because it does involve an exchange, and therefore an obligation. If there is an obligation attached, then it is not a true or genuine 'gift'. Thus, to be a gift the gift must either not be seen to be a gift, it must be disguised in some way (counterfeited), or it must be considered in terms that do not render it an obligation. Thus, although, of course, gifts are possible in one sense, it is *the* gift that is impossible. The gift in the singular should not exist because of the problem of the reciprocity of a return of the gift (Derrida 1992).[6] Thus, any recognition of the gift, in the sense of a recognition of the obligation to reciprocate with a counter-gift, spoils this notion of the absolute gift. It frustrates the opportunity to realize the prefect gift.

In addition, if we take another sense of giving seriously, that of death in the context of a 'giving of a life' say, again this connotes both an act of destruction and an act of faith (Derrida 1995). It is destructive and symbolic at one and the same time. So playing on this sense of the gift may also provide a resource to think about the nature of a different logic that motivates behaviour, and which could be articulated to the economy of excess and an alternative

---

[6] Thus, Derrida does not quite go so far as to deny the reciprocal return of the gift altogether in his formulations (see Naas 1997). And this is indicative of the difficulty continually at large in this chapter. On the one hand there is a position that resolutely denies the return of the gift and on the other that which in one way or another argues that this is either impossible and unsustainable, or that it requires at least a symbolic 'return' of some kind (and what Bourdieu (1977) would call the 'accumulation of symbolic capital'). The 'play' between these two contrasting conceptions around gift giving is what drives the analysis here and accounts for the ambiguity of its conclusions (see below).

conception of networks.[7] As we will see these considerations do not so much invoke just the breaking of the quality of *equivalence* thought to be involved with gift giving and receiving but with the very foundation of a gift mechanism that implies any kind of reciprocation.

4.4.1. Trust

What is suggested here is that it is exactly in the context of these ideas about gift giving and receiving that a different notion of trust might also be inscribed. As with the analysis of gifts, however, the conventional way of treating trust is also to render it in terms of an exchange. Thus, in the predominant TCA approach to economic coordination and governance (via markets and hierarchies) considered in Chapters 2 and 3: (a) trust arises to save on transaction costs—it is based upon a subjective calculation of the benefits derived from creating and sustaining a relationship relative to the costs of maintaining it or severing it, and (b) it is a response to the risks and uncertainties associated with economic exchange. The basis for calculative trust here is the subjective probability by which any agent assesses that another agent will perform a particular task or action, both before that agent can monitor the action (if, indeed, this can actually be done) and in a context in which it affects the agents own actions (see e.g. Gambetta 1998*a,b*; and in the specific case of networks, Jones *et al.* 1997).[8] In fact, Williamson distances

---

[7] Nor is death in this case quite a simple annihilation, since it also connotes the *adieu* of both a 'good-bye' and a 'hello' to something else. It suggests a different kind of knowledge—the knowledge of the 'beyond'. And it can further connote a 'duty'; for example, as in the case of 'he gave his life in the performance of his duty' (Derrida 1995). In performing such a 'duty', however, Derrida plays on this notion of death to suggest that it happens to accommodate the 'place of the other'—I die so that others may survive. In which case such a dying does not quite go unrealized or unrecognized. If this death is in the place of others, this implicitly establishes a social bond, even though it is a disguised or counterfeit one. Thus, what a network might itself be conceived to provide (give) is a radically new sense of knowledge and duty about behaviour and organization understood in this fashion.

[8] There is a vast literature on trust which has become a highly popular concern amongst those dealing with organizational relationships. For a representative sample of approaches and analyses, particularly as they pertain to the discussion of networks, see the chapters in Gambetta (1988); Kramer and Tyler (1996); Lane and Bachmann (1998); and Lazaric and Lorenz (1998); Bachmann *et al.* (2001). As far as can be judged, none of these deal with trust in quite the manner suggested in this chapter.

himself from this particular formulation within his overall pproach. He takes exception to any notion of a 'calculative trust'—the idea that trust arises as a means of safeguarding against the opportunism associated with risk (Williamson 1993). For Williamson, anything to do with risk is in principle 'calculable' and subject to contractual terms, thus it does not involve 'trust'. Trust is reserved for what appears to be economically trivial, non-commercial and personal relations (Williamson 1993, pp. 482–5). Trust is a 'personal passion' rather than a modality of economic action, and personal passions involve 'very special relations between family, friends, and lovers' (Williamson 1993, p. 484). As suggested above, it is the residual of a progressive and advancing calculative logic.

In these approaches then, trust is either confined to an economically uninteresting residual or rendered into a calculation in the image of an exchange (as a 'transaction'). But these approaches can be resisted by thinking of trust as occupying the space vacated by the absent gift exchange. Perhaps, then, that illusive quality 'trust' could be reconceptualized from a consideration of what goes on around the 'possible/impossible gift'? In this case trust is located in a space that operates according to quite a different logic to either the market or hierarchy. Trust is precisely a quality that serves to articulate that non-exchange based economic mechanism associated with coordination through networks, one driven by considerations of cooperation and loyalty on the part of economic agents—that is, as if by genuine gifts. This would be one of the key attributes for a pure network form of organization; an attribute that marks off the logic and rationality of a network from other forms of coordination and governance like markets or hierarchies.[9] The operation of the

---

[9] The literature on trust referred to above in footnote (8) provides an elaborate classification of different forms of trust. Not all of these are relevant to an analysis of network forms of organizations being considered here. Most are also designed to offer a contrast between what is argued to be a 'traditional' (and therefore limited) understanding of trust, and a 'new' more appropriate form. Amongst the most relevant of these for our purposes are the idea of 'blind trust versus reflexive trust' (Adler 2001); 'good will trust versus competence trust' (Das and Bing-Sheng 2001); and perhaps the most pervasive of all, versions of '(inter)personal trust versus institutional, systems or technical trust' (Luhmann 1979; Giddens 1990—in fact, Giddens and Luhmann try to link the personal and the institutional via the

non-reciprocated gift establishes a social bond that goes unrecognized as such by participants because it links to the counterfeit and disguised character of the action involved (see also footnote 7).

Interestingly, this formulation is somewhat similar to that suggested by Charles Sabel in a series of papers dealing with the nature of contemporary organization transformation in the US manufacturing sector, which are often discussed in terms of 'networks' or 'associations' (Sabel *et al.* 1990; Helper *et al.* 1997; Sabel and Zeitlin 1997—see also, Chapters 5 and 6 of this book). And Sabel (1990) is also at pains to deny the pertinence of conventional notions of trust for an understanding of the development of the quasi-horizontal and quasi-vertical disintegration of firms, something that Sabel elsewhere described as the development of the 'mobius-strip' company (Sabel 1991). Rather than invoking an idea of trust as that capacity which helps re-articulate such 'dispersed' activities arising in the context of new flexible value-added chains and subcontracting networks, Sabel introduces the term 'learning by monitoring' as a substitute explanatory category. The ever alert monitors learn about differences in manufacturing techniques and practices by close scrutiny of their partner firms and adapt their own behaviours accordingly. Thus, anything that might be called 'trust' that is established here is not unconditional, but highly conditional upon the continuous studied nature of monitoring between organizations or players. So they do not need to 'trust' anybody in an essentialist sense since the close monitoring does the same work for them (they are not 'trusting souls' in any universalistic sense).

Thus although on the surface this formulation might be considered akin to the way Williamson conceives his 'calculative agents'—Williamson describes the residual domain of personal trust as one in which there is 'an absence of monitoring' (Williamson 1993, pp. 483–4), hence monitoring and trust have nothing to do

idea of personal trust in systems or personal trust in technology). Some of these distinctions will be returned to in the chapter that follows this one on intra- and inter-organizational networks, but at this stage they are just mentioned to establish that trust is a widely used category in the analyses of networks, and one that does not necessarily conform to the usage developed in this chapter.

with one another—it turns out to be the reverse. Sabel is hostile to Williamson's overall project, and particularly to his idea of opportunism (see Chapter 3). Sabel suggests this implies an unrealistic 'science of suspicion', which if it were as ubiquitous as Williamson suggests would undermine all social organization, including market and hierarchies (see also Chapter 6).

However, the exact relationship between the idea of learning by monitoring, networking forms of organization, and trust in Sabel's interesting formulations needs to be considered in the light of his previous commitment to 'studied trust' as a key element in the development of new forms of economic organization (Sabel 1993). The general argument seems to be that trust is not a precondition for cooperation but rather a consequence of the learning embodied in the 'studied' nature of monitoring. Perhaps then, at the limit, we could dispense with the notion of trust altogether and substitute for it this idea of 'studied monitoring and learning' (operating along with an idea of 'strategy' as discussed shortly.

4.5. Consequences and Implications

Let us now explore some of the consequences of these conceptions for economic (non)calculation in networks. Here once again we conduct a rather general discussion of these implications, but in particular concentrate on those that highlight a potential application to analysing how network organizational relationships operate.

The first point to note is that the notion of a balance or equilibrium in network economic relationship would be undermined by the strict application of this approach. If by the act of giving, wealth is destroyed and for no apparent productive effect that is a radical unbalanced act on the part of the gift offerer since it does not render a counterpart act on the part of the recipient. Both the double-entry of the balance sheet so dear to accounting, and the idea of an equality of value being established in the act of exchange in economics, would be rendered conceptually problematic by this move (there is no notion of 'equivalence'). In addition notions of equilibrium and optimization are equally compromised.

Second, Bataille (1997) in particular draws on Mauss's ambiguous analysis of gift giving to suggest that the unproductive gift actually involved the destruction of objects that had little or no worth or wealth in a utility sense anyway (it involved the smashing of copper plates, or throwing objects into the sea, that have no obvious commercial use-value). This encouraged Derrida (1992) to raise the issue of the counterfeit nature of these relationships and mechanisms, as mentioned above. What is destroyed in these potlatches is almost worthless and has no economic (utility) value, so the whole process involves a disguised gift giving (in utility terms), involving counterfeit economic values. Rendered into a slightly different language, this means that the 'money' that would circulate these 'activities' (which are not exchanges, of course, but rather 'acts' or 'transfers') in a network context would be a counterfeit money from the start, necessarily disguising what it actually does.[10] From the point of view of a pure network logic, therefore, the acts and transfers involved in its articulation are not monetarized in the same way as are exchanges and transactions in a market situation. In addition, the disguised nature of this money means that it acts as a pure sign money. It represents no economic value or wealth in its utility sense. Money is a sign but not a representation (of something 'elsewhere') to the network. Clearly, this had a radical impact since it not only serves to undermine the conventional economic analysis of the restrictive economy, which operates to exactly link monetary financial totals to their true underlying economic values, but it also confirms a different logic (of money in this case) operating around networks.

A third implication invokes the consequences of this approach for the analysis of time in economic (non)calculation. All calculation presumes some division of time into discrete periods. It can then be treated just like any other number; a series of periods rendered into a potentially calculative modality. Economists are used to conceiving the nature of economic exchange as divided into just two

---

[10] Of course, this allows those who see economic relationships in a wider capitalist economy as necessarily involving an exploitative aspect to find in this the mechanism that disguises that exploitation (see Danby 2002).

domains—first barter which was later displaced by market exchange. Now we have a third and potentially rivalrous form; the non-productive absolute gift. Giving, in the sense discussed here for networks, is neither barter nor a 'free' market exchange.

So 'gifting' in its various forms offers another type of act (transferring, energizing, trusting), which complicates any rather simple and perhaps over-economistic analysis of economic exchange and time. If no return is expected, then the presents given are things very much of the present, just as much as they are things of presence. At this level the gift cannot easily be rendered into a time frame of lag, delay, and deferral (only an exchange-value involves stored up time). It is a radical act of the 'now'—it would mirror the spot market of conventional exchange.

However, the ambiguity of the gift allows some space for the cycle of return—indeed, the analyses of both Derrida and Bataille (whose approaches are being closely followed here) are redolent with notions of circles, cycles, and returns. As soon as there is an intention to do something—give a gift, say—a necessary temporal dimension would seem to be introduced (Wortham 1997, p. 401). Indeed, this is seen by many as a central aspect of the gift, one that opens up an aspect of trust in forward, debt-creating (trans)actions. The fact that, within conventional conceptions of the gift a reciprocal 'return' is promised sometime in the future, allows the operation of goodwill to at least partly secure that obligation. And this has been further exploited by Bourdieu to argue that the relational space opened up within gift transactions/transfers—both temporal and spatial—provides the rationale for the notion of 'strategy' to emerge and operate (Bourdieu 1977, p. 6). This notion of strategy also provides a means of linking the present to the future. It also provides a means by which the counterfeit nature of these events ('fake circulation') is given the opportunity to take hold. And if this is a kind of 'deliberate oversight' (or subterfuge even), then it needs a time interval for it to be made effective.

So, if we say that networks embody these characteristics they provide a space for genuinely strategic thinking and negotiations, something closed off by the market and hierarchy as modes of governance and coordination. Strictly speaking there is no possibility for strategic thinking or activity in neoclassical economics since behaviours there are fully proscribed by a deterministic rationalism, nor in a hierarchy where everything is proscribed by rules and procedures. Strategy substitutes for the strict adherence to rule in a networking environment. It allows for the operation of dexterity, tact, and *savoir-faire* (we return to this in Chapters 5 and 6 where tacit knowledge and game theory are discussed in the context of networks).

But why should networks conceived in this manner generate repeat operations, repeat transfers, or repeat interactions? Without the necessity of a genuine exchange and a reciprocal obligation to return the gift what is the incentive for the continuation of relationships involved in the network? Here it is what is *not given* in the gift that secures the incentive for a 'return' and the rationale for the operation of strategy—what Weiner (1992) has called 'the paradox of keeping-while-giving'. Some things cannot be given away, they are taboo. If everything were given in the gift, (or givable as a gift) then there would be no reason to continue to 'come back for more' (eventually the givable will become exhausted and things would stop). So part of the operation of the network, what makes it a network, is the anticipation or hope that something else might be offered in the next round of interactions. This provides the incentive to 'return' and a repeat interaction.

4.6. Goodwill, the Intangible, and Networks

But what are we 'giving for' and 'trusting about' in networks analysed by these means and through these terms? This is difficult to fully answer, but it would seem to have something to do with 'sharing' and 'good will'. Here it is not being suggested that gifting is non-rivalrous or non-competitive; it is very much both of these. But, such that it engenders any expectations on the parties involved these would be purely symbolically articulated, driven by an alternative logic of sharing and goodwill. These might sound clumsy and unrigorous terms, and it remains difficult to say exactly how they could be operationalized and rendered as such into a full account of any network operation.

Importantly, however, there is a clue as to how this might be approached since the category of 'goodwill' is already a well-established element in conventional financial accounting in that it constitutes one of the key components of the intangible assets of a firm. And the issue of intangible assets is threatening to become a central problem for those types of business activity that are often thought of in terms of network forms of organization, namely the so-called 'new-economy' ICT-based business models. This is treated more fully in Chapter 7, but here it will be useful to reflect upon goodwill as an intangible asset in the context of networked, new-economy type business activity and its accountability.

If goodwill is a key consequence of trust (as conventionally understood), then how should such goodwill be valued? Indeed, can it be valued in any sensible manner? The valuation of intangible assets has become an important focus for conventional economic analysis and accounting in the wake of the 'new-economy' boom. In part the issues revolve around how to properly measure the 'missing productivity' associated with new-economy type activity. The economist Robert Solow once rather famously remarked that: 'you can see the computer age everywhere but in the productivity statistics' (Solow 1987, p. 36), which drives home a point about the apparent absence of productivity growth associated with the advent of computers and ICTs. A response has been to press for the inclusion of intangible assets in the traditional 'growth accounting framework' used to analyse productivity changes in the economy (Yang and Brynjolfsson 2001). But this raises the difficult issue of exactly how to measure the value of such assets. One way to do this is to 'impute' the value of these as the difference between the book value of a companies assets (mainly made up of tangible assets) and its value on the stock exchange (which includes intangible 'e-capital' amongst other things—Hall 2000; Brynjolfson *et al.* 2001). However, this raises a potential circular argument. Should not stock market valuation logically be based upon some prior valuation of a company's total assets rather than used to value those assets? (see Blair and Wallman 2001). What the imputation approach does is try to preserve the 'efficient financial market' hypothesis. The stock market knows best; it knows more than individual accountants or managers and cannot be wrong in its valuations (in the long term). However, in the wake of the new-economy boom and collapse, and what is known more generally about financial bandwagons, bubbles and manias, this approach seems heroic to say the least. And the experience of the collapse of the telecoms boom in 2002 just goes to confirm this point. Thus, the conundrum of intangible asset valuation is hardly solved by this approach.

This, then, represents an example of the ambiguity built into the way the properties of 'networks' have been analysed in this chapter: the tension between a desire for a calculativeness of 'utility' on the one hand, combined with an approach that denies the possibility of utility calculation on the other. These issues can be summed for intangible asset valuation in relation to Fig. 4.1.

Tangible assets	Intangible assets
Liquid assets • Cash • Trade credit • etc.	Market access assets • Goodwill • Customer base • 'Quality' • ....?..........
Fixed assets • Structures • Machines • etc.	Knowledge assets • Managerial know-how and organizational assets • 'Firm specific' human capital • Business process redesign • ....?..........

← 'Shrinking' in the new-economy   'Expanding' in the new-economy →

Fig. 4.1. Network type business organizations balance sheet: the problem of asset valuation

On the left-hand side of the figure we have the usual company tangible assets divided conventionally into liquid and fixed assets. But this aspect of company assets is shrinking with the emergence of new-economy network type business, and such assets are themselves becoming difficult to value in the usual manner for these types of firms. What is expanding in the e-economy (and by implication for new network organizational arrangements in particular), are intangible assets given on the right-hand side of the figure. And these are even more difficult to independently 'value'. As can be seen from this side of the figure, these assets include a rather disparate and potentially ephemeral set of elements. Indeed, it is not altogether clear quite what should be included under the heading 'intangible assets' (items like convenience, customer service, and variety could easily be added). But a lot of these would seem to classically depend upon the operation of 'trust' as conventionally understood and discussed above.

Whatever one makes of this, however, it is these intangible assets that are growing in importance if an e-network type of economic mechanism is upon us. What this discussion has illustrated is the difficulty of dealing with the valuation of this in the context of 'networks' conceived as straddling the ambiguous domain between calculativeness and non-calculativeness. Indeed, the suggestion is that it is just the ambiguity expressed by this duality that gives rise to the problems of valuation highlighted. It illustrates one of the real problems of dealing with a pure sign money, one where there is no necessary representational relationship to a domain of 'real values'. Indeed, such a sign money constructs those very values in and of itself, which is what is signalled by the 'problem' of intangible asset valuation alluded to here.

4.7. Conclusion

This chapter has brought together a rather heterogeneous set of literatures and concerns that are not often considered together. The aim has been to test a kind of hypothesis; can we construct a radically different logic that might serve to articulate network forms of organization in clear distinction to that of either market or hierarchy? In doing this we have introduced what might be considered to be some rather unusual, even strange, formulations and juxtapositions. But this 'assemblage' was necessary to explore the hypothesis as set out.

However, has this been successful? Here one should probably remain sceptical and ambivalent. The key issue discussed in the chapter was whether the 'gift' could be reconceptualized so as to, (a) become detached from a conventional exchange relationship, and (b) form the centrepiece of a network operation. In this the chapter has been only partially successful. The economy of excess approach allows for a radical non-calculative space to be opened up for the gift and trust relations but it has been found difficult to sustain the full implications of this formulation. In particular, a number of features of networks that seem both desirable and central to their operation, like some form of deferral, strategic activity, goodwill, etc., all seem to require the re-imposition of a rather more conventional analytical and calculative stance. And this is reinforced by the difficulty experienced in valuing intangible assets around the notion of sign money.

However, there is probably enough unconventional analytical results that survive here to carry the radical approach to networks forward, something the second part of this book responds to. If the above analysis has any merit it points to the unique manner in which networks could operate. In the chapters that follow it is shown how networks are organized according to a particular set of norms and conventions. Convention theory stresses the key role of institutions in the conduct of economic life. And the notion of institutions is drawn very widely here; they are not just 'organizations' but involved the habits, norms, rules, routines, and so on, that constitute the conventions by which daily economic activity is conducted. This is explicitly taken up in Chapter 5.

What, then are the implications of this form of analysis for accountability in the context of networks? Clearly, it is the meaning and significance of the 'account' and accountability that will be most affected. Network organizations are required to produce an account like any other, if nothing else than to properly track cost centre expenditures and provide a public statement of their stewardship. But in so far as networks are also articulated by a different set of conventions and logics than are either markets or hierarchies, so they need their own particular accounting conventions as well. A 'gifting network' might work to encourage accessibility, compatibility, and flexibility in the conduct of economic relationships. It is with respect to 'accounting for trust' that the chapter has suggested this new set of conventions and meanings could be located. Quite how this will look in a practical sense has only been hinted at above. To provide some concrete illustration of this is the task set for the rest of the book.

But to finally sum up on this chapter, we might say that a network logic operates on the 'edge' of the reciprocated gift and the non-reciprocated gift. Any deferred return embodied in the gift of an economy of utilities obligates one individual to another and therefore creates a social debt between them, while a non-reciprocated gift of the economy of excess secures its social bond in an unrecognized and unrealized form by the slight of hand of the counterfeit and disguised engagement with the place of the 'beyond'.

Part 2

Applications and Empirical Comparisons

Part 2

Applications and
Empirical Comparisons

Chapter 5

Industrial Organization as Networks

5.1. Introduction

This chapter concentrates upon industrial organization. It looks at how the network model has been deployed in the specification and analysis of the relationships between firms and other agents that occupy the microeconomic field of economic organization. In the discussion of networks this aspect of their operation has been strongly emphasized and there is a vast literature that deals with the many features that characterize these relationships. However, it is not the intention in this chapter to provide another survey of this literature, other than to briefly introduce the main contours of that discussion in Section 5.2.

Rather, what is offered is, first, a commentary on some of the more interesting and challenging aspects for our understanding of how networks operate in this specific environment. Second, the discussion is directed at outlining what are argued to be the strengths of networks as opposed to other coordinating mechanisms, like market and hierarchy, in organizing inter-firm relationships. Third, for the most part, the chapter deals with theoretically informed issues. There is not a long catalogue of the empirical material on various forms of networks or the extent of networks in this area, though there are many references to instances where actual networks have been analysed to support the claims being made in the investigations referred to.

If it can be argued that network coordination represents a different and defensible model of coordination to either that of the market or hierarchy then both the nature of industrial organization and public policy directed towards industrial organization could be recast in the context of the growth of network forms of activity. Decentralized local industrial clusters and partnerships, quasi-public/private organizational forms, and 'unbundled' multidimensional firms and production plants would inhabit this particular economic universe. The previous chapters have outlined the nature of a logic that could claim to articulate such industrial organizational forms by designating the concepts of cooperation, solidarity, trust, and loyalty as a generalized set of 'network attributes' marking out the nature of a 'network order'.[1] In addition, in an attempt to more firmly ground this distinction theoretically, the notion of the 'non-reciprocated gift' was advanced in Chapter 4 as a way of overcoming the problem of conceiving all economic relationships in terms of an exchange. Of course, these considerations would provide a somewhat different theoretical grounding for industrial organization than that advanced by either hierarchical or market forms of organization. It is the consequences of this different theoretical grounding that we pursue further in this chapter.

As has already been argued, there are very real difficulties working with a single logic to try to understand all coordination problems. In the case of industrial organization this is something that the transaction cost framework in particular presses upon any analysis to accept. It is very tempting, for instance, to cast interorganizational networks in a transaction cost framework—to see the trust they are

---

[1] In Chapter 2, it may be recalled, altruism and reciprocity were also added as possible network attributes. Here I concentrate upon the four just mentioned since the subsequent analysis questioned the appropriateness of altruism and particularly reciprocity as genuine network attributes.

argued to embody, for example, as simply a response to potential opportunism (e.g. Gambetta 1988*a*; Bromiley and Cummings 1989)—but this temptation can and should be resisted. Thus, the general point outlined in Chapter 3 was to challenge the seeming ubiquity of the transaction cost framework for analysing all organizational situations, in both intra- and interorganizational settings.

Clearly, the above points also raise issues in the context of the contract theory approach to organizational coordination, one that brings together the transactions cost framework with agency theory. For transaction cost analysis (TCA) it is the properties of the transaction that determine the efficient governance structure. Agency theory is concerned with the question of how to align principal and agent interests. Both appeal to the notion of contracts as a solution to the twin problems of governance structure and interest alignment. Thus the firm, for instance, could be described as just a function of internal and external contracts (Reve 1990), where such a 'nexus of treaties' acts akin to a network.

The problem with such a contract approach is, however, precisely that which the network form of governance outlined earlier in this book is designed to address, that is, how organizational activity works that *cannot* be fully inscribed in—or proscribed by—formal contracts. It is well known, for instance, that all complex contracts are unavoidably incomplete. And without some other mechanism in the form of *credibility commitments*, contracts-as-promises are unsupportable. Thus, a first question becomes what is the basis for those behavioural responses that make up the credibility commitments typifying the coordination through networks as opposed to other coordination mechanisms? These we termed the 'network attributes', analysed in earlier chapters of this book.

But a major set of issues with the way this discussion was set up in Chapter 2 is that it attaches a certain set of attributes solely to one or other of the modes of coordination. In particular, the network order is considered to be articulated by the behavioural attributes of networks just mentioned: namely solidarity, loyalty, cooperation, trust, etc. But how far is this sustainable? Are not these also characteristics of hierarchies and markets as well, at least to some extent? And if not, all of them are typical features of these other coordinative mechanisms at least some will figure there strongly as their operational characteristics.

However, as we have seen, there are as many if not more problems with running all the coordinative mechanisms together into a single overarching conceptual 'networking structure' that is argued to characterize the entire socio-economic domain or capture all its salient organizational features. Thus, we are analytically caught in a bind it would seem. On the one hand not wanting to reduce all coordinative or governance activity to a single form or analytical logic, yet on the other hand accepting that the complex nature of organizational existence does not easily lend itself to identifying particular and unique attributes for any single coordinative mechanism alone. This was the dilemma alluded to and focused on in Chapter 4.

This chapter takes up many of these issues again, this time around the nature of economic organizational structures. The idea is to tease out what might be an added series of features and characteristics of networks specifically in the context of intra- and interorganizational relationships. In the main part, this will concentrate on interorganizational formations since these have been the ones to which most attention has been directed in respect to industrial networks. In part, this will raise again issues about loyalty and trust since these are often argued to be the main attributes of networks (as well as of markets) in respect to interorganizational relations.

5.2. A New Network Industrial System?
Cooperation, Trust, and Firm Organization

This section examines the long-term relationships between main firms and their subcontractors and suppliers, which are often characterized in network terms. The relationships here tend to be informal and cooperative in nature, relying on a trust between the main firm and its suppliers. They are neither straightforwardly hierarchically organized via orders and administrative edict, nor strictly straightforward market relationship where the main firm continually searches for the least-cost supplier and only maintains a short-term arm's length 'buyer/seller' relationship with its suppliers. The stimulus for this change comes from technological developments and the need to increase flexibility by the client firms. Such developments, it is often suggested, are leading to the disintegration of the vertically hierarchical character of firms as more and more of the production of manufactured parts needed for in-house assembly are located in subcontracting firms. This saves the main firms from investing in specialist machinery that they might not have been able to make full use of. The main firms often keep the design function in-house, however, using the subcontracting firms to produce to their specific plans (though increasingly, even design functions are being decentralized and subcontracted out amongst the network participants— see Helper *et al.* 2000, and below).

In the conventional story, to overcome the possibility of opportunism trust between the companies is needed. In addition, and to create this trust at least in part, both the subcontracting and the client firms seek to diversify their client base in order to reduce the risk of dependency on any single main firm. All manner of mechanisms operate to secure the idea of a 'partnership' between the firms; mutual dependency and adaptation, discussion and negotiation, honesty, long-term commitments, quality control, benchmarking, common knowledge shared between them, etc. Two very important aspects of this are the flows of *knowledge* or *information* that the network encourages (and not just an exchange of information about prices), and the flows of *personnel* between the client and subcontracting firms, involving the mutual training in the production practices of each of the firms. This reinforces the point that where it was a lack of communication between the parties this can easily threaten to undermine the fragile level of cooperation established. Cooperative networks thrive on communication and information flows between their members. And these new systems seem to work because they are the most *efficient* way of organizing the production of the particular range of products involved. The relationships will be more efficient in providing satisfactory outcomes than those typifying either the vertically or horizontally integrated firm. They may also be more profitable in the long run for all the elements concerned, though again, this is in no way guaranteed.

Applications and Empirical Comparisons

But according to the Anglo-American pioneers of this kind of analysis, such as Hirst, Piore, Sabel and Zeitlin, these examples are not unique (e.g. Piore and Sabel 1984; Hirst and Zeitlin 1989, 1991). These authors argued that the changes just outlined are the tip of a major transformation in the organization of production that promises to engulf much of the advanced industrial economies. They argue that we have experienced a systemic transformation in the way industrial production is being organized. This is summed up under the terms 'mass production versus flexible specialization'. Much of mass production process technology has given way to a flexibly specialized process technology and business strategy.

Flexible specialization involves the production of small batch outputs. It is niche-orientated and 'fashion' driven. It implies non-standardized and specialist demand from consumers. It calls for short production runs, requiring flexible machinery and a highly skilled and flexible labour force. Increasingly it is being undertaken in small to medium sized plants. As a result it can lead to the disintegration of the vertically integrated company and the refocusing of the horizontally diversified company. The most appropriate mechanism linking the kinds of firms that will produce most efficiently in this kind of an environment can best be described as the network type structure. Often this type of production takes place in highly integrated 'industrial districts' which in some cases eventually expanded to become new regional economies, it is argued.

Johnson and Lawrence (1988) describe these developments as the generation of 'value adding partnerships' (see also Chapter 7), seen as a network of interdependent and mutually supportive elements neither formally hierarchically organized nor simply articulated by price relationships. The need for greater flexibility is recognized as central to the reasons for the development of the extended partnership idea. New flexible technologies are seen as an important adjunct to, but not as the sole reason for, the changes in the production processes just described. Along with these changes goes a redefinition of the management problem and its outlook. But there is no single unambiguous 'model' that guarantees success for such a trust forming and securing mechanism.

One additional point that should be noted from these examples is the way market type relationships, although not formally the object of the analyses, still remain at least partly present within the explanations of how these examples of networks operate. Thus we are dealing with an overlapping area when looking at these economic activities. Network and market relationships *coexist* (along with hierarchical ones), though it is the network type relationships that are highlighted as potentially the most important and the ones that impart the other coexisting relationships with their particular specificity.

The above analysis concentrated on the nature of the relationships *between* firms in the newly evolving production environment. But it also involved some implications for how we might view the nature of the firm itself. We have already mentioned the case of vertical (dis)integration in the above discussion. According to Williamson's well-known theory about vertical integration, it developed (in a period of mass-production) to reap the scale economies to be had as transactions costs were eliminated with the successive integration of more and more production activity within the (expanding) boundaries of the master firm (Chapter 3). The 'external costs' of market transactions were thereby eliminated as these were 'internalized' under an increasingly hierarchical and bureaucratic coordinating mechanism. With the break up of mass-production, however, this process could be in reverse. But will it result in an increasing resort to purely market transactions?

Those committed to the idea of a new era of network firms think not. For instance, Sabel (1989) has suggested that one of the new organizational forms developing in the wake of the true mass production firm could be termed a 'quasi-disintegrated firm'. This acts as a systems integrator and specialization consortia within a collaborative manufacturing environment. Sabel's early examples of this were taken from the reorganized European car manufacturing companies, particularly BMW, Fiat, and Volkswagen (Sabel *et al.* 1990). A quasi-vertically disintegrated firm is one where an increasing range of part product processes are 'externalized' from the main firm, and located either in their own affiliated organizations or within separated supplier firms. The main firm may keep some of the overall design and R & D functions, but as mentioned above even these are increasingly being located in those organizational units with responsibility for the production of their own discrete part of the overall manufacture. In this way the functions of conception *and* execution are being re-merged in the variable (sub)units. These subunits are also taking on more of the production process proper, with their own flexible process technologies. The main firm is thus able to hedge its technological bets under this kind of an arrangement for fear of getting burdened with a technology that quickly becomes outdated or redundant.

Under this kind of an arrangement the main firm must reorganize to cope with a 'snap-on' goods type production process, as the output elements from the related firms appear and are finally assembled. It also begins to appear as little more than an organizing, and possibly financial, centre for the extended network of suppliers and subcontractors. It becomes the systems integrator, organizing the specialist consortia of subunits over which it has no direct control. But the manufacturing system becomes *collaborative* under these conditions. None of its elements can afford to completely go their own way, yet nor do they want to become totally dependent upon one single dominant firm. Thus, increased trust and cooperation can be fostered by this kind of arrangement. The way this type of system operates is close to an 'internal network'. Indeed Sabel suggests it becomes difficult to specify a clear dividing line between where one firm ends and another one begins. There is no clear boundary around the firm; no internal network to pitch against an external one. It becomes like a continual loop with a twist in it, so that what is at one time the 'outside' is at another the 'inside' of the network. This has been designated the 'mobius-strip' firm, with no clear demarcation between its 'inside' and its 'outside' (or what may at one time or one place appear to be 'outside' at another appears to be 'inside').

Many of the attributes of networks operate and thrive in this kind of an environment. The relationships between the subunits is too delicate to leave completely to market type arrangements, with their constant search for new cheaper suppliers or the ruthless attempt to reduce existing supplier output costs, it is suggested. In any case a long-term collaborative relationship needs to be forged, in which there is a constant exchange of ideas and personnel, requiring trust and loyalty *as well as competition*. The constant search for better process and product technologies forges a new common interest, one shared by all the members of the consortia. But it does not mean that a healthy rivalry between them is absent. It just means that competition is redefined—it is not necessarily strict market competition. Indeed this approach implicates a necessary balance between competition and cooperation for industrial success.

Given this broad-bush description of the main themes of the chapter in how it approaches network types of organizational structures conceived in an industrial setting, the rest of the chapter takes a series of key elements in the picture it paints and analyses them separately. These issues are as follows: the role of knowledge; the question of what 'self-organization' means; the role of 'complexity' and the evolution of networks (as opposed to their deliberate organization); the relationship between flexibility and diversification or variety; the characteristics of strategic alliances and corporate interlocks; and finally the nature of embeddedness and strong and weak ties.

5.3. Knowledge and Innovation in Networks

Industrial networks are argued to pre-eminently involve the creation and circulation of *knowledges*. Indeed, some have argued that this is the main rationale of these kinds of networks so that, for instance, the industrial districts of loosely integrative firms outlined above are little more than 'knowledge economies' or can be characterized as 'intelligent regions' (Cooke and Morgan 1998). In particular, networks in this regard have been argued to enhance the *innovative capacity* of the systems they engender; they encourage technological advance in a way that neither hierarchical or strictly market arrangements can. This has two main aspects. First it is viewed in the context of the role of 'institutions'—conceived as configurative arrangements of norms, routines, and habits that impart certain types of behavioural capacities to the agents involved in, or making up, these networked institutional spaces. Second, it is considered in terms of broad 'systems of innovation' or 'technological systems' traditionally viewed as functioning in a national context, but which are increasingly being reconsidered in an international environment (Leoncini and Montresor 2000). In the next sections, we treat these two aspects in an interlinked fashion. Given the vast literature on both issues this discussion picks out a few key points, developing themes already outlined in the previous main section. In addition, a good deal of the fuller discussion of these matters appears in Chapter 7, concentrating there on the international inflection of knowledge networks. That chapter also tackles the role of ICTs in connection to networks. Here we deal with the more formal aspects of knowledge in the first instance, and one pitched very much in a national context.

5.4. Networks as Institutions

In this section, the argument begins by analysing knowledge networks as an organizational form that displays many of the characteristics of 'institutions'. These characteristics are outlined in a moment. It then goes on to criticize this by taking up issues of dynamic change as posed in the context of these institutional mechanisms.

But first, what is meant by the term 'institution'? This has a number of features.

1. A set of rules and constraints that shape human action through inducing a particular pattern of human behaviour; an order of appropriate activities, clustered around procedures for their maintenance in the face of threats from self-interest and from exit and entry pressures that might modify them. Such constraints take the form of formal written rules and codes of conduct, which may be transformed by negotiation or political action and may represent a framework within which human interaction takes place.
2. They constitute and legitimize participant agents and political actors and provide them with consistent behavioural rules,

conceptions of reality and standards of assessment and the basis for purposeful action.

3. The role of institutions, then, is to reduce uncertainty by establishing a stable structure of human interaction by limiting the menus of action given to agents. They stabilize the environment for action.

4. Given an environment, they perform the function of shaping the visions of the world. They shape the interactions of networks and behavioural patterns and help establish the identity of agents.

5. But they also change with the evolution of the environment in which they exist, since they are forms of human action. They co-evolve with the external environment through internal adaptation and endogenous dynamic change.

6. Thus, institutionalism denotes a process of attaining a patterned social order by deliberate coordinated action and governance.

Clearly there are many types of knowledge that could be dealt with in this institutional context. These are usually divided into two broad categories, however; codified knowledge and tacit knowledge.[2] *Codified knowledge* bundles up somewhat different phenomena; (a) scientific knowledges, that is, theoretically grounded and publicly reproducible knowledge used to transform material and social processes; (b) knowledge defined as intellectual property such as patents, copyrights, trademarks, licences, scores and scripts, etc.; and (c) routinized knowledge, sometimes designated as 'information' or 'data' that can be gathered, aggregated, marketed, and disseminated by various means and through various institutional routes. The other kind of knowledge, *tacit knowledge*, is that which cannot be explicitly codified but which rests very much in implicit personal or institutional practices often associated with craft like skills, awareness of reputations, hands on techniques, etc. (Ancori *et al.* 2000; Cowan *et al.* 2000). Thus, tacit knowledge cannot be

---

[2] This distinction between codified and tacit knowledge was first introduced by Polanyi (1967). For the purposes of this chapter a code is defined as a structured symbolic representation of something that can be processed and communicated according to some instruction.

written down or copied. So a further difference between these is that the first type is easily transmissible to others while the second is not.[3]

Both of these broad types of knowledge are thought to be particularly amenable to networking type operations, particularly tacit knowledge. Although some of the results of knowledge production can be readily marketed, the market mechanism as such is ill-suited to maximize productive outputs because of the 'public good' nature of knowledge (to maximize the production and use of knowledge requires non-excludability, non-rivalry and transparency, features the market is not always best at providing). And hierarchy is thought to be too inflexible to readily adapt and accommodate to the fast pace of technical advance that characterizes knowledge-based industries.

However, communication networks should be distinguished from social networks in this respect. Communication networks are better at dealing with routinized knowledge, and they can be important in respect to the dissemination of scientific knowledge. The Internet is the classic contemporary example of a communication network, whose connection to social networks is analysed in great detail in the Chapter 7. On the other hand, social networks are

---

[3] It should be noted that for ANT theorists considered in Chapter 3 this distinction is meaningless. Tacit knowledge cannot be disassociated from codified knowledge. This is because scientific knowledge cannot of itself be diffused or systematically transferred. It rests in definite actor-network structures of research which only *replicate* scientific knowledge through these structures, involving combinations of laboratories and instruments (Latour 1987). For Latour scientific knowledge is always in the making, reality is only that which resists, a trial that is continually being resisted. It cannot 'harden' except in dramatic, fleeting moments of sudden challenge and controversy, struggle and trials of strength. But such experimental trials do not produce or reproduce the same result—another trial constructs another reality relation and another reality. Trials must be followed by more trials.

In a similar vein, Allen (2002) has proposed the undermining of the dual notions of explicit and tacit knowledge with an appeal to, first, a Foucauldian notion of power/knowledge to highlight the always combined nature of these knowledges as located in definite but different institutional practices, and then the symbolics of knowledge set within an entanglement of abstractions, expressions, significations, and representational registers. Knowledge, here, is an effect of these assemblages, where the tacit/explicit distinction dissolves. However, it is unclear whether this dispenses with the distinction rather than just redefines it or reinterprets it in another language. Also, one must be careful in finally overemphasizing the 'symbolic' moment in knowledge production as against its organizational determinants.

best at dealing with tacit knowledge. Tacit knowledge depends upon being 'in place' in the network. Given networks thrive on closely connected relationship between agents, tacit knowledge can be learned and passed on to others. But it clearly favours insiders at the expense of outsiders.

This issue of the relationship between insiders and outsiders is important for the general functioning and health of network forms of coordination and governance, as has been stressed in other chapters (e.g. Chapters 3, 6–8). It poses the problems of trust, effective participation, free riding, and compliance. Networks by their very nature are exclusive communities—you are either in them or outside of them. If the objective is to avoid a closure, which would seem essential from the point of view of the production of new knowledge, then mechanisms to prevent stagnation as the insiders monopolize the network and use it to their advantage against the outsiders would seem essential. This is where mechanisms to encourage effective negotiated governance between partners, self monitoring of their activities, learning by doing amongst members, and the permit of new entrants become crucial. Without these features knowledge based networks will not perform better than either the market of hierarchy, and activities will tend to favour the already known over the new. The implication is that knowledge networks need to be strongly governed by these mechanisms. Weak governance will lead to disorder, undesirable social costs and a lack of dynamic innovation. Weak governance undermines strong coordination (see Chapters 2, 6, and 7, and below).

These problems are particularly acute when it comes to the non-transmissible tacit knowledge, since these are by their very nature less amenable to effective coordination and governance. Indeed, if these types of knowledge are genuinely un-codifiable and non-transmissible then it is difficult to see how any form of effective coordination or governance could emerge. If such knowledges are so tacit that they are uncommunicable then they are completely private and secret. They are not amenable to any form of 'public' governance, and one suspects a network involving them could not operate under such conditions. Of course, at one level all knowledge is tacit in that it requires at least some 'hands on experience' to operationalize it. This is just as true of publicly available scientific knowledge (which needs to be interpreted, redeployed in a different environment or for a different purpose, etc.) as it is of knowledge about how to play a musical instrument (which is often put forward as an extreme example of the tacitness of learning and knowledge).[4]

As a response to this conundrum we need to introduce some conception of the way agents can actually communicate even if in the first instance they cannot (or do not wish to) completely understand one another. Sabel (2001) has termed such a pragmatic solution 'pidgin conversations'. This is a kind of half language, a colloquial dialogue within and across groups with proximate knowledge that makes intelligible differences between them even as they do not quite 'speak' the same language. Such pidgin conversations encourage deliberative self-reflection, reinterpretation and a re-examination of accepted ideas, so that new knowledges can emerge even within fields where deep tacit practices prevail.

This way of thinking about knowledge, and particularly tacit knowledge, clearly parts company with a tradition of thinking about these matters going under the heading of 'the economics of knowledge'. In the economic approach to knowledge, *knowledge* is treated as a form of *information*. Indeed, a clear distinction is not made between these two categories. So what is the difference between them?

Information is 'passive', 'static', and 'discrete'. It is something that already exists to be accessed and marshalled for a purpose. *Knowledge*, on the other hand, requires the application of a cognitive capacity, it demands an interpretation, an understanding, and a deployment or use. It is an active category. As information is a 'presence', knowledge is a 'process'. Knowledge increases understandings and meanings. It implies a labour of conceptualization and a theorization to generate it.[5] Thus, while information is 'captured',

---

[4] Of course, this abstracts from the notion of 'talent'—the intelligence, ability, and proclivity to make use of one's cognitive abilities.

[5] This distinction is different to that advanced by Cowan *et al*. (2000). For them information is ' . . . a message containing structured data, the receipt of which causes some action by the recipient agent—without implying that the nature of that action is determined solely and uniquely by the message itself. [. . .] The term "knowledge" is simply the label affixed to the state of the agent's entire cognitive

knowledge is 'produced'. In addition, knowledge is not discrete like information. It demands a connectivity, so it appears in the form of a loosely patterned structure (Boulding 1955).

Without this distinction knowledge is treated as information, and both are viewed as very much like any other economic good (Ancori *et al.* 2000). There is a given quantity of it that can be unearthed if only sufficient resources are devoted to this task. It has discernible and measurable characteristics. The generation of knowledge presents a similar problem as posed by the access to information. It is only constrained by the cost of finding it or producing it. If costs are too high, or too large relative to the benefits, then there is no incentive for agents to 'acquire' either information or knowledge.[6] Whilst this might work for the idea of information discussed above—there is a stock of it that needs accessing which costs money—it cannot work for knowledge where a calculation of its extent beforehand is impossible. In principle knowledge would seem to be infinitely expandable. Of course, to expand new knowledge does involve resources, and therefore its generation is constrained at any one time. But there would be a different main constraint on knowledge production, which has to do with the central cognitive (interpretative, conceptual) element in its make up.[7]

context' (p. 216). To my mind this distinction does not quite enable Cowan *et al.* to fully escape conflating information and knowledge into the typical economistic framework of a single 'good' that can be accumulated, distributed, appropriated, etc., that is, into something that necessarily implies an economic exchange. In addition, their approach places a central emphasis on institutional codification as a condition for knowledge production, thus it cannot escape the habits, norms, routines, etc., that such a codification implies. And the practice of codification itself takes on a cost–benefit aspect, so it is the supply and demand for codification that determines its 'price' and hence the 'cost' (and ultimately the 'benefits') of new knowledge. See the main text for a critique of this, though it is recognized that Cowan *et al.* do actually advance a sophisticated and nuanced position.

[6] An interesting reprise on the economistic analytical approach is provided by Kogut (1998) who suggests that the value-productivity of a firm is directly related to the quality of the knowledge embedded in the principles by which cooperation among firms is coordinated and supported in the extended networks of firms. In this case then the firm is a coordinator of knowledge rather than a processor of information.

[7] This plays on one of the paradoxes of the 'knowledge as information' conception; that knowledge/information is at one and the same time infinite but also scarce.

Thus, amongst other things, the economistic approach does not recognize that what flows between organizations, especially where industrial activity is concerned, is often tacit knowledge rather than simply 'information', and that such knowledge production is above all a cognitive act. Second, it fails to recognize that the key to organizational design is that it can generate different, new, or additional knowledges rather than just redistributing existing information between the parties involved.[8] Finally, it begs a central question about the differences between the logic of the market, of hierarchy and of other coordinating devices. They are not all on a par in terms of their logic of operation as coordination devices so that they cannot all be reduced to a question of the distribution of information or some other essential principle of their operation. However, if 'knowledge networks' are to do any real business in terms of constructing genuinely new knowledge, they must involve this different sense of what knowledge is and how the network itself encourages innovation through 'learning by monitoring' and 'pidgin conversations'.

5.5. Are Knowledge Networks Effective as Institutions?

The definition of institutional characteristics given above and the subsequent analysis of knowledge networks raises an issue as to whether these networks (indeed, any networks) can be adequately characterized as institutions, or adequately considered within the confines of an institution. Apart from codes the other key features of institutions in the knowledge network context are the habits, routines, conventions and norms of the network (Lazaric 2000).

---

[8] This is akin to what Ancori *et al.* (2000) term a complex transformation/ transmission problem. Knowledge for them is a kind of transformation mechanism; first as information is transformed into knowledge via the codification mechanism, then as it is transferred between individuals, then as between individuals and the organization and vice versa, then as appearing as a form of commodification. The capacity of the organization, the individual, and the system to assimilate knowledge depends upon the interplay of epistemic social constructionism and concrete contextualized organizational settings. As a result, knowledge cannot be considered independently of the process through which it is obtained (pp. 218–19).

Habits arise as a result of the bounded rationality and a lack of full attentiveness to all potential situations. The expedient of habit means complex tasks can be rendered simpler. Crucial elements of the situation can be taken for granted. Problems are 'automatically' broken down into parts small enough to be cognitively grasped and posed as separate solutions, then made amenable to aggregation so as to comprehensively manage the overall original situation. *Routines* give these habits an organizational existence. Routines ' . . . establish connections between the parts and simultaneously place limits on the operation of each part as necessary to maintain the integrity of the whole. Thereby they limit the possibilities of self-dealing that specialization affords.' (Helper *et al.* 2000, p. 462). Conventions and norms complete this picture of a patterned social order. *Conventions* are the generally accepted informal rules or frames of reference that order behaviour between agents, while *norms* provide a means for standardizing and benchmarking differences so as to provide a metric of comparison and evaluation between agents.[9]

The questions raised by this list, and the previous discussion of codes, are that they tend to emphasize the known over the unknown. They are about how things are done now rather than how they might be done differently in the future. Thus, there is the danger of building an organizational inertia into such a system. Existing practices become 'institutionalized' in the negative sense of that term. In addition, this discussion raises issues about 'path dependency'— the way present configurations of activity have been locked into an institutionalized pattern inherited from the past. Once a technological pathway is established, for instance, it becomes difficult to escape its limiting and routinized possibilities, which inhibit further adaptation and innovation. A process of cognitive and organizational self-entrapment ensues.

[9] We might add *rules* to this list of institutional attributes as the *formal* limiting mechanisms by which repetitive action is organized, and *custom* as a socially and collectively sanctioned action pattern that secures acceptable behaviour. But these two features are more the prerogative of a wider social action rather than particular to institutional action as concentrated on here. In addition norms are also often spoken about as the socially sanctioned acceptability standards for general behaviour.

Applications and Empirical Comparisons

Both of these concerns mean that institutionalized patterns of behaviour organized around codes, routines, norms, habits, rules and custom create severe problems of adaptation to changing circumstances. They could almost guarantee organizational failure rather than success. This comes about, then, when a strict interpretation of the protocols of institutionalization is adhered to. To place 'knowledge networks' just in the context of an institutional analysis could simply serve to undermine the very rationale for those networks.[10]

Clearly, the way to get round this problem is the one developed in the analysis above—to allow 'history to erupt' to break through the confines of a strictly narrow institutionalist view of knowledge production (or more accurately, its potential non-production). This means that, at best, the domain of institutions needs to be expanded to allow for this dynamic to partly undermine its effects while at the same time preserving the benefits of characterizing knowledge in institutional terms. Quite how, and to what extent, the ordering effects of the 'institutional complex' can be cast aside in a rush to allow the free flow of experimental openness is something examined in the following sections (see also Chapters 3 and 8 where these issues are posed in slightly different terms in connection to ANT and post-ANT developments).

Finally, in this discussion of knowledge and networks it is important to recognize that not all networks dealing with knowledge are actually involved with the production of new knowledge and innovatory activity. Indeed, even those networks that are discussed explicitly in the context of innovation and new knowledge may also be doing something else. These networks also *divide* (Riles 2001). They divide both spatially and legally; spatially in the sense that some of those in the network will have full access to the knowledge so produced, and some will not, depending where they are in the network; legally in the sense that questions of ownership (patents,

---

[10] This potential downside to institutionalized networks is often recognized but seldom posed analytically. See for instance, in a completely different context, the way the World Bank has adopted the terminology of 'Norms and Networks' as an informal aid to development in its *2002 World Development Report* (World Bank 2002, ch. 9). But this is firmly celebratory and does not recognize the dangers associated with norms and networks as just outlined here.

licences, copyrights, etc.) over outputs and products are also acutely posed. The study of how actual networks operate indicates that these 'inequalities' in networks are inevitable. Variation in the pattern of technological specialization and learning of firms in the network depend upon their different positions within it (Shachar and Zuscovitch 1990). Whatever arrangements there are to cooperate and collectively share outputs it is impossible for some not to be advantaged, or to take better advantage, than others.

The overall burden of this discussion of 'networks of knowledge production' has been to consolidate the idea that knowledge is not simply an exchange. If the analysis is to advance much from a crude information-is-knowledge position there is a need to recognize that all manner of non-reciprocal gifting is involved in these networks, as suggested in a more abstract context in Chapter 4.

5.6. Evolution, Biology, Complexity, and the Self-Organization of Networks

The above discussion of the way knowledge is generated in industrial networks relates directly to how networks are often considered in terms of evolutionary or biological theories of organization. Evolutionary and biological approaches to networks are usually based upon three principles. The first takes the notion of 'routines' considered above as analogous to the 'genes' of the network. These provide the heredity of the organization; the repetitive activities of routines guaranteeing coherence between individual and collective behaviour, and allowing a certain predictability in outcomes. The second principle is that of 'mutation', which involves the generation of diversity as searching behaviours explore and test new routines. This is the capacity of the network to generate new knowledge, characterized as 'collaborative learning by monitoring' and 'pidgin conversations' in the above discussion. The third principle would be that of 'selection'; a process by which routines and mutations are picked and shaped by cognitive interventions and the dealings with interpretative ambiguity (imitation, benchmarking, joint problem solving and quality targeting, simultaneous design, shortcoming comparisons, etc.). The network then becomes a locus where competencies around these features are continuously built, managed, combined, tested, selected, nested, contested, etc., in an evolutionary process of creation and adaptation. Learning, then, is not seen in this context as just a process of adaptation but it also conditions future actions by shaping the environment through the results of its own activity.

In fact, this description is a little too simple. As is pointed out in a moment it collapses two somewhat different conceptions of the 'evolutionary economy'. And it further poses the question of how far this process can be considered as a self-organizing one as opposed to a consciously organized one? In previous chapters networks have been characterized in both these terms (e.g. Chapter 2 in particular). In fact they sit rather ambiguously, and some would argue uneasily, between the two. The reason for this has in large part to do with the level of abstraction at which the discussion is pitched and in part to do with exactly which analogy of the system one begins with. Two main analogies are discussed here: the 'Darwinian self-selection biological' analogy on the one hand and the 'evolutionary population ecology' analogy on the other (Foster 1997, 2000). Both of these claim to say something about how self-organization works, which is the focus here.

The Darwinian self-selection analogy is in some ways the more conventional of the two. It is 'biological' in origin, concerned with how competition between atomistic units (the 'genes' of the system, which may be 'selfish') produces evolutionary adaptation and change. This neatly fits with the *homo economicus* of traditional economic theory. Fitness (profit) is maximized while adverse mutations (inefficiencies) are minimized as competitive selection processes steer the system towards a potential, if only temporary, equilibrium with optimal properties. This process of competition can limit variety as the weak are eliminated and the strong and more efficient rewarded. As a result, homogeneity emerges and economic evolution would, at least temporarily, cease. Built into this process is a conception of equilibrium and disequilibrium. Sometimes this is modelled through the simulation and calibration mechanisms of non-linear dynamics (e.g. Etheridge and Sriram 1993). It lends itself neatly to the strategies of game theory and an evolutionary stable strategy of the Nash equilibrium type. This conception is akin to the working of a market system as outlined in Chapter 2.

Against this Foster wants to pitch his version of 'evolutionary population ecology'. This stresses the notion of mutualism (cooperative trade and contracting) over competition as the dynamic of the system. This does not rely on well-developed markets, but on a continual, spontaneous generation of novelty—the work of *homo creativus*, capturing the creative and adaptive aspects of human behaviour and thereby cutting any necessary 'biological' link between selection and variety. Novelty and variety generation become decisive, with competitive selection becoming *dependent* upon this primary aspect not its progenitor. It is not the market system that generates variety—that is, secured by the creativity, innovation, and entrepreneurialism shown by adaptive agents. Rather, the market system presents opportunities to *test out* variety and novelty. Selective competition follows varietization, not the other way around. There is no equilibrium or disequilibrium operating here, only non-equilibrium involving complex feedback loops that encourage the internalization of selection and adaptation.

This latter conception is what Foster calls genuine evolutionary self-organization. For him it is not an analogy like the biological model discussed previously but describes a real process of the transformation of materials, energy, and information; which are the historically enduring properties of all dissipative systems, he suggests. The 'spice of life' of this system, variety, is never fixed. Variety at the individual level leads to further variety as individuals form into cooperative organizations.[11] Thus we have the process of economic self-organization and the cumulative formation of organized complexity which—although originally couched in market terms in this formulation—lends itself nicely to being reconceived in network terms. And variety is *endogenously* created here, not the result of an encounter with an external environment as in the biological case.

---

[11] And these behaviours can generate a group dynamic that enhance the evolution of social norms in the direction of collective action solutions to common resource problems (see Ostrom 2000).

Indeed, this endogeneity is one of the defining features of *self*-organization. There is no arranged external stimulus. Such that order can be thought of here as it happens not because of selection but despite it, a function instead of the spontaneous propagation that is self-organization. The learning that is involved in these systems is not, then, equivalent to the classic systems–environment model, where the adaptation of the system to its environment is controlled externally and according to which the adaptation of the system occurs in the course of the learning process. Rather this is replaced by a *systemic closure*. This closure is operational in so far as the effects produced by the system are the reasons for the maintenance of systemic organization. *Where there is sufficient complexity, the system performs internal self-organization and exerts self-control.*[12] The information the system provides thereby on its environment is a system-internal construct. Any reference to an 'outside' is merely a special case of self-reference (Krohn *et al.* 1990, p. 7).

But there must be some 'energy' within the system that drives it. This is provided by the 'work' that the members of the network contribute, which is of two kinds. First there is strict 'internal' work; combining and recombining the existing configuration of elements and agents. But then there is another kind of work which involves the internalization of the 'external' agents and elements; suppliers, customers, partners, and new members. Only if there is a constant injection of the energy provided by these two interrelated means will the system/network thrive (be a 'dissipative structure'). In turn, this means that the recruitment of new energy—by motivating the internal stakeholders, by shaking up the organization, by providing new sets of challenges—becomes a key issue. Generally the more turbulent the internal environment, the more energy there is being produced and used up, and the more robust is the network. So the key to the recruitment of new energy from 'outside', as it were, is

[12] This conception is allied to (but is not the same as) chaos theory. Chaos emerges even when there is no change in the external environment. It is an internal property of the system where instability over time depends upon initial parameter values without the influence of outside factors. But, for network theories—in particular, in the case of ANT analysed in Chapter 3, there is a pattern (an actor-network) to be uncovered from seemingly chaotic systems. Chaos becomes a kind of order.

what is going on 'inside'. And that energy must be recognized and reconfigured internally (so as to preserve the endogenous character of genuine self-organization—though see below).

However, there are some thresholds—upper and lower boundaries—to the extent of this turmoil if the system/network is not to collapse. To establish order, there must be neither too many connections nor too few. Too few, and the network energy is low, so collapse threatens. But too many connections—at the limit full connectivity with every element connected to every other one—and the system becomes hopelessly unstable (Simon 1996). Instead what is needed is a system in which there are loosely coupled connections (a 'decompositional hierarchy') so that most components receive inputs from only a few of the system's/network's other components enabling change to be isolated into local neighbourhoods. This controls the rate of change and establishes an order in the network/system.

Clearly, stable states are thus delicately balanced. The more connections there are, that is, the greater the potential network energy, the more likely it is that the internal system will be thrown into turmoil. And there is a tendency for the system to gravitate towards maximum connectivity—towards the 'edge of chaos'—since this gives it the advantage of maximum energy. But if there are too many of these connections, when the system is perturbed, elements/agents will fly off from one 'attractor' to another, or create a new attractor (an attractor is a limited range of occupied network's state space). This accounts, then, for both the idea of change in these kinds of networks—they evolve as the system moves from one attractor to another creating new connections—and why the question of stability and order are the flip side of this evolution. The system is always delicately poised between stability and disorder. It can also theoretically account for Granovetter's 'the strength of loose ties' idea. Looser and less dense connections are a strength, necessary for stability and network robustness. This is discussed further below.

But, this also demonstrates one of the unsolved conundrums of the complexity/self-organizing principle of network organization pitched in these terms. The need for there to be some 'management' of the system to prevent it moving too closely to the 'edge of chaos' would seem to be both a necessary and a redundant feature of networks conceived in this manner. Systems 'automatically' evolve towards this point—a point where small and large avalanches of co-evolutionary change cascade—because this state gives them a selective advantage. Getting near here (but not past it!) provides a competitive advantage over those systems that do not reach it. At this point small changes in behaviour lead to widely different 'fitness levels'—peaking and tumbling to very low fitness levels. So, the key to organizational success is to learn how to manage this trend towards the edge of chaos; to stay near it but not to let things become truly chaotic; to find an intermediate region which maximizes system fitness by combining sustainable levels of flexibility and stability. Above this was discussed in the context of the idea of 'connectedness'. But if they are genuinely self-organizing then there would be no reason for this kind of managerial intervention. The fact that this is contemplated and a seeming reasonable requirement to prevent the 'descent into chaos' raises a genuine issue as to their self-organizing status. Admittedly, if left entirely to themselves these systems would, one suspects, eventually return from chaos, but at what cost and under what circumstances? The temptation to managerially intervene, in an attempt to avoid this cost, is clearly present, and indeed is the main way that this complexity/self-organizational discussion has entered the managerial and organizational literature (e.g. Anderson 1999).

5.7. Neural Networks

In the context of learning and knowledge there is another form that this self-organizational process takes in the literature, that of 'neural networks', where this problem may not be quite so acute. Neural networks are adaptive networks (neural nets) in which 'outputs' can be greater than the 'inputs'. They involve computer programmable algorithms under which information is accumulated in programmed objects or nodes that are capable of 'learning' through many iterations using simulated or real data (Johnson and Picton 1996; Garson 1998). Neural networks are so named because their initial formulation was inspired by analogies to the neural architecture of the human brain as applied to problems of cognition and learning. They still retain much of the terminological roots of their biological and cognitive beginnings, though their application is no longer confined to just these areas. They are called networks because their structure is conceived as linking a set of input nodes to nodes in a hidden middle layer (involving processing entities known as 'neurons') to nodes in an output layer. The multiple connections between input layers and output layers are weighted according to the strength of the connections, adjusted to store the preprogrammed experimental 'knowledge' and make it available for the analysis of new data inputs. The key to their ability to learn is that neural networks are systems capable of changing internal structure to reflect new input patterns, and they do this without any direct intervention to change the nature of their computational algorithms. They learn from examples by a process of 'back propagation', which redesignate the weights connecting the inputs to the hidden middle layer of neurons and then on to the output layer. This gives them their 'self-organizing' character.

But these systems do not offer anything obvious in terms of how industrial organization might function. At best they can only operate as a loose metaphor for the learning properties of network type organizational relationships. In addition they lack causal properties. Neural networks are useful as classificatory devices and can be used for predictive purposes but they do not tell investigators anything directly about what causes what in their (non-linear) input–output system. Thus the neural network metaphor is of limited usefulness for the purposes of the analysis of this book. It is better seen as a form of economic modelling or empirical testing procedure (see the papers in Anderson *et al.* 1998).

Finally, from this discussion, the capacity for self-organization (self-organizationalness) of networks might be best thought not so much through the traditional lens of specialization and tacitness, but through that of varietization and formalization. Too much specialization of functions by agents in networks reduces their capacity for pragmatic self-reflectiveness, and too greater taciticity increases the possibility of cognitive entrapment. On the other hand an emphasis on variety and diversity open up opportunities for agents, and formalization of otherwise tacit practices equally enables concurrent learning between parties, encouraging mutual innovation. This has important implications for the types of industrial districts mentioned in Section 5.2 of this chapter, and which are further analysed in Chapter 7. Traditionally the old 'craft based' industrial districts relied upon a specialization of functions for their competitive advantage (hence the emphasis on 'flexible specialization'). But the new districts need to emphasize 'pragmatic varietization' if they are to preserve their self-organizational flavour and retain their competitive advantage against the large oligopolistic and hierarchically organized international firm on the one hand, or if they are not to retreat before market forms of coordination on the other (see Chapter 7).

5.8. Complexity and Social Systems

All these considerations are sometimes brought under another conceptual umbrella, that of 'complexity'. Complexity is the general term used to refer to self-reinforcing dynamic systems with many feedback mechanisms. The non-linearity of complex systems means that small amounts of changes in inputs can have dramatic and unexpected effects on outputs. Formally, complexity is equated with the number of different items or elements that must be dealt with simultaneously by the organization (Anderson 1999). But its distinctive feature is to stress the world as a system in construction, a dynamic formulation encouraging the notion of continual process of spontaneous emergence (Thrift 1999). Multiple possible outcomes are typically associated with mathematically inscribed non-linear modelling techniques, a lot of the features of which were described above. Turbulence and uncertainty abound in this environment, often further described as 'open systems ecologies' where perpetual novelty results. Filling one niche simply provides new niches, and small perturbations can affect the future of multiple combinations of events, as discussed above. This is the image of a 'networked society' writ large in information and system terms.

Furthermore, this provided an opportunity to briefly look at another approach to self-organization that can connect to network operations even though it was not directly developed in that context. What it is connected to, however, are questions of governance and 'steering', and particularly self-governing systems. The social systems approach most closely associated with the names of Niklas Luhmann (1997) and Gunther Teubner (1993, 1996) is concerned with the macro societal level of social coordination and governance. They are particularly concerned to elaborate the problems associated with the governance and coordination of different social systems displaying different 'logics of observation'.[13] These systems may be economic, political, or legal systems, organizations and even individuals. Each of these systems orients itself according to its own distinctions, its own constructions of reality, its own observational codes. They constitute autonomous spheres of meaning, employing distinct and divergent codes and programmes in observing and handling events in their environment (they conform to what Teubner calls 'polycontextuality'—Teubner 1997, 2001a,b; Paterson and Teubner 1998). Thus economic systems, for instance, observe with economic distinctions in mind, such as what is, or can be, paid for, or what is profitable, or what is economically efficient, etc. Legal systems observe with the distinction of what is legal and what is illegal, what is prosecutable or not, what is actionable and what is not, etc. The political system observes with political distinctions in mind based upon the relation between government and opposition in regard to public opinion, that is, as between having and not having access to official power. Individual systems operate on moral and solidaristic distinctions, observing on the basis of what is good and what is bad, who has status and esteem and who has not, etc.

The problem for this approach is that no single governance centre can overcome these differences in observational logic and govern or steer from a single coherent position. This is because reactions to any 'external intervention' are only produced through the independent inner logics of the different systems, which are blind to external intentions. The constitutive differentiation of society into different

[13] This visual metaphor is a crucial one. Observational choice depends upon a position already occupied in a social system. It provides a perspective on phenomenon, on causes of events and crises, and on relationships within the system.

(sub)systems means that they all operate according to their own distinctions, thereby continually reproducing new differences. This means that the only steering possible is self-steering by the individual systems themselves, according to their inner logics. This self-governing process of systems is, however, subject to pressures for the 'reduction of differences' (cf. the discussion of homogenization and varietization above). But the differences to be reduced or minimized can be seen as differences only if they are continually observed and reproduced. This is guaranteed by the enclosed nature of the individual system's logics. Thus, any capacity for governance is limited to the possibility of influencing the conditions under which self-steering operates. But this is continually frustrated, even as it takes an indirect and abstract form of operating on the techniques of social self-regulation, self-learning and voluntary compliance embodied in the different systems. New perturbations, new differentiations, new irritations, new provocations, new unexpected events, continually arise (Teubner 2001a,b—see also Chapter 7). However, some limited coordination may be possible for a time as organizational co-evolution and mutual adaptation proceed through a framework of controlled self-control, self-learning, and supervised self-regulation, but very much as a consequence of rather contingent events which will, as a consequence, soon dissipate (Paterson and Teubner 1998). Clearly, it would be inviting to interpret both the internal logics of different social (sub)systems and the relationships between these systems (such that they are) in network terms, something this social system approach has not been slow to realize.

5.9. Interorganizational Technological Networks and Partnerships

It is the area of technology and innovation that the network form has strongly appeared in terms of interorganizational relationships. By all accounts the number of collaborative interorganizational networks (sometimes termed 'strategic alliances') has steadily grown since the 1980s. In fact, one of the features of these networks is that they are more interinstitutional in nature since they often involve more than just firms. Public research institutes, government departments, academic institutions, and individual researchers all participate with firms in these situations. Their main objective is to create and further the adoption of innovations.

This links to the idea of a 'knowledge based society', and all the issues associated with knowledge and information mentioned earlier. In particular a knowledge based society is one where the conception, creation, and utilization of knowledge are run together in a continuous interaction, rather than these stages being conceived as separate both chronologically and institutionally. It is here that the network form of organization is argued to come into its own, since it lends itself to this kind of continuous interaction more comfortably than do either market or hierarchical relationships. The argument is that in advanced knowledge based technological sectors like molecular biotechnology, software production, specialist information and communication technologies (ICT) providers, etc., small *dedicated firms*, linked into vertical and horizontal collaborative network chains and clusters, are best placed to capitalize on basic research and new scientific developments, and are best at translating these into industrial sectors. The traditional *diversified firm* on the other hand, linked into well established production areas like organic chemicals, petrochemicals, computers, pharmaceuticals etc., are not adept enough to pick up and run with the rapidly evolving trends in these new knowledge based fields.

But would this network type of operation be anything more than an intermediate and temporary form of organization? As the dedicated small firms continued their collaboration with the large diversified firm (LDF), this latter could construct a knowledge based and absorptive capacity of its own, aided by the public research institutions. The small dedicated firms, originally emerging to bridge the institutional gap between the LDF and the public research institution, would thus be squeezed, eventually disappear, and industrial organization would return to the basic dichotomy between market and hierarchy.

Of course, this is a long-term hypothesis, and one that it is probably too early to pronounce upon. But there seems no strong evidence that such a counter-trend is yet underway. Indeed, there are strong indications of the continual strength of the small networked firm in advanced technological sectors and other innovation based activities. Indeed, there is an incentive for the LDF not to undermine the benefits it gains from collaborating with the small-dedicated firms in a networking context. The alternative, for the large firms to invest heavily and irreversibly in the same field, represents a high-risk commitment on their part. Collaboration constitutes a more flexible and reversible strategy. The LDFs are better suited to continue to combine different competencies and complementary assets to produce final products. Thus, the likelihood is for the networking firms to continue in these areas, particularly where scientific and technological advance is rapid.

Technological and other partnerships can be of various kinds. As these are strategic alliances they are primarily designed to enhance the long-term competitive position of parties in terms of product performance rather than as just being cost cutting exercises. And they involve different combinations of coordination and governance. Arranged along the dimension of more to less organizational independence (loose to tight governance). Hagedoorn (1990) and Hagedoorn and Schakenraad (1990) provide the following taxonomy (drawn from the MERIT data bank on cooperative agreements).

First are joint ventures and specially set up research consortia that share R&D expenditures, usually for specific objectives or distinctive research programmes. These are popular and grew rapidly during the 1980s. They allow a high degree of organizational independence for the parties involved. Second, there are more specific research pacts covering agreements that regulate technological sharing and product development costs. These imply a stronger commitment of companies and a higher degree of organizational interdependence between them. Third are direct investments, usually taking the form of equity stakes in other companies. Taking a minority holding in small high-tech companies allows for some direct managerial involvement in partner companies without a complete absorption of those companies. This allows for all the advantages mentioned above in terms of avoiding risks associated with technological lock-ins while actively collaborating in leading edge technological developments. These organizational structures involve more direct forms of governance. Cross-licensing and mutual second-sourcing provide a fourth category where organizational independence is less and governance stronger. These agreements involve the swapping of technological information and transferring product technologies, the licensing of patented information/technology and the transfer of technical specifications. They are highly restrictive in terms of the detail of the technology involved but grant wider ranging opportunities for partners to exploit that technology as suits their purpose. A fifth category is that of customer–supplier relations. Here inter-firm cooperation takes the form of the leading firm organization of component supply and assembly production by secondary firms, the outsourcing of some component design and production tasks under lead-firm direction, and the establishment of co-marketing arrangements. Close contact regarding quality control, supply planning, benchmarking, etc., ensures process technological sharing and some strategic technological cooperation. Given the lead-firm/supplier/assembly–firm relationships, the level of organizational interdependence is small, governance being organized with a greater degree of centralization (see also Chapter 7 on supply chain management in an international context, Section 7.6). Finally, we have research contracts as a form of R&D cooperation where the lead firm contracts another party to perform a particular and discrete research task on its behalf in return for a fee. This is a case of little organizational independence in the inter-firm cooperation with almost complete closed governance.

5.10. Venture Capital and Networking

It is not only in the area of interorganizational production and technological relationships that networks are thought to thrive but also in respect to certain aspects of financial relations. This is particularly so in the case of venture capital that provides finance for small and medium sized start-up companies, often in the fast growing high-tech and commercial sectors. Venture capital is most strongly developed in the United States, where it has been important in stimulating the economic activity of Silicon Valley companies in California and 'Route 128' companies around Boston in Massachusetts (Zider 1998; Castilla *et al.* 2000). Venture capital does not play a central role in financing basic R & D type activity; that is left to large companies often working in cooperation with the public funded agencies. Rather, venture capital is short-term money designed to bridge the gap between the results of R & D and the full market launch of products and companies. Venture capitalist firms—often referred to as 'funds'—operate as a kind of intermediary between established financial institutions and the start-up SMEs. They take capital from investment banks and private equity funds and in turn invest it under their own auspices in a range of companies that are not yet mature enough for full stock market floatation. They then manage the portfolio of venture capital assets under their control until the companies are ready for floatation on Stock Markets. Clearly, this is a risky business, so it thrives on the local and intimate knowledge derived from close association with a specific geographical area or sector of business. All this rather naturally lends itself to be considered in network terms, at least while the venture capital firm remains involved and before floatation.

But venture capital firms do not spend much time on the day to day activity of advising and managing the actual businesses with which they are involved. Rather they treat them as one element in an overall portfolio of assets that need to be managed, often according to strict financial criteria. Deals drive this process, so that it is buying and selling assets according to well defined performance criteria that tends to dominate, something mirrored by the wider financial arrangements in Anglo-American style financial systems. Most attention is devoted to those reasonably performing companies located in the middle of the range. Poorly performing companies are sold on; high-flyers are left alone.

A second form of venture capital is provided by so-called 'business angels'. These constitute informal networks of usually wealthy individuals who typically contribute seed capital, on-going managerial advice and support for businesses in which they themselves have had some experience. These operate along classic network lines (Mason and Harrison 1995; Steiner and Greenwood 2000). The angels are either still active older business people, in which case only part-time help can be offered, or those who have retired with a high net-worth. They tend to be willing to invest in areas or companies that the institutional venture capitalist industry misses for one reason or another. And they offer a much more 'hands on' role than do official venture capitalist operations.

But these networks suffer from low visibility. Search costs are high, on the part of both the angels and those looking for seed-corn investment. The ultra-informality of the network in this case works against its efficiency and robustness. This has led the focus to shift to a final organizational form of networking venture capital; the 'business introduction service'. These are semi-official bodies, often attached to local enterprise agencies of local authorities, that promote awareness of business opportunities amongst local start-ups and informal investors, local business owners and professional intermediaries (e.g. accountants, bankers, solicitors, marketing consultants). These agencies have the advantage of a higher and an institutionalized visibility, which adds to their credibility and trust. But they also require funding, and a very active approach towards 'match-making'. Passive public agencies waiting for new investors and investment opportunities to arrive quickly go under and fail. The network of contacts has to be continually fostered and re-invigorated.

The latter two forms of business venturing tend to operate in very local contexts. But as a consequence, the coverage of their activity is patchy. And this is also the case, if not more so, with the official venture capitalist industry. Venture capital funds in the United Kingdom, for instance, have tended to operate almost exclusively in the core regions of London and the South-East of England. Peripheral and lagging regions are badly served. And this spatial focus has been found in other countries. In addition, much ostensible venture capital activity is not that at all. It has tended to support expansionary financing, leverage buy-outs, and management buy-outs, etc. Thus, a lot of networked venture capital has fallen under the spell of the rather traditional market of hierarchical forms of provision.

5.11. 'Embeddedness' and Weak and Strong Ties

One of the key terms deployed in the analysis of interorganizational networks is that of 'embeddedness'. This has its contemporary origins in the work of Mark Granovetter discussed in Chapters 2 and 3 earlier (Granovetter 1973, 1985, 1992). Broadly speaking embeddedness refers to the way that socio-economic action and outcomes are affected by the dyadic relations between parties and the overall network structure in which actors are placed. Of course, this emphasis on the social context in which action and outcomes are placed did not arise just with Granovetter writings in the 1970s but has a long provenance in sociology stretching back to Durkheim's concept of the division of labour (Grabher 1993) and can be found in the work of Schumpeter (1950) and Polanyi (1957). The modern approach, however, has served to emphasize the *ongoing* process of construction and reconstruction of interactions in a network context, linking embeddedness to a continuous process of evolutionary change and complexity as outlined earlier in this chapter.

Embeddedness is closely associated with another concept introduced by Granovetter, that of 'weak ties'. Networks benefit from these weak or loose ties in a number of ways. They prevent the 'locking-in' of close and strong organizational couplings. These are argued to inhibit interactive learning and innovation as actors are given the opportunity to search for other linkages in the network if they are not committed strongly to any single set of relationships. In addition, weak ties help against the establishment of exclusive networks of closely knit insiders who look with suspicion on outsiders and thereby jealously guard their own privileged access to the network resources at all costs. To thrive networks need to share those resources beyond an immediate circle of favoured partners. Weaker ties to distant actors prevent an untimely closure of the network. And finally, this allows for some redundancy or slack, so that ineffective ties and relationships can be terminated, and new ones kindled, but in an environment that does not mean a wholesale clean sweep and the beginning from scratch again if things do go wrong. Some ties are maintained and re-activated, while it allows for completely new ones to be established without the necessary demise of the whole network structure.

This discussion of embeddedness and of weak (and strong) ties enables us to revisit some of the issues originally raised in Chapter 2 around the formal model of networks in Section 2.5. Weak/strong ties, for instance, can be used in two slightly different senses. First they refer to the *intensity* of a connection in terms of the robustness with which the parties are related; what degree of commitment is there from both parties? Second, they refer to the *value* of the connection in terms of the richness of the contacts, information, resources, etc., made available by the relationship. In addition, there is a question of the *size* of the network, measured by its density. Network density can be defined as the ratio of the actual number of dyadic connections between companies in a network of companies (say k) to the theoretically possible number of connections, $\frac{1}{2}n(n-1)$, where n is the number of firms in the network. The higher the ratio $k/\frac{1}{2}n(n-1)$ the higher the density of the network. At the limit, where every firm is connected to every other this ratio equals 1. In addition, there is the attribute of *diversity* to networks; the kinds of connections that are made to different individuals/firms or clusters of individuals/firms, so that not all connections are simply duplicates but ones that add variety and diversity to relationships and thus enable the accessing of different resources. This attribute is clearly closely related to the value quality just mentioned.

Granovetter emphasizes that size matters when it adds to the diversity of the network. More ties by themselves are not useful. And the greater the density of ties, over some optimal level, can also prove to be detrimental. Both of these can produce the overstrong ties that paradoxically lead to the weaknesses associated with lock-ins, etc., mentioned above (and expressed as the danger of moving too close to the 'edge of chaos' in the above discussion of complexity). This plays off the sense of the value of diversity. But this does not say much about the intensity of the ties, and how to manage these in the interests of the overall strength of the network to cope with unexpected events, shocks, change, etc. It is only if increasing size adds to diversity that it is positively viewed. This is what Burt (of SNA connection, see Chapter 3) has phrased as the effectiveness of 'structural holes' in networks (Burt 1992). Structural holes refer to the idea that there should not be too much overlap between network participants and clusters which simply duplicate connections to resources, and that therefore the objective should be to minimize the number of ties to each similar cluster or participant. Again, this gives some organizational meat to the abstract bones of the 'edge of chaos' thesis discussed above.

Clearly, this notion of 'managing the network' relates to the idea of the *efficiency* of the network in terms of keeping redundancy to a minimum (see Chapter 3). Redundancy is the term associated with an excess of duplicated and unnecessary connections.[14] This is costly in that it leads to overstrong ties and an overall weakness of the network. Better to seek weak(er) ties which are a strength. Sparser or thinner connections are stronger than denser, closer and thicker ones.

But there are a number of complications to this story which do not so much completely undermine it so as to provide some added texture to its basic premises. One issue is that inter-firm networks are not just about accessing a single resource like 'information' or 'knowledge' but involve the accessing of multiple resources all at the same time. They are multidimensional in scope. Services of various kinds are involved (crucially including financial resources), other goods, political influence, even emotional support in some cases. Thus, there is a potential for 'overload' in the management of such multidimensional networks, where it may be sensible to actively build in some excess redundancy just to ensure that, with so much going on, there is a scope to bolster the system as things go astray or focus is lost. As mentioned above redundancy in a network is useful for lubricating the wheels of change. This is particularly so when it involves key links in the structure, the absence of which could otherwise lead to a rapid undermining of the network. Efficiency, by

---

[14] The notion of redundancy operating here refers to the form and extent of connections in a network. In Chapter 3 redundancy is used in a slightly different sense to refer to the cascading of conceptions of social organization when an 'open-systems' approach is adopted towards organizational analysis. Whilst these two conceptions are clearly connected they are not quite the same. We return to the issue of redundancy in Chapter 8.

increasing dependency, also increases vulnerability, and can thus contribute to, rather than decrease, the liabilities associated with newness (Steier and Greenwood 2000). In addition, in respect to the rather neglected issue of the intensity of the network, the amount of contact can be crucial in terms of the frequency of interaction. This again relates to the potential overload problems, which in turn raises issues of the efficacy of some built in redundancy in relations between participants. It may not be a weakness to oversupply the amount of contact if this consolidates the intensity of commitments amongst the (key) player connections in the network. Finally, 'embeddedness' may have a further dual specificity in multidimensional networks. In an attempt to empirically establish the nature of the connections between manufacturing and financial firms, for instance, Brian Uzzi has emphasized the benefits of *network complementarity* in synthesizing the ties between different organizational entities (Uzzi 1996, 1997, 1999). Network complementarity relates to an integrated mix of embedded ties and arm's-length market type ties. The most robust networks and those that promoted coordinated adaptation were those that combined a judicious mix of these two different kinds of ties; a hybrid of networks and markets. Arm's-length ties enabled the manufacturing firms to reap the benefits of scanning the market for the best deals and broker information among banks, and thus avoid the overattentiveness to local resources and inherited conventions. On the other hand, embedded ties offered all the advantages of collaborative knowledge and the longer term facilities of partnering. The range of available action was maximized by combining these two.

5.12. Conclusions

What is to be gained in our understanding of industrial organization if we take the network form of organization seriously in a microeconomic context? This has been the issue confronted in this chapter. It is one of the most robust areas where networks are considered important, so it has been worthwhile concentrating on the specific strengths of the analysis as applied to various aspects of inter-firm relationships. It is impossible to avoid a discussion of these topics in the context of knowledge production, the role of variety, the nature of self-organization, and the general approaches to the grander understandings of economic organization from a non-economistic vantage point.

Perhaps the key overarching theme for all of these aspects of the discussion is to be found in their connection to the contemporary transformation of industrial organization. In this chapter, we have not concentrated directly on the ICT elements of this transformation. These are explicitly addressed in Chapter 7 (where their importance is argued to have been exaggerated). Rather in this chapter we have highlighted the basic economic organizational features of that transformation, dealing with its socio-economic characteristics and determinants rather than its technological ones. This is to stress the primacy of socio-economic relationships over technological ones.

In doing this, we have seen how the network form of organization is thriving in this new environment. Indeed, the network form is often argued to be in the forefront of this transformation. It represents the new leading edge organizational structure that will eclipse both hierarchy and market. Whilst we would not wish to go this far—it is the *relationship between* these three modes of organization that is being recast, not the eclipse of one by any other, so that the changing but complementary relationships between them is what is at stake—the analysis offered in this chapter has served to highlight the necessity of taking networks very seriously in this new context. Indeed, the argument has been that we need to take this organizational structure much more seriously than has often been the case. And this reinforces the necessity of examining the nature of this organizational structure in terms of its particular logic and the limits to its organizational embrace, which is pursued elsewhere in the book but which is also something this chapter has added to. For instance, we have seen that the relationships that are involved in articulating industrial networks cannot be simply reduced to ones of reciprocal exchange. Knowledge, complexity, self-organization, neural analogies, systems theory all demand a richer and more complex set of conceptual terms to relate them to networks. And these are better understood in the light of the analysis conducted in Chapter 4.

Chapter 6

Political Networks and the Politics of Network Governance

6.1. Introduction

This chapter concentrates upon two related aspects of networks that have to do with their political dimension.

The first of these is the way the political domain itself has sometimes been considered in terms of a network. Thus, either politics as a whole, or more often certain discrete ways that political expression is organized, can be understood in network terms. This involves five further related ideas: (a) first, that either elites or experts actually run politics or account for a major element in political power; or (b) it can be interpreted as the means by which social interests, or the 'social partners', are mobilized into a structure that actually conducts the business of government and governance somewhat independently of, or parallel to, the main axis of representative politics; (c) third, that this has more to do with 'associations' so that the field of politics is made up of various private and public associations which act as a definite political formation, and these take on a network character in the way they are linked together; (d) fourth, there is the operation of non-governmental organizations (NGOs) that characterize bottom-up political 'networks of dissent' and which are quintessentially organized in network forms; and finally (e) that all of these are instances of a generic trend in governance terms, the development of which are known as 'policy networks' which account for interest intermediation in the formation of public policy making. We will investigate these five network-type political structures in turn, but beginning with their overall characterization as instances of 'policy networks'.

The second way politics is introduced into this chapter is to ask a slightly different question that is 'what are the politics of networks?' In this case, we briefly analyse the decision-making nature of network organizational structures, to ask for instance, whether they are democratic or authoritarian, how the relationship between various networks is organized politically, etc.?

Clearly these two aspects are closely related and we treat them together for the most part, but bring out their two different emphases whenever possible. In addition, we consider these issues in the context of their relationships to other coordination and governance systems. Networks, then, are treated as just one of a number of 'vehicles for governance'.[1]

6.2. Networks of Political Power and Authority

The usual way of thinking about political representation in liberal democratic societies is via the notion of a hierarchical set of layered governmental institutions culminating in the sovereignty of a parliament. Thus, we have local government bodies of various types, each subordinate to some higher level. This is overlayed by a set of

---

[1] Stoker (1998) defines political governance as being ' . . . ultimately concerned with creating the conditions for ordered rule and collective action' (p. 17). See also Chapter 2.

central government apparatuses, administrative departments of the state, the government itself, the Cabinet, and finally the sovereignty of a parliament or the legislature. These central government institutions are themselves also organized hierarchically, with sometimes complex relations of subordination and superordination between them, but with the final 'pinnacle of power' situated in a parliament— the sovereignty of parliament (a parliament that still shares some of its authority with residual and marginal powers of the monarchy in the UK system—in republican and federal systems somewhat more complicated divisions of power operate but they share much of the same imagery as outlined here). This downward flow of power is paralleled by an upward flow of representation, so that it is 'the people' that ultimately vest the democratically elected parliament with its legitimacy to rule over it. In traditional democratic theory, then, the key concepts of representation and sovereignty go hand in hand. 'The people' are somehow divided into constituencies with an interest. These interests are then represented in the relevant legislative arena via their constituency representative. Political parties are the instruments of this representational mechanism. They mediate between the people, their interests (all political parties claim to represent an interest), the legislative arena, the government, and the sovereignty of parliament.

But against this orthodox conception can be posed a somewhat different and perhaps parallel mechanism that might be thought to capture another aspect of the way governance is organized. This mobilizes the notions of 'policy networks' involving 'elites', 'corporatism', 'associationalism', and NGOs as mentioned above. Policy is increasingly said to be produced through negotiation and agreements—either in pluralist 'policy networks' involving semi-autonomous parliamentary committees and bureaucratic agencies inhabited by experts and specialized policy analysts, or through neo-corporatist consultation ('concertation') between governments and peak associations of capital, labour, and other societal interests. In addition, in some areas or countries, important aspects of socio-political governance have been delegated to negotiations between 'self-governing' organizations or associations of providers and consumers of collectively financed services. Finally, the politics of dissent presents a deliberately alternative style of organizational mode focused around NGOs. So it is with how these policy networks operate that we concentrate on in this chapter so as to illustrate the differences between networking governance and traditional representational governance.

6.3. Policy Networks and the Formation of Public Policy

Two main forms of policy network have been identified in the literature: 'policy community' and 'issue network' (Jordan and Schubert 1992; Thatcher 1998). A *policy community* is characterized by a largely stable set of interdependent participants, co-existing in a bounded network, who build up a set of shared values and norms and hence form a community into which it is difficult to break (the 'insiders' keep out the 'outsiders'). Incremental change is typical of this form, stable interactions and lasting configurations predominating. Policy-making is segmented into well-defined subsystems involving a limited and privileged participation. On the other hand, the idea of an *issues-network* involves a more open and fragmented network structure. In this case, a wide circle of 'policy activists' drawn from a range of interest groups, government personnel, academics, and concerned individuals—who are constantly changing—form loosely articulated network groups around specialized *ad hoc* issues of public concern and policy making. Fundamental change is more possible here, as issues come and go and the make up of groups alters. Power and dependency relationships are diffused and the locus of decision-making difficult to trace.

More or less permanent or ongoing policy networks tend to exercise negative coordination, that is, stopping things they do not like or that threaten their perceived interests. This is less likely in one-off situations because these have less of a history and are less formally constituted. Often the former type need an 'outsider', say a research institute or an important and able 'active mobilizer' amongst the participants to galvanize decision-making and enable parties to overcome individual competitive objections so as to see common advantage in cooperating. But, as just mentioned, this is difficult to organize in the case of these insider groupings and they present formidable obstacles to achieving cooperation. Interactions amongst a relatively small set of permanent and active participants make decision-making easier because these develop a shared normative or cognitive orientation.

While these two forms provided an early classification, they were soon joined by a range of other alternative claims to describing policy networks: 'pressure pluralism'; 'competitive pluralism'; 'state corporatism'; 'corporate pluralism'; 'captured statism'; 'negotiated economy'; 'clientelism'; 'associationalism'; 'professional normalization', and more besides (Jordan and Schubert 1992; Rhodes and Marsh 1992; van Waarden 1992; Thatcher 1998). This explosion of epithets was in part a response to the perceived weakness of the policy community/issues network duality. It covered only part of the policy-making process, rather ignoring agenda setting aspects, the original distribution of power, technological and economic factors, the macro institutional context, and an explicit address to questions of change (Atkinson and Coleman 1992). The other forms just mentioned brought in many of these issues by adding a wider set of contextualizing features into the policy network structure, in particular, questions of overall state form and potential macro interest-group management.

But why should the general issue of policy networks, and this increasing range of claims to describe them, have taken such a hold on political analysis? In part, this has to do with a set of changes in the way societies were perceived to operate. Amongst the features here are:

- . . . 'The emergence of the *organized society*, or society based on organized collectivities;
- a trend in most reasonably sophisticated political systems of *sectorization* in policy making;
- the increased mobilization of competing interests which leads to *overcrowded policy making*;
- increased *scope of state policy making*—perhaps as a result of the electoral "auction" which forces political parties to appear to offer solutions to everything;
- *decentralization* or the *fragmentation of the state*. There are few state goals but an aggregation of departmental interests;

- *blurring of boundaries* between public and private. Policy making tends to be made between factions of the state and clientelistic interest groups'.   (Jordan and Schubert 1992, p. 11)

In this context, the whole policy-making process becomes a more fragmented and relatively open system made up of competing interests vying for their voice to be heard and their influence to be felt. These systems involve a complex and sometimes unstable combination of competition and coordination, negotiation and the exercise of power, independence and interdependency, and consultation and the exercise of pressure politics. Even within governments, interdepartmental coordination between semi-autonomous lower level units is increasingly designed to be solved through bilateral or multilateral negotiations amongst the participants, rather than through the hierarchical direction of chief executives (like the so-called 'joined-up-government' in the United Kingdom). In addition, public service provision often depends on interorganizational cooperation within networks of formally autonomous or *de facto* independent semi-public and private sector organizations.

Thus, there is a range of approaches to understanding the nature of these policy networks. But for the rest of this section, we concentrate on just the four mentioned in the opening remarks; namely, elites, corporatism, associationalism, and NGOs. These are themselves something of generic terms with a number of variants but they are different enough to give a flavour of the overall range of characterizations.

6.3.1. Elites

We have already come across this term in Chapter 3 in the context of the discussion of interlocking directorates. This is a clear example of an elite group—a financial-industrial oligarchy some would say—whose activity is to manage a good deal of the economic resources of a country. Personal ties and a shared cultural outlook mean that they wield a great deal of power, perhaps unaccountable power. In addition, in as much as they share convictions and a similar outlook with political elites, they can influence—some would say unduly influence—political processes as well.

Elite networks are different from 'democratic' policy networks in that they can be based upon birth or inherited influence. And it is the role of elites in the informal governance and coordination of power that explicitly raises the problem of the lack of accountability of that power within important areas of social life. Elites can serve to circumvent 'the proper conduct of democratic politics' (as seen from the point of view of the traditional sketch of politics that opened this chapter), by organizing influence behind the scenes, bringing their own interests to bear unduly on decisions, and so on. In these cases, the manner in which elites are classically thought to work is via all the characteristics that constitute networks as described in Chapter 2. They combine a select and small-scale group, held together by reciprocal bonds of loyalty and trust. But elites are genuine 'inegalitarian' networks. They are marked out by birth or status, which also gives them a decidedly hierarchical feel.

Thus, we can see that elite theories of politics would postulate another type of influence on the political arena, which could largely escape the operation of the representation–sovereignty couple outlined above. In fact, elites are not well integrated into an explicit policy network analytical framework precisely because they do seem to hark back to an older era of political organization, one where power and influence were the direct result of birth or inherited wealth rather than those of 'negotiated interests'. And this is exactly what corporatist theories of government are argued to address.

6.3.2. Corporatism

Corporatism is a political theory stressing the way large interest groups—the 'social partners' as they are sometimes referred to—combine informally in a cooperative manner to regulate and govern central aspects of social life. Thus, we might see the government bargaining with the organizations of large and small industrialists, with agricultural interests, with the financial sector, and with organized labour, or some other important social groups like consumers or environmentalists, to establish a *modus vivendi* on an important social, political, or economic issue. It generates cooperation by means of bargaining and negotiation between formally specified and recognized actors. As a result, the actors in the system must respect certain interest positions of other parties, pursue certain substantive goals, and follow certain agreed procedures for future interactions. But this procedure means that parties must resist unilateral actions and must observe mutual obligations, otherwise the network would degenerate.

Some analysts have seen whole countries partly or largely governed along these lines, where the social partners or interest groups are integrated into an established regulatory order that can dampen potential conflicts between them before they break out into a more open conflict. In this way, a consensus can be built up informally, and the business of government conducted in a more conciliatory manner as a result. The point here is that once again, this process tends to bypass the normal channels of political lobbying and representation. It operates a kind of macro-scale network in the conduct of governing a country.

The status of corporatism in the current period is unclear. Some see it as a failed and outmoded form of governance, something that typified the inflexible and rigid systems of economic management operating during the 1970s and 1980s, which was swept away by a neoliberal turn in policy matters in the 1990s. In fact, there were genuine advantages to such a corporatist regime of economic governance, not least a generally superior economic performance for those countries (mainly in continental northern Europe) that had most closely embraced its organizational framework (Thompson 1993*a,b*, ch. 5; Thompson 1996). However, whether these macro-corporatist arrangements did actually break up in the 1990s also remains controversial. Others have found they survived and indeed, reinvented themselves as part of a turn towards 'social compacts' designed to protect vulnerable sections of the population otherwise subject to the increasing insecurities and uncertainties associated with 'globalization', or in the context of the revival of 'diversified' regional economies and industrial districts (see Chapters 5 and 7). Thus, there may have been a revival of this form of economic neocorporatism—and, therefore, macro network type governance—since the mid-1990s, though one found most prominently in the smaller or more vulnerable states of Europe (Hirst and Thompson 1999, ch. 6; Crouch *et al.* 2001).

6.3.3. Associationalism

The third form of this alternative political conception that is considered here is associationalism. This represents a more pluralistic version of corporatism (see Streeck and Schmitter 1985; Hollingsworth *et al.* 1994). This particular approach stresses the myriad of political associations in which people invest their political allegiances, energies, and 'sovereignties'. It challenges the idea that there is a single dimension to sovereignty, organized along the hierarchical lines mentioned above. Rather, it stresses the dispersion of sovereignty, and with it the representative mechanism that supports it. Thus, from this perspective, sovereignty is dispersed throughout the series of 'political' organizations to which any individual might owe an allegiance. These organizations go to govern the range of private interests existing in any society. There is thus a plurality of sites where the sovereignty of the people rests, some of which may not even be considered political in the usual sense, for example, places of employment or social clubs.

Written somewhat larger, this idea has been promoted as a model for a particular kind of 'negotiated state'. This involves the articulation of voluntary self-governing association into a general macro structure of power—what Paul Hirst has termed 'associative democracy' (Hirst 1994, 1997—see also below). With this model, the semi-autonomous democratically organized associations, conducting their business on behalf of their members, rely upon state finances and are conditioned in what they can do by state law. This is not directly hierarchically organized or coordinated, however. Policy choices are not pre-empted by the unilateral prerogative of a hierarchical authority but are shaped by the constellations of preferences negotiated amongst the associated network members. In addition, this conception opens up private interest governance to a public accountability, in part as a consequence of the granting of public monies to the self-organizing associations on the basis that they will deliver a certain level of service to their members (so that they are to be made accountable for their expenditures), but also in terms of the way state law acts as a 'tribunal of last resort' that adjudicates in disputes between private associations.

6.3.4. NGO networks of dissent

A final somewhat different deployment of the idea of networks operating in this field involves the role of NGOs in network governance (e.g. Reinicke and Deng 2000). These appear as something of a counterweight to the essentially 'participatory communities' just described. NGO networks provide the 'other' of the elite and establishment influence on governance, although in some ways they are a variant of the notion of 'associationalism' just considered. NGOs are essentially private interest associations, but ones concerned with campaigning and propaganda for a particular purpose. Their objective is to change public policy, usually by mobilizing public opinion and putting pressure on the established policy frameworks from the outside.

And it is here that two key aspects of NGO activity arise. The first of these concerns a problem of their legitimacy. On whose behalf do they speak and how can they be made accountable? The second problem facing NGOs is whether they are effective and make any difference to the issue areas in which they concentrate their activities. This has always presented NGOs with a real dilemma. Should they stay 'outside' the political mainstream and remain part of a pressure politics, or should they cooperate and become part of the policy network environment as described above? Of course, the issues and dilemmas that are brought out here and which face NGOs in an acute manner, are problems and issues that are faced by all types of networks, and are discussed further below.

But how can we conceptualize the broad way decision-making is organized in these kinds of networks? This is the controversial issue considered in the remaining sections of this chapter. To begin with, a contrast can be drawn between two overall approaches, which themselves rather depend upon how the operation of networks are themselves conceived.

First, we have a conception that says networks are fundamentally no different to any other institutional mechanism in how their internal business is conducted. Networks involve differences of power and authority in terms of those agents and participants that are members, so it all amounts to the deployment of these power or authority capacities. All the usual modalities of bargaining and negotiation can come into play here; the operation of guile and cunning, not declaring one's total hand, the operation of rhetorical and persuasive skills, the deployment of talent and skill in making alliances, etc. So no outcome can be quite predicted in advance, despite the fact that some will have an obvious superior advantage over others, and can use their greater power to their own ends.

On the other hand, we have a conception that rests upon the idea that these organizational networks are fundamentally different to other institutional mechanisms. In this case, in each of these sites, a consensual, cooperative, collaborative ethic is argued to operate. Thus, again what we have is a kind of elongated, 'flat' framework for political representation, working through a plurality of organizational and associative forms, operating something akin to a network, that governs private interests increasingly in a public manner.

The implications of these differences for network decision-making are explored later in this chapter.

6.4. Multi-level Governance

In recent years, a different though related conception of policy networks has entered the discussion of political governance. This is the notion of 'multi-level governance'. Multi-level governance refers to the particular problem of coordinating the activities of different layered dimensions of governance. In a macro context, this can involve relations between local, regional, national, supra national, and transnational bodies. In the absence of overarching political mechanisms of hegemonic imposition, this requires the skills of negotiation and bargaining between parties situated at the different levels in a familiar pattern to that just discussed in the case of policy networks.

These kinds of administrative arrangements are thought to strongly typify certain aspects of EU decision-making ('joint decision systems', 'expert committees', 'open methods of coordination'—see below) where on the one hand, *horizontal* policy coordination at the local, regional, national, transnational, and supranational levels has been conducted through bilateral and multilateral negotiation on such issues as environmental pollution, economic integration, and communication regulation, while on the other hand, *vertical* policy coordination requires a similar pattern of behaviour but now organizing relationships *between* these administrative levels. One key element in this multilevel governance conception is the *re-allocation of authority mechanisms* between the different levels, either under a principle like that of subsidiarity in the EU case, or the dispersal of policy-making powers in the case of decentralization or devolution in other contexts (Hooghe and Marks 2001). Both trajectories mean the reconfiguration of existing jurisdictions and the creation of new ones, with authority capacities being reformulated accordingly.

Clearly, this re-allocation of decision-making jurisdictions could result in just a new hierarchy rather than the mutual dependency, asymmetrical dependence, or relative independence that would be most characteristic of network forms of relationship. And a good deal of formal looking institutional arrangements may actually operate informally, which can be easily underestimated or misunderstood, so these could be a cover for a real recentralization, undermining the scope for the network policy dynamics to actually shape outcomes.

However, power sharing across multiple jurisdictions is thought to be more efficient in grounding policy decisions in a credible commitment environment since it can better reflect the heterogeneity of preferences of different constituencies situated at the different levels. The monopoly appropriation of decision-making authority by central state bodies looks vulnerable to these competing interests and constituencies. Multiple jurisdictions also allow for some jurisdictional competition, which can be good for governance and regulatory innovation.

Hooghe and Marks suggest that there are two types of multilevel governance. The first conceives of the dispersion of authority to a limited set of non-overlapping jurisdictions at a limited number of levels. These jurisdictions bundle authority into quite large packages, and they are relatively stable. This is the *semi-federalist option*, or one that lends itself easily to intergovernmental relations. The second type pictures governance as a complex, fluid patchwork of innumerable overlapping jurisdictions. These jurisdictions are lean and flexible, coming and going as demands change, and their competencies are also highly fungible. This is the *polycentric option*, with overlapping geographical territories and functional domains. The whole idea is for this to be flexible and to respond to changing citizen expectations and preferences, and to be sensitive to functional requirements as they evolve. It is the second of these types, then, that most easily lends itself to be envisaged in classic networking terms, but the first type can also be interpreted in this light as well, though it would seem to operate more formally.

6.5. Network Forms of Governance and Game Theory

It is often claimed that game-theoretic analyses of strategic interaction lend themselves readily to analysing the decision-making processes in these network-like structures of governance. Network forms of governance involve the coordination of the interdependent choices of multiple units of government, or the interactions between government agencies and organizations in the non-governmental sectors. This arises as a response to the ever-denser patterns of interdependence and interference that increasingly cut across pre-established demarcations of organizational, political, and sectoral boundaries and levels, as mentioned above as a defining feature for the growth of interest in policy networks.

But before we get on to questions of interdependence between players, it will be worthwhile describing the 'base-case' of the non-cooperating Prisoner Dilemma (PD) type game since this acts as a founding framework for subsequent refinements and extensions.

6.5.1. Generating 'cooperation' in a game theory context

Game theory is a technique for analysing the strategic interactions between different participants in any bargaining or negotiating situation. Thus, in principle, it lends itself nicely to the issues being discussed in this chapter, which have to do with how multiple participants in a decision-making environment can possibly reach an agreement, given that they have different and competing interests and objectives at stake. There are a number of very formal and mathematically specifiable models that develop these relationships between players. Here, we concentrate upon some intuitive results that arise from game theory, and ones that suit the particular problems of political decision-making in network types of environment that are being discussed in this chapter.

Of particular importance in this environment is the relationship between cooperation and trust in game theory situations. Clearly, if distrust is complete, cooperation will fail. History is legion with the consequences of such breakups of trust and cooperation. We could also enumerate cases where trust is very one-sided, which might also lead to a break up of cooperation. The extreme case of one-sided trust is where it is blind for one party. In this case, there is a clear incentive for the other party to engage in deception or to become opportunistic. However, repeated instances of deceit can only last for so long before they are uncovered, and cooperation undermined (see Chapter 2).

Broadly speaking, a classic PD game theory situation is one where there are a number of players who are suspicious of one another because they have different interests at stake in the negotiations. Thus, they are reluctant to either show their full hand in a negotiation, or to agree to something and follow it through when there is the possibility that the other party will renege on the agreement, or will actually follow another course of action altogether. Such competition between players, where they are always looking to reap an advantage from the weaknesses of the other player, or as the other players sticks to an agreement whilst the rest do not, present problems of establishing trust between them and a cooperative outlook. And there are good reasons to show that when players are set up in this manner, there will be no cooperation between them and they stick solely to looking after their immediate conflicting interests. This is particularly so when the players are not able to communicate with one another directly, only through the unfolding sequence of their own suspicious behaviours.

For cooperation and trust to emerge under these circumstances, there is the need for a principle of choice based on collective interests. In its absence, the temptation to 'go it alone' remains strong. The question asked of this in the case of decision-making networks is which party would withdraw from the network first and for what reason? Unfortunately, there is no completely convincing rational solution to this kind of a dispute, which highlights the difficulty of reaching a cooperative 'compromise' under the circumstances described. Without trust, individual interests override collective ones. But the collective outcome, some form of a 'cooperative compromise' could provide a better result overall. It could mean that each of the individual players were to gain more than if they insist on their go-it-alone strategies.

But it should be noted here that any conditional cooperation that can be forged amongst the players in these situations emerges solely from a desire to maximize their individual long-term payoffs.[2] Thus, one of the crucial assumptions of this example of game theory as applied to decision-making is players begin with a set of already known interests and the questions asked are how these can be maximized, how do they interact, or how might the interests be modified in the process of that interaction? However, why begin with a situation in which interests are already fully known before entering into any negotiation or relationship? It could be that the negotiation or relationship itself *establishes* those interests. Players may not fully know their 'interests' before they enter into any negotiation. Similarly as members of networks. The activity engaged in could at least in part determine what are conceived to be the interests at stake and how they are made manifest.

As it stands, however, the players are assumed to be akin to actors who act as rational egoists, maximizing their expected individual utility functions. What is more, these utility functions are quite independent of one another. In this situation, players do not care whether other players achieve or do not achieve any gains from the cooperative relationship. Strictly speaking, therefore, it rules out

---

[2] Cooperative solidarity as (the outcome of) a 'selfish' strategy will thus depend upon a number of conditions:

(a) the relation between individual contributions and their expected benefits;
(b) the probability of gaining the expected benefit even without cooperative endeavours and sacrifices;
(c) the opportunity costs of the strategy. Solidarity will occur only if total benefits exceed total costs. If this produces a net benefit, the opportunity cost (the cost of the alternative foregone) of not cooperating will be negative, and 'rational' individuals would not decide on that option; and finally,
(d) the ease of monitoring the other parties' actions, that is, can non-cooperation and opportunism be detected?

the analysis of situations characterized by common but mixed interests (but see below where this analysis is taken further by introducing mixed interest situations).

However, there is an important way to express the manner in which cooperation could come about in these rather artificial situations; it may *evolve* over time as players become used to one another (Axelrod 1981, 1984). It is with the idea of repetition of actions and reactions that some of the issues associated with the establishment of trust and cooperation are usually explored. Axelrod explores examples of Tit for Tat (TFT) games, involving a policy of cooperating on the first move and then doing whatever the other player does on the following move. Thus, this example uses the notion of a *strategy* (a decision rule) based upon the history of the game. Given consistency of behaviour and the continuation of interactions, cooperation can emerge gradually. Cooperation here is the result of a number of conditions; random signals and their interpretations being confined to a 'cluster' of interactions amongst a repeatedly connected group; there is testing out of those interpretations to increase conviction and lessen misunderstandings; the gradual learning of the rules and norms is allowed; and the solidification of a mutual interest in cooperation emerges as a result. These are the classic descriptive characteristics of a network.

Thus, the important message of this analysis is that cooperation does not necessarily have to be either 'taught' or 'imposed'. The crucial issue at stake is the need for a 'cooperative outlook' to be fostered. According to Axelrod, this can come about if the game is played over and over again. If the expectation is that the players will have to deal with each other repeatedly and frequently, this can counter the temptation to defect or counter-defect. Thus, from this perspective, the foundation of cooperation is not necessarily trust, but rather the durability of the relationships involved. It develops spontaneously (and possibly tacitly) between reciprocating parties. The *reputation* of the parties for cooperation rather than for competition becomes *expected* and 'socially embedded' as a result.[3]

---

[3] One way this kind of evolved cooperation might be made manifest is through the notion of a 'regime'. A regime is the institutionalization of principles, norms, rules, and decision-making procedures around specific policy areas where actor

These types of game situations—involving moral dilemmas and tactical choices, although rather artificially specified here—pervade a good many real life and more complex situations. Although illustrating the problem of generating cooperation in the context of game theory, the point is that similar situations and problems can arise in a broader network context. The PD game raises subtle problems of trust and suspicion. A player who trusts the other to behave cooperatively has a reasonable justification for doing likewise, but one who suspects that the other may defect has only one reasonable course of action, namely to also defect. For this reason, there is a tendency for pairs of players to adopt increasingly similar patterns of play when the game is repeated a number of times—if they have been faced with a similar situation before and acted cooperatively then. Thus, if you start out with an initial (trusting) disposition to cooperate, it is likely that you will actually end up cooperating, as the same situation repeats itself on a number of occasions. What it means, however, is that 'repeat transactions'—the repetition of day to day cooperative activity—tends to self-reinforce that very cooperation and secure it in a robust manner, even as it is based upon individualistic self-interested calculations.

In game theoretic terms, this means that the services of coordination and governance needed to organize increasingly fragmented domains of government and policy delivery could be conceived as dependent upon a number of conditions. First, self-coordination achieved either through mutual anticipation and unilateral adjustment ('noncooperative games') or through negotiated agreements ('cooperative games') in the image of the PD and the TFT games just described (which are examples of so called 'unstructured n-person games'). Second, through 'complex connected games' where the game is better viewed as involving multi-actor constellations in which the overall network structure of relationships is very important to the outcome (Scharpf 1993). In the latter case, of course, the policy issue of 'structural reform' is posed as the decision consequences of existing game configurations emerge which are deemed less than satisfactory.

expectations converge. Such regimes can assist the development of cooperation by improving the quality and flow of information, reducing uncertainty and the incentive for opportunist defection, and promoting mechanisms for monitoring compliance (Krasner 1983; Keohane 1984; de Senarclens 1993).

Applications and Empirical Comparisons

But can game theory be used to provide a rigorous way of thinking about network operations rather than as just a suggestive way? Is it more than a metaphor? Can it become a genuine model in the political realm? The first thing to note is that not all situations involve PD type competitive games as described above. Many are of the Assurance game type, where it is a matter of negotiated games in repeat situations (of which TFT is a transitional type). But formally, such repeat games display many more potential equilibrium solutions, which means that narrowing these down to manageable proportions is very difficult. While simple models do not work very well as genuine illustrations of the complexity of political decision-making, complex models are too difficult to handle empirically and operationally. For instance, can complex actors, aggregated in one way or another, be considered as a single unitary actor?

So the issue is whether stable generalizable solutions that might offer predictive possibilities have reliably emerged from this type of analysis, or is it all one-off adhocery with no general answer to the trust problem implicit in the exploration of game theoretic models? (Sabel 1993). Elinor Ostrom has provided some evidence that formal game theory models do provide the possibility for understanding institutional arrangements that reinforce rules and 'guarantee' ongoing cooperation, like guarding and monitoring the rules of coordination and governance in situations of common resource management (Ostrom 1990; Ostrom and Gardener 1993). Thus, there seems to be something to learn from this about which network type institutional structures might be most effective, and therefore help in the design of such institutions. This could also help in the organization of structural and regulatory reform.

But there remains the problem of operationalizing the game. Here the techniques of social network analysis (SNA) have often been combined with Game Theory. SNA is used to establish a relatively stable network and identify the 'clusters' that can then be used to formalize the players in the Game context. But often these two cannot be easily or directly mapped on to one another. This requires the addition of a lot of 'thick description' to make the analysis stick. However, the use of SNA techniques does enable the experimentation with different rules and even with different games to compare outcomes (say in respect to information flows that actually circulate amongst network actors).

So how are negotiations organized in self-organizing networks? This partly depends upon whether the actors are forced to deal with each other and cannot exit, or whether there is a low cost exit solution. In the first case this could result in the formation of stable but relatively suspicious and uncooperative coalitions, while in the latter it is either a case of cooperation *or* exit, so for those who remain, cooperation is the likely result. Hence this could be analysed analogously to the weak and strong ties of Granovetter (1973)—see also Chapter 5. But any high degree of vulnerability also encourages trust between participants because they feel jointly threatened.

6.6. Social Capital

The importance afforded to trust in network situations associated with political decision-making and the effective operation of politics more generally is something demonstrated by the discussion of social capital. Social capital expresses the degree of citizen involvement in community affairs, which, it is argued, powerfully influences the performance of government and social institutions (Coleman 1990, 1998; Putnam 1993a[4]). In recent years, it has been taken up by such organizations as the World Bank and the OECD, which have tended to use it as another way of encouraging 'community values' and 'good governance'.[5] Civic traditions, it is suggested, like local networking, in which agreed norms of behaviour and trust between participants are encouraged, generate social connectedness and social participation, enabling participants to act together more effectively in the pursuit of shared objectives. Put simply, the argument is that the more people

[4] Putnam defines social capital as ' . . . features of social organization, such as networks, norms, and trust that facilitate coordination and cooperation for mutual benefit. Social capital enhances the benefits of investment in physical and human capital', Putnam (1993a, p. 1).

[5] The World Bank describes it thus: ' . . . The institutions, relationships and norms that shape the quality and quantity of a society's social interactions' (World Bank 2002). The OECD thus ' . . . networks together with shared norms and understandings that facilitate cooperation within or among groups' (OECD 2001).

are connected to one another, the more they trust one another and the more this serves civic ends.

The UK government has also become interested in social capital, which it sees as a natural compliment to its emphasis on 'inclusion', social engagement, and economic performance. The Performance and Innovation Unit (part of the Cabinet Office) draws a distinction between three types of social capital:

- *bonding* social capital—characterized by strong bonds (or 'social glue'), for example, among family members or among members of an ethnic group;
- *bridging* social capital—characterized by weaker, less dense but more cross-cutting ties ('social oil'), for example, between business associates, acquaintances, friends from different ethnic groups, friends of friends, etc.;
- *linking* social capital—characterized by connections between those with different levels of power or social status, for example, links between the political elite and the general public or between individuals from different classes . . .   (Aldridge *et al.* 2002, pp. 11–12.)

Clearly, there is a simple logic at play here, which many have found a compelling one. In one of its most celebrated manifestations, Frances Fukuyama (1995) finds in social capitals' underlying logic the key to the *cultural* determinants of the whole of social progress and economic prosperity. His argument speaks against the idea of a purely 'economic' explanation for prosperity, fore-grounding the social virtues of trust and association as a better basis for the making and sustaining of wealth, prosperity, and economic competitiveness. Fukuyama argues that it is this combination of economic rationalism and traditional community values that best exemplify the robustness of liberal democracies, underpinned by self-organizing relationships of networks and trust. And these combinations are something that are differentially registered in different societies, resulting in their differential capacities for stability and the sustaining of a dynamic 'modernity'. For Fukuyama (1992), of equal if not greater importance than the economic progress made possible by these combinations of rational economic action and traditional virtues of civic communitarianism, are the political implications of social capital. Social capital provides the means by which the political project of the 'ultimate triumph of liberal democratic society and the end of (Hegelian) history' could be forged (Fukuyama 1992). Spontaneous sociability and a healthy capitalist economy go together; sufficient social capital in the underlying society permits businesses, corporations, networks, and the like to self-organize, throwing off the mantles of authoritarianism and state intervention. The self-organizing proclivity so generated is exactly what is necessary to make democratic political institutions work, and finally triumph.

Whilst not all those committed to the idea of social capital would go quite so far as embracing Fukuyama's full programmatic 'end of history' argument, the approach has set up an intense debate about how much social capital different societies manifest, whether it is declining or growing, how to nurture it, and what are its precise political and economic consequences, if any.

In his *qualitative* work, Putnam (1993*b*) provides a similar analysis to those theorists like Sabel and Scharpf reviewed elsewhere in this chapter, and others who have championed the 'industrial district' literature discussed in Chapters 5 and 7. Putnam points to the effectiveness of regional governance in Italy, where there was a thoroughgoing reform in the 1970s that established strong regional governments. He found that some of these worked well while others did not and asks why there was this differential response. Two types of regions are identified.

The first are the 'civic regions', of which Emilia-Romagna in the north is a prime example. Here there are many active community organizations, where citizens are engaged by public issues, not by patronage. They are seen to trust one another to act fairly and to obey the law. Leaders in these communities are relatively honest and committed to equality. Social and political networks are organized horizontally, not vertically (hierarchically). These 'civic communities' value solidarity, civic participation, and integrity. Here democracy works.

On the other hand, there are the 'uncivic regions' like Calabria and Sicily in the south. The very concept of citizenship is stunted here. Engagement in social and cultural associations is meagre. Public affairs are considered someone else's business (like 'the bosses' or 'the politicians'). Whilst almost everyone agrees that laws are there to be broken, fearing others' lawlessness, everyone demands stricter discipline. As a result, there is a pervasive atmosphere of authoritarianism. Trapped in these interlocking vicious circles, nearly everyone feels powerless, exploited, and unhappy. Unsurprisingly, here representative government is less effective than in the more civic communities.

Putnam argues that the civic roots of these traditions run very deep. They can be traced back many hundreds of years. At the core of the civic regions is a dense and enduring heritage of organized networks for civic solidarity; guilds, religious fraternities, neighbourhood associations, town societies, cooperatives, mutual aid societies, communal fraternization, etc. Networks are seen as not just crucial to economic collaboration in these contexts but extended to the necessary political support for such economic performance (Putnam 1993*b*—see also Boix and Posner 1998). Putnam argues that the more successful regions did not become civil because they were rich; they became rich because they were civic.

In his *quantitative* work, Putnam (Putnam 1993*a*) makes social capital and civic engagement a multivariate function of education, age, race, time and generational effects, the penetration and types of communications media, family stability, group membership, and other independent variables. These are measured by the results of the US General Social Survey, various polls, attitude surveys, and proxy indicators of social engagement (Putnam 1995, 2000). The outcome of his work using these methods is to find a significant decline in social capital in the United States and the destruction of trust (although it is recognized that the United States may still maintain higher absolute levels of social engagement than many other advanced countries). One problem here is whether all of this actually measures the levels of trust rather than the attitudes of Americans towards trust; what they 'feel' rather than what they 'do', or how they 'act' (see also footnote 6).

A similar problem confronts those attempts to use attitude surveys to measure the direct effects of social capital on economic outcomes. Although Whiteley (1997) found that social capital had an important and highly significant impact on economic growth in a sample of thirty-four countries over a twenty-two year period (1970–92), one at least as important as the influence of human capital or education, his analysis relies upon the World Values Survey (WVS) and a generalized measure of trust derived from it. And La Porta *et al.* (1997) also used this measure in their analysis of trust in large corporations.[6] After an extensive cross country multivariate analysis, they found that trust promoted cooperation especially in large corporations, helping in the formation of 'horizontal networks of cooperation' between organization members which was crucial to company performance. Interestingly, they also found that trust in family members was low (which Fukuyama also argues), so they conclude that strong family ties are detrimental to economic development and institutional experimentation. This tends to contradict the importance of Aldridge *et al.*'s (2002) first type of social capital mentioned above—bonding social capital. Family ties indicate to a more hierarchical set of relationships, which inhibits the political advantages of social capital already discussed. Finally, in a SNA inspired analysis of the extent and consequences of social capital in a single firm, Tsai and Goshal (1998) found that the intra-firm networks established formally and informally within a large multinational electronics company (with fifteen separate business units) facilitated inter-unit resource exchange sufficient to make a real contribution to product innovation and value creation.

One issue thrown up by this discussion of the existence and effects of social capital is whether it can be fostered and created. For Putnam, social capital in the Italian regions he studied (Putnam 1993*b*) was the direct result of the civic traditions originating in the nineteenth century, and he also stresses the older civic traditions in the United States, which are now under threat (Putnam 2000). Thus, from him social capital is a commodity deeply embedded in the history of societies, and once undermined is very difficult to recreate. On the other hand, Coleman (1998) has a more contingent conception of social capital, the level of which can change over time dependent upon

[6] These measured trust as the willingness of the average citizen to trust others including members of their own families, fellow citizens, and people in general, based upon surveys of attitudes in the various countries. The actual question in the WVS was 'Generally speaking, would you say that most people can be trusted, or that you can't be too careful in dealing with people?' (La Porta *et al.* 1997, p. 333). See also Aldridge *et al.* 2002, table 3, p. 15 and table 4, p. 19, which use the same survey methods in the United Kingdom context.

interactions between social actors. Here social capital can be created and destroyed in the short run, just like other forms of capital, so it is relatively easy to create either a virtuous cycle of economic prosperity and trust or a vicious cycle of decline and mistrust. This rather depends upon the nature of third party influence or enforcement agencies, and the potential contribution that more hierarchical forms of authority could contribute to the production of trust (Braithwaite and Levi 1999). From this perspective, it is possible to create or destroy social capital dependent upon the wider political context, and in principle institutional design can be fostered to enhance it. Below we revisit this discussion in terms of the importance of the 'shadow of hierarchy' in the reproduction of viable policy networks (see also Chapter 7).

Defenders of the social capital idea have reacted to Putnam's concerns about its destruction and long-term decline with the idea that this might just be a sign of its *transformation*. Direct, informal social engagement may be giving way to new indirect and more formal types. 'Bonding social capital' is giving way to 'bridging social capital'. Here developments like cheaper travel and Internet access are seen as possible instruments for this transformation, along with a new emphasis on legal redress, rights charters, performance indicators, and the like, which provide a more individualized citizenry with the means to civic engagement under radically changed social and cultural circumstances. In addition, various public policy initiatives to encourage 'linking social capital' could be pointed to (see below).[7]

A further issue associated with the concept of social capital is that it implies a notion of capital directly analogous to that of physical or financial capital. It is presumably something that can be accumulated and invested and used efficiently to produce a surplus that can somehow be appropriated. Clearly this raises a host of issues, akin to the debate about 'human capital', which it mirrors. If networks, for example, are effectively 'commons' to be shared, this does not sit too

[7] The question of the effect of the Internet on civic engagement is considered in Chapter 7. There it is argued that this development has had little effect and that its impact has been exaggerated.

easily with all the traditional notions around capital (where it can be 'appropriated', 'used-up', 'run down', and 'exhausted'). In addition, it does not chime at all with the notion of networks as driven by an alternative logic of the 'non-exchange gift relationship' explored in Chapter 4.

And the immediately preceding discussion raises a further underlying problem posed by the PD example considered above; what is the *rationality* of social cooperation? Note that rationality is posed in quite individualistic terms by the examples examined above—as a means to a given end. The kind of rationality operating here is an instrumentally calculative kind. This idea of rationality links objectives to actions by way of decisions about means to an end. It is individualistically rational and logical in these terms. But there are other quite legitimate descriptions of rational behaviour that do not operate in quite this manner. For instance, to recognize that there are all sorts of reasons why different types of social and economic agents make decisions, largely constrained by the conditions they face. In the case of human agents, this is because of the activity of *thinking*, which may not be 'rationalistic' in a calculative ends/means sense. This particular approach does not necessarily rely upon an individualistic logic of utility calculation that assesses the costs and benefits of all options before making a decision based solely upon that logic. For instance, we have already seen that networks can be built on symbolic and discursive relations (rhetoric and persuasion), which may not be 'rational' in the sense just described. But that does not mean these are 'irrational' either. In addition, the very terms used to describe the means of network organization—trust, honesty, altruism, loyalty, solidarity, and cooperation—need not be thought of in rationalistic terms either. Trust, for instance, could simply describe a personality disposition; a cooperative outlook and a state of mind (Coleman 1982; Lewis and Weigert 1985). Suppose, then, that we assume from the outset that humans are naturally trusting rather than that trust is absent and that calculations of self-interest drive the motivation of social agents. Thus, we might suggest that trust is a *precondition* for any form of *social* life. The implications of this are further explored below.

Applications and Empirical Comparisons

But there are final issues thrown up by this discussion of social capital and the active engagement of citizens in community duties or networking relationships. Does the network form of governance raise completely new issues of 'citizenship'? To pose this in a slightly different language and intellectual space than that offered by Putnam serves to highlight a somewhat different take on these matters, though an analogous one. From a Foucauldian perspective, for instance, networks are conceived as regulative technologies that, though not necessarily 'rationally' articulated in a means–ends sense, are nonetheless imbued with their own rationalities. Thus, they might also imply a particular vision of the active, social, and moral citizen as a bearer of a 'regulated freedom', a particular form of what Foucault has termed 'governmentality'. Networks could thus serve to open up a new 'fictive space' in which the active self-fulfilling subjects engage with a particular field of economic choice. For instance, the newly flexible production systems discussed in Chapter 5 imply a set of techniques, and workers that exercise their own discretion, delineating networks of activities where individual 'initiative', 'flexibility', 'judgement', and 'entrepreneurialism' are celebrated. Above all these processes, by fragmenting the hierarchically organized firm, introduce a new emphasis of 'consumption' into the firm and between semi-autonomous organizational entities. Separate activities consume costs, and the monitoring of these consumption-cost centres becomes the prime mode of network governance. The consumer as a personage is also directly implicated in the organizational network of production as that production is increasingly subject to the dictates of marketing and consumption. This may be heralding a new rather more general triptych of 'network-citizen-consumer'—recall the emphasis on the various Citizens Charters so popular with the Conservative government of John Major in the United Kingdom. However, as pointed out above, this also opens up a slightly different space of citizenship, one in which the behavioural and ethical virtues of loyalty, trust, and cooperation are actively celebrated. It is perhaps this idea of economic citizenry that becomes an attractive one in a period when both the market and hierarchy are losing much of their attraction as coordinative mechanisms.

6.7. A Preliminary Evaluation of Political Networks

So far in this chapter, we have explored a number of alternative but connected approaches to the understanding of political organization, contrasting them to an 'orthodox' position. Each of these approaches displays some of the features of a network structure. Each of them also gives us insight into the actual way politics works. Clearly, they do not exhaust the insights; as argued in a moment the orthodox representational position continues to have much to offer. Perhaps the best way of viewing the relationship between the two is as complementary. They run very much in parallel to each other, highlighting particular aspects of a complex whole (see Section 6.8).

But let us step back a little from the formal presentation of the policy network model to critically evaluate it. A first point is to ask whether these networks are essentially undemocratic? Clearly they do not totally conform to traditional notions of 'representative democracy'. Elites, for instance, may become cliques—groups or bodies of partial and unrepresentative interests who, because they cooperate closely and share a common social or economic outlook, can exercise great power and influence. But that power and influence is unaccountable in any obvious democratic fashion. Networks of interlocking directorates, for example, may weld together men and women of high finance and industrial muscle who decide matters between themselves informally. Those decisions then have a profound impact on the economy and beyond. But how can any collective influence be effective if the power so controlled is neither visible nor accountable? Indeed, how can elected representatives properly conduct their own legitimate business if they face similar obstacles? The 'establishment'—operating as a network of influential opinion formers, agenda setters, and decision takers with a shared social, educational, and cultural background—may act to usurp and undermine genuine democratic government. If one happens to be in a network that may work to your advantage, but if you are one of those left out you may just have to put up with it.

A second and related set of criticisms of networks conceived in this way focuses upon the 'informal rationality' that pervades these types of coordinating mechanisms. This is contrasted to the 'procedural rationality' that is thought to typify both the hierarchy and the market model. The advantage of procedural rationality is that it tends to be open, explicit, and rule driven. It is either bureaucratic or contractual. Thus, it is not so obviously open to possible manipulation and abuse as an informal rationality might be. Informal rationality relies much more upon the operation of discretion. It allows the agents in the network to decide as suits their purpose and whim. The fact that the network does rely more on discretion leads to the awkward problem of potential corruption. Who is to monitor and police informal networks? Of course, corruption and abuse are not immune from the market or hierarchy either, far from it. But there would seem to be more scope, in principle, for this to arise if discretion becomes the dominant form of network operation. For instance, in some ways the Mafia is the perfect network structure (Gambetta 1998*a,b*). It relies upon trust, loyalty, solidarity, etc. (but not honesty!), and would seem to operate with a wide scope for pragmatic discretion.

Policy networks are often viewed as opportunity structures in which political exchange takes place between those 'in the loop' (Thatcher 1998, p. 391). Thus, the question arises as to what exactly is exchanged in this process. Clearly, nothing obviously alienable like money or a commodity is exchanged in these networks (other than if they are corrupt), so it is something like information or the transfer of 'influence resources'—promises to use part of your information or influence in the interests of the other party, and vice versa. But what ensures promises will be kept? One answer is 'embedded trust' (Pappi and Henning 1998, p. 565), which echoes all the conventional analysis of exchange-based approaches to networks outlined in Chapters 2 and 3 and critically interrogated in Chapter 4. Based upon pre-existing connections that define a loose configuration of influence, those with more connections can reach a wider circle of actors and can therefore have greater opportunity to negotiate mutually advantageous trades and exercise influence. SNA techniques are often used to establish the extent of these networks but they often operate ultra-informally, which makes it difficult to pin down their personnel and extent. They can also be analysed through a TCA framework. Policy networks reduce uncertainty and transaction costs, it is suggested. So transaction costs can act as access barriers to networks; elimination of transaction costs reduces these barriers, thereby opening networks up so that participation is encouraged until the point where the cost of transacting for the marginal participant by being within the network is equal to the benefit derived from being a member. See Chapters 3 and 4 for criticisms of this way of conceiving networks.[8]

In fact, we might well take this critique of networks even further. Above it was suggested that the attributes of a robust, cohesive, and long-term network were to be found in the notions of trust, loyalty, honesty, and the like. But one could point to networks where just the opposite characteristics were present. Thus, some networks might work on the basis of fear and suspicion. This can be particularly the case if groups of otherwise competing 'insiders' are faced with an even greater threat from a group of 'outsiders'. In this case, the insiders can generate an (possibly only temporary) alliance in the form of a network, to try and deal with the threatening outsiders and defend themselves. Despite the mutual suspicions between them, it is the insiders' greater fear of the outsiders that leads them to establish and sustain a working network between themselves. Something along these lines led to the formation and sustaining of many lobbying networks of British firms when faced with the threat from foreign, particularly Japanese, competitive suppliers in the 1970s and 1980s.

Finally, it may be that 'policy networks' are now being eclipsed by new forms of policy making that have drawn the whole process further into either the framework of hierarchical organization (or more

---

[8] But TCA could introduce a useful corrective in the context of the 'public sector reform' movement in places like the United Kingdom. This movement has resulted in a number of public–private partnerships in which large parts of the former public sector are handed over to the private sector to be run as private corporations, whilst the infrastructure remains in public ownership. This has led to an enormous build up of 'transactions costs': first in the form of consultants' fees to assess the feasibility of such moves, then in the form of the contract between the government and the private company to run the activity (these often run into several hundred pages), and finally in the form of monitoring and surveillance costs to assess performance (further regulatory Quangos). In the face of this, a moment's reflection on Williamson's analysis would indicate that there are good reasons why it is sensible to 'internalize' activity within a single organization rather than to have it 'externally' run by the market, so as to save on transaction costs.

into the ambit of market power, which is examined below). The first move in this direction is exemplified by the emergence of what in the United Kingdom is called the Quangos (quasi-governmental organizations). These organizations, which have been imposed upon the policy-making process from above, arose as the public domain was compartmentalized into a myriad of agencies, boards, and trust in conjunction with the imposition of quasi privatized quality standards, audits, and managerialist direction resulting from the 'reform' of the public sector (Skelcher 1998). These boards, trust and agencies 'compete' with one another in terms of meeting their targets for service provision as they are ordered into hierarchical league tables of *ex post* performance. The result is an odd combination of competition and command, where the ultimate authority has increasingly been appropriated into a command (and hierarchical) style of operation.

The second aspect of these moves is the development of the role of specialist advisers and policy units attached to departments of government designed to give 'private advice' on policy matters directly to government ministers. This bypasses both the traditional policy networks and the traditional advice and responsibility of Ministry Civil Servants.

Both of these developments concentrate policy-making power centrally. The creation of the policy units and the quasi-governmental trusts, agencies, and boards is not democratically organized and the personnel who are appointed to them are not elected or subject to the usual terms of accountability.[9] They have become the fiefdoms of politicians and the government in particular. In many ways these new arrangements undermine the more widely dispersed subagency 'policy networks' where a larger range of interests were involved in policy making and decisions.

6.8. Political Networks, Hierarchies, and the Market

Often, networks exist in the shadow of the market, majoritarian rule, or hierarchical authority—which actually enhances the effectiveness

---

[9] Skelcher (1998) estimated there were 70,000 *appointments* to these *Quangos* by the late 1990s.

of both networks and these other governance modes, and the outcomes emerging from their interactions. In this sense networks have proved to be effective governance mechanisms as they complement other forms. This idea of a 'shadow of hierarchy' relies upon the ability of a hierarchical authority to affect lower level interactions without coordinating these directly or unilaterally (a kind of 'action as a (vertical) distance'—see Chapter 3). It builds upon a distinction between a *hierarchical authority structure* (something difficult to avoid in matters of governance) and *hierarchical direction* operating to override decision preferences of other actors (Scharpf 1997). The former rests upon a threat, while the latter rests upon an intervention. Clearly, where there are networks of self-organization and self-government existing in the shadow of the state, we have a case of a hierarchical authority structure but one where the state does not necessarily directly intervene to coordinate decisions and the activity of the networks in any detail. Rather, it establishes the rules under which those networks operate. On the other hand, 'negotiating states' as such are an example of more overt direction, where the state intervenes to establish collective outcomes by negotiating as a party with the other associations of social partners, or acts as an 'honest broker' to bring these together under its auspices. As we have seen, this is sometimes expressed as 'private-interest government'— where the state enforces compulsory membership and shepherds the parties into negotiations (Streek and Schmitter 1985; Hollingsworth *et al.* 1994).

But this gives rise to ideas about how to manage these networks, which is the distinctive contribution of the so-called Dutch School of network analysis (Kickert *et al.* 1997). Whilst this approach celebrates the self-organizing and self-governing characteristics of policy networks, it also wants to ask how to manage these relationships, particularly how governments can manage them. One would expect self-organizing and self-governing networks to resist such steering and to jealously guard their own autonomously generated decision-making environments. Adopting such a managerial perspective on networks could then be seen as undermining the rationale of networks, and this remains a real possibility. But such a stance might actually enhance their long-term viability by providing the conditions for a sensible extension or support for their autonomy (thereby preventing network closure).

In addition, Sabel suggests that what is needed is a semi-hierarchical 'constitutional order' that provides the framework in which consultation and negotiation take place, sets the rules of the game, and resolves disputes between parties. Within this 'deliberative forum', a sense of collective participative management is set up. This guarantees flexibility, collective adaptability, mutual trust (rather than individual trust—see Chapter 4), in a way difficult to establish in either straightforward hierarchical or market situations.

And this suggestion is reinforced by the whole idea of associational democracy. Associationalism in this sense is not something exactly akin to the private interest governance of Schmitter and Streeck (though they sometimes use the same word—associational) because that is meant to be a description of things as they are already found in the political arena—one of the claims to say how existing policy networks are actually formulated and organized. Associationalism and associational democracy, on the other hand, are aspirational and normative suggestions as to how political decisional-making could, and indeed should, be organized so as to overcome what are argued to be inadequacies of contemporary social governance.

But as well as this 'shadow of hierarchy/state' we might also have the 'shadow of the past' and a 'shadow of the future' that hang over networks. The 'shadow of hierarchy' operates vertically, so to speak, whereas the shadows of the past and the future operate horizontally. The shadow of the past produces a certain disposition in the present amongst the players, based upon their experiences of past interactions. The shadow of the future involves the anticipation of what will happen as a consequence of various positions and moves adopted now, so there is a conception of the prospects resulting from present moves, which will cast a shadow forwards into the future. This means that decisions about present behaviours can be caught within these twin perceptual constraints.

The important analytical implications of these issues can be judged from the following contrast. Supposing we consider a number of players (A, B, C, etc.) in a network who are at first traditionally conceived as having strictly *independent* utility functions of the form $Ua = Va$; $Ub = Vb$, etc., where the Us are the utility of players A, B, etc. and Vs the pay-offs to the players. In this case—the selfish case— players are concerned only with their absolute advantage. Thus, they do not care what they or other players might achieve, or might not achieve, from cooperating with each other. This is analogous to the position in the PD game analyses above. It rules out cases where players have common or mixed interests.

But in contrast to this we might suggest that utility functions are *interdependent*, where common and mixed interests become signifi- cant, so that the relative position of advantage gains becomes impor- tant. Here any attempt to forge cooperation between players in the network might be dependent upon the perceived changes in rel- ative capabilities that the cooperation would bring about. If this were the case, the utility function for participant A would not just involve the term Va, but also an additional term Wb designating the partner player B's payoff (Grieco 1990). One way of thinking about Wb would be to view it as 'negatively' contributing to the player A's utility, so that if the capability 'gap' between the two players were to increase, the individual player A would feel threatened. In this case, the utility function becomes:

$$Ua = Va - k(Wb - Va); \quad 0 < k \qquad (6.1)$$

with k representing the network player A's coefficient of sensitivity to potential capability advantages or disadvantages perceived to arise as a result of cooperating with B. Note that with this formulation it is only gaps in gains favouring partners that reduces the utility a player enjoys from cooperation. Thus, this could lead the relatively disad- vantaged player to avoid cooperation altogether, even though the joint action promised it at least some individual absolute gain. This would happen if the gain gap ($k(Wb - Va)$) were sufficiently in its disfavour to outweigh the absolute individual gain (Va).[10]

---

[10] Of course, the reverse could happen. It could be that the gain gap is positively inscribed as between participants. In this case A's utility function would take the following form: $Ua = Va + k(Wb - Va)$. But this seems an unlikely case since it means that player A would actively encourage other players to gain an advantage over them since this positively adds to the player A's utility. See below in the main text for a more sensible way of formulating a positive relationship between player utilities.

Applications and Empirical Comparisons

Clearly, in these examples, the network players' utilities are at least partially interdependent so that one player's utility is affected by another's. This is a case of what has, in a different context, been called 'defensive positionalism' (Thompson 1998). But it also implies a suspicious attitude on the part of the players as they approach cooperation in a network—something that Sabel (1993) mentioned above suggests is an unfortunate, though nevertheless strong, characteristic of the analysis of network situations conceived in traditional game-theory terms.

These models, then, rely on a 'politics of suspicion' and a lack of goodwill on the part of players. In effect they begin from a selfish position of radical non-cooperation, non-trust, and non-interdependency, and ask how cooperation, trust, and interdependency can be built up. But the issue is that most network situations begin from positions that already display some cooperation, trust, and interdependency features, or begin with these attributes at least partly in place in some manner (otherwise, they could hardly exist as 'social' networks). Therefore, there is a need to begin from a different position, one that recognizes the already prior existence of these attributes in some form or another.[11]

Let us suppose, then, that the aim is to maximize the utility of the network system as a whole. It is further assumed for convenience that the utility of this system in time period 1 (Us_1), is additive of the utilities of the individual members of the network, A, B, C, etc.:

$$Us_1 = Ua_1 + Ub_1 + Uc_1 + \cdots + Un_1 \tag{6.2}$$

and that the utility of each individual player is itself now a combination of their own absolute advantage in this period and some

---

[11] This is a point to be made about all game theory approaches. They begin from a position of radical non-cooperation and ask how cooperation is built up without realizing that the actual world is made up of already existing cooperations. In addition, the problem with game theory is that it has become such a ubiquitous technique that a further prior question tends to get lost: 'Is this a game-ish situation?' Before the technique is used this question needs to be asked because many situations to which game theory is applied are just not that game-ish if examined closely. This applies in particular to those situations where there are clear fixed administrative rules for the conduct of relationships and business between the parties involved. Clear 'rules of engagement' between parties eliminate the capacity for bargaining and strategy. They undermine a space for the operation of discretion.

inherited goodwill derived from the cooperative nature of the network in the 'previous' period. Thus:

$$Ua_1 = Va_1 + j(Us_{t-1}); \quad 0 < j \qquad (6.3)$$

and

$$Ub_1 = Vb_1 + h(Us_{t-1}); \quad 0 < h \qquad (6.4)$$

where j and h are the goodwill sensitivity indicators for network members A and B, respectively, inherited from the previous time period (Us_{t-1}). Thus, we can rewrite the network system utility function in the present period as:

$$Us_1 = [Va_1 + j(Us_{t-1})] + [Vb_1 + h(Us_{t-1})]$$
$$+ \cdots + [Vn_1 + \infty(Us_{t-1})] \qquad (6.5)$$

This way of characterizing the network situation has the advantage of making it dynamic by building in some inherited activity from the past. Clearly the goodwill sensitivity factor is the crucial one. It represents a number of features of the network: the cooperation, trust, and interdependency benefits already built into any system that claims to be social. The 'goodwill coefficients' express the individual players' attitudes towards these features. Thus, the analytical issue from this point of view is not to ask how cooperation, trust, and interdependency can be built from nothing, but how can the network system and the members in it be encouraged to be more trustworthy or trusting, or differently trustworthy or trusting; or how can different forms of cooperation and interdependency be fostered; or how can the existing network system be modified to better suit players' interests and expectations, etc.

An interesting gloss on this way of conceiving the operation of networks broadly dealing with political decision-making is to see them as involving the activity of 'persuasion'. This is part of a way of characterizing the work that networks do as involving expectations of how others will behave—now and in the future—not as the result of a calculation or the reciprocal assessment of an advantage, but based upon an appeal to underlying norms, principles, and values that are shared by the participants in a 'conversation' (see also, Chapter 4). This is a form of rational persuasion that involves the changing of people's minds, their choices of alternatives, etc., independently of their calculations about the strategy of other players (Keohane 2001).

Such a stance towards the work of networks also helps in understanding how a more general approach to negotiation and bargaining within networks might be conceived, one organized around the notion of 'directly deliberative polyarchy' (Sabel and Cohen 2001). This is part of an attempt to characterize the European Union as an evolving political entity. Sabel and Cohen suggest that the EU's specialist expert committee system ('comitology') and the development of open methods of coordination (OMC) amount to a form of large-scale networking activity—almost 'network governance'.[12] While as yet this has been mainly confined to welfare and employment matters, it is something that is expanding in significance as a way of regulating the EU polity more widely. The overall system involves 'learning by doing' in which collaborative problem solving predominates, and a process of mutual capacitation between the parties unfolds. According to Sabel and Cohen, the different combinations of comitology and OMC dealing with different areas and functions calls into being a range of different 'publics' which in combination define the EU polity. Thus, this does not rely on a traditional conception of the 'demos', and whilst it is broadly inclusive, it is not an example of a 'deliberative democracy'. It is a deliberative *polyarchy* made up of the combinations of publics so created. Once

---

[12] Comitology refers to the systems of expert committees appointed by member states that advise the Commission and draft regulatory proposals for a vast range of EU activity. They operate by consensus, self-reflective deliberative debate, comparison and benchmarking across the different states, establishing rules and technical specifications. These specifications most often provide a framework within which member states compare and elaborate their own final regulations. OMC has more to do with procedures for integration, associated with economic development and social inclusion. It involves public–private partnerships, NGOs, relevant statutory authorities, and local social partners. They operate through iterative, critical comparisons of local initiatives, moving between the Commission and national implementation plans in a cycle of consultation, strategy making, guideline establishment, implementation monitoring and surveillance, and the re-assessment of priorities. The classic example of this is the European Employment Strategy.

again, this model undermines the traditional conception of representation and sovereignty with which we opened up this chapter. It involves another variant of the dispersed notion of sovereignty.

And in many ways this process could be seen to be mirrored in the United Kingdom as a consequence of the fragmentation of the traditional 'Westminster model' of political governance. This does not so much involve the hesitant moves towards devolution in the UK case, although it involves this in part, but has more to do with the fragmentation of the direct policy-making process. As mentioned above, the United Kingdom has been one of the homes for the development of the 'policy network' approach to coordination and governance, but this may now have been overtaken by subsequent events that have often been summed up under the broad term 'managerialism'. As discussed above, the United Kingdom has seen the proliferation of quangos as various semi-private/semi-public partnerships, trusts, agencies and boards have been charged with policy making and policy implementation activities, organized around performance targeting and quality control procedures. But this regime has now been joined by a growing number of 'policy units' attached to Departments of Government, that report directly to Ministers, thus adding another layer to the overall policy-making process. Whether this increasingly complex regime is another example of a 'directly deliberative polyarchy' remains controversial. On the surface it looks more like an attempt to take the policy making process much closer to the hierarchical model. So it may be that policy networks in the traditional sense are being squeezed in the United Kingdom from a newly reinvigorated hierarchical trend. The 'shadow of hierarchy' is growing and intensifying.

But, of course, policy networks are also being squeezed from a different angle, from the 'shadow of the market'. From this point of view, managerialism is a somewhat contradictory process. It involves not only a strengthening of hierarchical control but also the introduction of a number of market-inspired innovations to bolster this. Large swathes of the traditional public sector have been privatized or radically commercialized. Competition between agencies, the development of public–private partnerships, more accurate pricing of public services, competitive tendering, and the like, are the modalities of this particular part of the process. In the United Kingdom, for instance, the National Health Service is little more than a large 'command economy' where resources are allocated centrally, and most prices set centrally, but where its 'branches'—the health surgeries, trusts, and boards—'compete' with one another to provide the actual output, under the guidance of benchmarked norms, targets, and quality indicators. This looks suspiciously like a form of 'market socialism'. Whatever else it is it does not look very much like a network structure.

6.9. Conclusion

This chapter has taken a broad-brush look at the way the concept of network has been appropriated into the realm of political analysis and political policy making. The key concept highlighted was that of 'policy network', which has been used as a general term to designate a wide range of different forms of political coordination and governance. The debate about the appropriateness of these different designations; elites, associations, corporatisms, etc., provided the opportunity to examine the way they are argued to invoke the notion of network as an organizing principle for their operation.

In addition, the chapter served to open up a slightly more formal analysis of how the technique of game theory could be aligned both to an analysis of the political domain and to that of network operation in particular. In this respect, the main issue has been whether game theory models are anything more than just that; models. Can they be sensibly operationalized to provide genuine characterizations of the networking political process or are they destined to remain little more than metaphors; interesting analytical devices but with few realistic pay-off situations in the messy world of real political policy making? Here the argument was that, on balance, these models do genuinely tell us something about the decision-making process so they are worth studying for their analytical insights. But they need to be approached with caution.

The chapter has also highlighted the way politics and economics are closely linked in the formation and understanding of policy networks. Clearly, the game theory techniques examined here in a broadly political register are heavily deployed in the straightforward analysis of more obvious economic networks (and in other economic contexts involving strategic decision-making). But there are the additional linkages between economics and politics written into the idea of industrial districts (examined more closely in Chapters 5 and 7) and in respect to policy making across Europe and in the United Kingdom. The idea of 'social capital' offered another clear example of this linkage, tied up closely as it is to the context of comparative economic performance.

But the overall conclusion of the chapter must be that policy networks are under severe pressure. They are caught in a pincer movement between an increasingly confident 'shadow of hierarchy' on the one hand and an equally strident 'shadow of the market' on the other. Indeed, whilst one might say that policy networks have always been placed under a shadow of hierarchy—and rightly so since they need this as a regulatory condition and to maintain the necessary 'openness' of their operations—the contemporary turn in their activities is to reappropriate this business back into the traditional mainstream of policy making *within* government in a much more forceful way than has been experienced in recent decades. More and more of the policy-making process seem to be being brought back 'in-house'.

In addition, of course, the market also hovers over this in two ways. First as more and more of the traditional public sector business has been directly privatized or semi-privatized. And second, as that remaining public sector business has been itself subject to the dictates of a marketized regime of internal scrutiny and performance assessment.

These twin moves, then, may be heralding the demise of the policy network paradigm, or significant aspects of it, not only in the United Kingdom but also throughout Europe and the United States of America where similar pressures and moves have been felt over recent years.

Chapter 7

Networks and the International System

7.1. Introduction

One of the fastest expanding areas for the deployment of the network metaphor is with respect to the growth of international organizational relationships, involving economic, technological, political, and other governance and coordinating activity. This chapter discusses the way the network model operates in a number of discrete but linked areas. The link between them is provided by the term 'globalization', which they all claim to address and exemplify.

In the first place, we review a group of issues gathered around transnational interactions associated with new information and communications technologies (ICTs) like the Internet. Within the domain of network studies there is a fascination with the effect of the world wide web (www) on a whole range of political, social, and cultural relations—which it is worth investigating further.

Second, the idea of globalization is increasingly being reformulated in network terms. In this context, we begin with the relationship between the 'core and the periphery' in the international system.

Applications and Empirical Comparisons

This is argued to provide a linchpin for a number of subsequent specific areas that have developed out of the basic 'core periphery' model. One of these is a growing literature analysing the idea of 'global cities', which is being empirically interrogated with the aid of many of the techniques already discussed in earlier chapters, like social network analysis (SNA) and actor-network theory (ANT) (Chapter 3), but also involving new techniques for mapping interactions between cities.

Then we move on to the idea of 'commodity or value chain' analysis, which has to do with the processes and consequences of the internationalization of production and distribution. Commodity chains are presented as a mechanism for integrating international production networks and governing cross border production activities. This can be extended to revisit the discussion of interorganizational alliances, joint-production networks and partnerships, and international intra-organizational relationships, first considered in Chapter 5. Here the contrast is between the essentially domestic network relationship discussed in Chapter 5 and the explicitly international focus in this chapter, where the character of the TNC network organizational form is the focus. In addition, there are the more aggregated issues of international trade and migration, and questions of their consequences for the global economy. Here we include some discussion of the nature of globalization itself and particularly what impact this is having on industrial districts, regional economies, national systems of innovation and business, the 'transitional economies', etc. All this has also been conceived in network terms.

Finally, an important element in this growth of concerns involving networks is an extension of the discussion of the politics of international economic governance to reimagine or reinterpret it in network terms. As was discussed in the previous chapter, the idea of 'policy networks' (Reinicke and Deng 2000) is becoming a strong element in this reformulation, as is the related notion of 'multi-level governance' (Hooghe and Marks 2001). But policy networks and multilevel governance have been supplemented by other ideas with a slightly longer pedigree, such as 'epistemic communities' (conceived as a form of 'international regime'—see Krasner 1983, and Chapter 6, footnote 3).

The overall tone of this analysis will be to take all these areas seriously but at the same time to question whether, (a) they are quite as significant as is often claimed, and (b) in particular, to stress the continued salience of the national territory as a site for these forms of activity and as the key component in the structure of their interactions.

Much of the analysis in this area presumes that the 'global transnational networks' being constructed by growing international integration and interdependence are rapidly eroding the pertinence of national borders for governance and coordination, which are, as a consequence, being reconfigured through new 'informal' mechanisms beyond the reach of the nation-state (e.g. in the form of 'supraterritoriality', Scholte 2000).[1] This will be interrogated for each of the issue areas just mentioned in the investigations that follow.

7.2. The Internet and the WWW

Probably the most forceful exponent of the radical importance of the Internet in reshaping the whole nature of domestic—but more importantly, international—social and economic relationships is Manuel Castells. His thesis about the 'network society' was first fully announced in the 1996 book *The Rise of the Network Society* (RNS) (Castells 1996), and the thesis was more or less restated in *The Internet Galaxy* five years later (Castells 2001). These books are about the economic and social dynamics of the new information age. What are the effects of the new information technologies on the contemporary world? To quote from the inside cover of *The Rise of the Network Society (RNS)*:

The global economy is now characterized by almost instantaneous flow and exchange of information, capital and cultural communication. These flows order and condition both consumption and production. The networks themselves reflect and create distinctive cultures. Both they and

---

[1] 'The difference between globality and internationality needs in particular to be stressed. Whereas international relations are *inter*territorial relations, global relations are *supra*territorial relations. International relations are *cross*-border exchanges *over* distance, while global relations are *trans*-border exchanges *without* distance' (p. 49, emphasis in the original).

the traffic they carry are largely outside national regulation. Our dependence on the new modes of information flows gives enormous power to those in a position to control them to control us.

Similarly sentiments emerge in the *Internet Galaxy* (*IG*), which concentrates more on the history and significance of the www though its basic themes overlap with the earlier book (the following is again taken from the inside cover):

The popular and commercial diffusion of the Internet has been extraordinary—instigating and enabling changes in virtually every area of human activity and society. We have new systems of communication, new businesses, new media and sources of information, new forms of political and cultural expression, new forms of teaching and learning, and new communities.

In both these cases it is the image of a network that informs the analytical description of the shape that the new society wrought by these technological changes is creating. This 'network society' displays all the attributes of a virtual reality and a systemic volatility, where innovation is continuous, risk endemic, space and time shrinking, crises and marginalization rife, etc. This 'internationalized network society' continually undercuts the ability of nation states to control it, recasting them as bit players in a fast evolving transnationalized environment of increasingly privatized and individualized personal relationships.

There are three preliminary points to make about this imagery. The first is that it reproduces much of what has been dealt with in detail in earlier chapters so there will be no need to re-elaborate its full content again here. In particular, the basic discussion of network order in Chapter 2, the discussion of intra- and interorganizational relationships, the nature of knowledge that circulated around networks and their self-organizing character from Chapter 5, and the political underpinnings and resonance of networks from Chapter 6 will all find an echo here. Second, the imagery is resolutely 'technologically deterministic' in tone and content; its meta-theoretical pretensions, whilst sensitive to the socio-economic context or framework for social analysis (see below) make technological advance the *sin qua non* of the new information economy and network society it invokes (cf. Friedmann 2000). Third, whilst there is much to commend in Castells' detailed treatment of these issues, the burden of the following critical engagement will be to argue that the thesis remains an exaggerated one. Indeed, in the case of the 'network society' the argument is that it is just plain wrong.

Interestingly, Castells does not devote much time to defining networks in his books. The term crops up continually and is used liberally, but it is taken very much for granted in the texts. There are a few key concepts that are deployed throughout both books: 'network', 'network enterprise', 'networking logic', and of course 'network society'. These are defined as follows:

- '*A network* is a set of interconnected nodes . . . *Networks* are open structures, able to expand without limit, integrating new nodes as long as they are able to communicate with the network, namely as long as they share the same communication codes (e.g. values and performance goals). A network-based social structure is a highly dynamic, open system, susceptible to innovating without threatening its balance.' (*RNS*, p. 270)
- '. . . the *network enterprise* [is] the organizational form built around business projects resulting from the cooperation between different components of different firms, networking among themselves for the duration of a given business project, and reconfiguring their networks for the implementation of each project.' (*IG*, p. 67)
- '. . . *networking logic* of any system or set of relationships [are those] using these new information technologies. The morphology of the network seems to be well adapted to increasing complexity of interaction and to unpredictable patterns of development arising from the creative power of such interactions.' (*RNS*, p. 61)
- 'I propose the hypothesis that the *network society* is characterized by the breaking down of rhythmicity, either biological or social, associated with the notion of the life cycle' (*RNS*, p. 446). This has to do with the arrival of something Castells calls 'timeless time': 'I propose the idea of timeless time, as I label the dominant temporality of our society, occurs when the characteristics of a given context, namely, the informational

paradigm and the *network society*, induce systemic perturbations in the sequential order of phenomena performed in that context. This perturbation may take the form of compressing the occurrence of phenomena, aiming at instantaneity, or else by introducing random discontinuity in the sequence. Elimination of sequence creates undifferentiated time, which is tantamount to eternity.' (*RNS*, p. 464)

A central assessment of these conjectures and hypothesis, which Castells to his credit does try to empirically verify, must turn on whether there is a 'new information economy' and a network society that goes with it. This is, of course, the subject of intense comment and debate. Here I concentrate on just one aspect of this, but it is a central one: the advent of ICTs and their impact on the idea of globalization.

Let us stick to the Internet for a moment. Do we have an internationalized e-economy? (Baily and Lawrence 2001). Of course, in large part this depends upon how one defines the idea of a 'new economy'. The difficulties here are legion. Just to give two examples, the US Council of Economic Advisors (2002) restricts its analysis very much to the dominance of ICTs (p. 58–60), whereas an analysis for The Bank of England by Wadhwani (2001) includes a wider set of structural changes, including 'globalization', intensifying product market competition, financial market liberalization, changes in the labour market flexibility, and other factors (p. 495). Both these argue that there is a 'new economy' in the United States and possibly the United Kingdom, but not elsewhere. In addition McGuckin and van Ark (2002), for the US Conference Board see a new economy only appearing in the United States, as US productivity figures soar away from the rest of the world. None of these analyses, then, would unequivocally support the idea of an internationalized new economy, 'e' or otherwise.

But let us tackle this from a slightly different angle. In 2001, the estimated global e-commerce turnover was between US\$400 bn and US\$500 bn. Adding in m-commerce revenue to this (financial e-business) contributes another US\$150 bn. Thus a reasonable estimate of total e-business would be somewhere between US\$550 bn and US$650 bn.[2] World GDP in 2001 was estimated to be some-where between US$47,000 bn and US$50,000 bn. Taking an aver-age of each of these estimates ($600 bn and $48,500 bn) means total e-business revenue was just about 1.25 per cent of world GDP in 2001. But this is obviously not comparing like with like. Revenue figures are not strictly comparable with GDP, which is a value-added measure. Revenues can be many times GDP. Thus even the figures so far would seriously *overestimate* the importance of the ICT sector. It has been estimated that on average *company* value-added is between 20 and 30 per cent of their sales revenues (Wolf 2002). Taking 25 per cent as an estimate means that the value-added of total e-commerce was only US$150 bn in 2001. Comparing this to GDP gives a figure of just 0.3 per cent of world income. Putting this another way 99.7 per cent of the global economy was made up of 'old-economy' or 'non-e' economic activity. And even if total e-business was twice as much as this (it is very difficult to get accu-rate figures: Fraumeni 2001 and UNCTAD 2001 discuss the issues) it still means that e-business would have been just 0.6 per cent of total world output. Thus, the 'weightless economy' hardly exists.[3]

What is more, total e-business is made up of a number of different components or 'layers' (see University of Texas: Internet Economy Indicators—www.internetindicators.com). The first of these is 'Infrastructure Provision' (telecom companies, Internet Service Providers (ISPs), Internet backbone carriers, end use equipment manufacturers), the second is 'Internet Application Infrastructure' (software products and services, transactions intermediaries, service consultancies that design, build, and maintain websites); then there

---

[2] These figures are rough calculations derived from www.net-profit.co.uk; www.internetindicators.com; Fraumeni 2001, table 1; and United Nations Conference of Trade and Development 2001. See below in the main text for caveats and commentary.

[3] There exist many wild 'estimates' forecasting a spectacular growth of IT business in the future, particularly B2B (see for instance comments in Fraumeni 2001 and Lucking-Reiley and Spulber 2001). Since most of these forecasts are produced by management consultants who have a vested interest in 'boosting' the importance of the sector, these need to be taken with extreme caution. In addition, most of these estimates were made before the crash of the IT sector stock values, before the downturn in the US economy, and before the events of September 2001. And OECD (2002) provides later figures that show no dramatic increases in ICT activity.

is 'Internet Intermediary Activity' (advertising, the maintenance of membership organizations); and finally 'Internet Commerce' itself, made up of companies conducting web-based commercial transactions like B2B, B2C and m-commerce. It is this final level that attracts the attention and is the public face of the Internet, but it only comprises a third of the total in terms of revenues and employment. If the global e-commerce revenue figures quoted above *included* revenues from these various layers (this is difficult to determine from the raw data) then the real 'business' conducted just over the Internet is even smaller than the percentages calculated so far, possibly as low as 0.01 per cent of global GDP. On the other hand, if they *exclude* these layers, then value added is potentially three times as much as the initial estimates, that is, between 1.2 and 2.4 per cent of global GDP. Whatever estimate one takes, however, e-business remains trivial.

In addition, B2B, B2C and m-commerce are heavily concentrated in the United States. Eighty five percent of total revenues in 2000 were generated in the United States (calculated from International Comparative Data, www.net-profit co.uk). Thus, for all real intents and purposes the Internet economy—such that it is—is a uniquely American experience.

So what do people (Americans) do on line? On an average day in late 2000, some 60 million Americans went on-line (there were about 106 million with Internet access—all the following statistics are taken from www.pewinternet.org/reports/). The ten most popular things people did were; send email (49 per cent), surf the web for fun (23 per cent), get news (22 per cent), look for information on a hobby (19 per cent), check the weather (17 per cent), look for political news/information (17 per cent), do research for their job (16 per cent), do a search to answer a specific question (15 per cent), get financial information (13 per cent), research a product or service before buying it (13 per cent). The ten least popular activities were; buying or selling financial instruments; making a phone call; going to a dating website; buying groceries (all 1 per cent), participating in an on-line auction; looking for a place to live; gambling (all 2 per cent), and visiting an on-line support group (3 per cent). Things like going to an on-line chat room were not popular (4 per cent), nor was banking on-line (4 per cent) or buying a product (5 per cent). (The order of these daily activities were similarly mirrored by *all* activity over the net—see www.pewinternet.org/reports/ 'Overall Internet Population'.)

What are we to make of these activities? Clearly, most people are using the Internet to do the most mundane of existing tasks slightly more easily. They are above all else keeping up with already existing contacts by sending e-mails, not experimenting much with chatrooms, support groups, dating sites, etc., where they would likely meet new contacts and genuinely 'network'. Nor are they doing much buying or selling. Although there was some activity surfing to find information about products and services very little of this turned into the actual purchase of anything *via the net*. Thus, while people may be 'globally connected' by the Internet, they seem to be 'locally orientated' with respect to its use. And up to now at least, it has presumably not changed their lives that much. And this impression is confirmed if we look at whether the Internet makes people more sociable, more community minded, more trustworthy of others, better citizens, etc., that is, all those attributes that are often thought to be features of network type structures. Studies have found that, while those who use the Internet may *already be* more sociable and friendly, the use of the medium changes very little in terms of these 'civic aspects' of their lives (Uslaner 2000; Howard *et al.* 2001). It does not enhance 'community values' (or 'social capital'—see Chapter 6) in any substantial way. What Internet use shows is that social capital is more a prerequisite for, rather than a result of, effective computer-mediated communication (Putnam 2000; Kavanaugh and Patterson 2001; Wellman *et al.* 2001).

Of course it would be wrong to suggest it is only the Internet that comprises the 'new economy'. In principle it involves much more than this: information technologies are expected to affect the entire manufacturing and service sectors. It affects the 'old economy' as well as the 'new' one. This is not the place to assess these claims in any detail but a basic problem with the thesis has been to find the productivity benefits that would be expected to have emerged across the entire economy if there had been such an IT revolution. Again, the evidence here is at best mixed (Thompson 2003). As of 1999 there was still no clear indication that the productivity growth in the United States was in any way historically exceptional for that economy overall. Whilst there had been a prodigious growth in productivity in the computer-manufacturing sector (between 1995 and 1999 a 42 per cent *annual growth rate* in output per hour), this sector comprised less that 1.5 per cent of overall US output. Productivity in the overall manufacturing sector was increasing at about 5 per cent per annum in the late 1990s, but the record for the rest of the economy, particularly the service sector, remained modest (though see Baily and Lawrence 2001, and McKinsey and Company 2001). Recent estimates have been more upbeat about the US position (Council on Competitiveness 2001; Council of Economic Advisors 2002), and there is some evidence that IT led productivity growth is developing in other OECD countries as well after significantly lagging behind the United States (Daveri 2000; Gust and Marquez 2000—though see Roeger 2001; McMorrow and Roeger 2001 for a detailed analysis of how far the European Union has lagged behind the United States and the reasons for this, and Oulton's 2001 detailed study of the United Kingdom which reaches similar conclusions). However, there is little systematic evidence of significant spillover effects from ICT investment into the economy as a whole, which is one of the reasons for the concentration on the possible role of 'intangibles' discussed in Chapter 4. Thus, the reasons for the lack of a clear productivity miracle in the United States and elsewhere as a direct result of ICT investment, and whether such a miracle will emerge in the near future, still remain unclear (Graham 2001).

At the global level, B2B revenue comprises 85 per cent of total e-business revenues (www.net-profit.co.uk; International Comparative data). Thus what is going on in this sector is key to the economic effects of the Internet. If we examine the business strategies that it engenders these mainly involve reaping cost efficiencies from the automation of transactions between businesses (e.g. Wise and Morrison 2000; Lucking-Reiley and Spulber 2001). In particular, while the establishment of intermediation agencies—on-line exchanges—provided a first cut at cost reduction, there is intense discussion as to whether these will themselves be eclipsed by more direct B2B trading (Wise and Morrison 2000; Kogut 2003). However, whatever one makes of these arguments, two issues are clear. First, these moves may just as likely undermine any 'networking' relationships already established between main producers and their suppliers as to reinforce or encourage such networking relationships. Cheaper new suppliers found via the ICT exchanges might usurp established networks of suppliers. Second, these moves look suspiciously like a rather traditional business strategy, even as tied up with all the new imagery. That is, as just another move in the relentless downward pressure put on supplier cost margins in an attempt to take out yet more 'fat' from the supply chain. There is little that looks radically new here.[4]

Thus, it is difficult to know what the long-term implication of e-business will be in terms of its impact on networks. Leamer and Storper (2001) argue that there is a difference between those businesses that require a 'handshake' for the conduct of their activities and those that merely require a 'conversation', which can be conducted with the aid of ICTs at a distance. If, however, new activities increase the complexity of design and production this might increase the need for face to face contact. In addition the inevitable incompleteness of contracts will always imply the necessity for handshake transactions and regular face to face contact to iron out difficulties. ICTs complement this; they do not displace it. Information for detailed product specifications, the organization of production schedules, and the monitoring of quality standards cannot all be codified in advance. There is no quick technical fix for the monitoring of all of this. It requires the continuation of proximity, the clustering of activities where they can be controlled and monitored through handshake transactions (see also Council on Competitiveness 2001 for the rationale for 'clustering' as a consequence of this).

---

[4] Some would challenge this as a *future* model for all new businesses, however. For instance with respect to a particular and limited business sector, the US and UK advertising industry, Grabher has argued these are adopting a completely new business organizational style—the 'project model'—that is emblematic of wider changes in networking structures that will infect all business relationships as a result of the emergence of ICTs (Grabher 2001). Such a 'project model' of time limited collaborative relationships between parties to complete a specific task may be all very well for 'creative' enterprises in the advertising sector, but it does not look an attractive or viable option for the production of complex manufacturing goods, for instance, which require the establishment of enduring and long-term relationships. But note how it chimes with Castells' idea of the 'network enterprise' defined above.

There is a limit to the diversification and dispersion of production. Networks continue to do their work 'locally'. Just-in-time production process technologies (which make full use of ICTs) concentrate supplier plants around assembly plants, and centralization has grown here in recent years (Klier 1999). ICT dependent financial service industries remain tethered to a few huge cities as agglomeration economies continue to focus activities around existing centres (Venables 2001).

Finally, the advent of widespread use of ICTs should not lead us to believe that distances and time have become unimportant (or that time is now 'instantaneous'—cf. Castells and Scholte above). For instance, although there has been a significant reduction in the costs of conducting international trade (Baldwin and Martin 1999), there still remains an active trade off between time and cost (Hummels 2000), and distance continues to remain a formidable barrier to trade and other economic activity (Venables 2001; Thompson 2002).[5]

7.3. Patterns of International Interaction, Globalization, and Networks

None of this should be thought to underestimate the growth of international interactions along such dimensions as travel, telephone usage, Internet connections, educational links, or scientific and technological knowledge networks. These are all often seen as a manifestation of increased 'globalization', and they are increasingly interpreted through the metaphor of 'networks'. It is the way globalization and networks are linked together through a particular filter that operationalizes the relationship between the dimensions just mentioned that is investigated in this section. For the most part this filter is associated with a certain 'mapping' of the international interconnections arrayed along

[5] It should be remembered that 80 per cent of world trade is still merchandize trade (agricultural goods, minerals and manufactures), which requires a physical movement across space. Only 20 per cent is service trade, including financial services, which is more amenable to ICT penetration (WTO 2001, tables 1.3 and 1.4). These proportions have remained more or less stable since 1975.

these dimensions of activity, and interpreting this as a strong indicator of 'globalization' (Hargittai and Centeno 2001—which is an introduction to the Special Issue of the *American Behavioural Scientist* titled 'Mapping Globalization' dealing with these dimensions of international connectivity). This approach has strong affiliations with the SNA discussed in Chapter 3. But it also has other determinants, in particular the neo-Marxist 'world systems' model originally closely associated with theorists like Andre Gunder Frank (1979), Samir Amin (1974), Giovanni Arrighi (1978), and Immanuel Wallerstein (1974). Perhaps the best known contemporary inheritors of this underlying position are Gary Gereffi (Gereffi and Korzeniewicz 1994) and Christopher Chase-Dunn (1989).

It is important to trace the legacy of this approach since it casts a long shadow over its contemporary analytical register, and helps explain the strengths and—as will be emphasized later—the serious weaknesses of the approach. As suggested, the underlying analytical framework in which it operates is variously referred to as a 'neoMarxist', 'dependency', 'structuralist', 'centre–periphery', or 'world systems' approach.[6] This model is resolutely 'systemically global' in character. It sees the international system as just that, a highly integrated *system* where all the parts of the world economy, polity, and society are drawn together into a relationship of superordination and subordination operationalized through an exploitative mechanism organized around variously conceived concentric rings, stretching from the 'periphery', into the 'semi-periphery', and finally to the 'centre/core'. At heart this system relies upon an exploitative *economic* relationship, one by which surpluses generated at the periphery are progressively sucked into the centre (via a mechanism of 'unequal exchange' or 'unfair trade'), with economic and political power flowing in the opposite direction.[7]

Although this model has been adapted to suit the contemporary conditions of 'global capitalism' its neoMarxist intellectual credentials and terminology should not be forgotten. These helped shape the

---

[6] Obviously there are differences between all these but they share more than they differ and they have a common lineage with the founding authors just mentioned.

[7] With respect to the idea of 'globalization' as explicitly linked to this position, see Hoogvelt (1997).

manner of the analysis and its results. Laid over the periphery-centre imagery, for instance, is a conception of these relationships as akin to networks stretching around and through the international system. Networks have become the contemporary terminology of choice for this approach. Networks serve as the multifarious conduits through which the 'surpluses'—or flows of resources—move from the peripheries to the centres on the one hand, while on the other hand influence and authority move simultaneously in the opposite direction, from the centre/core to the periphery.

Second, the approach lends itself nicely to a geographical interpretation. It readily displays a spatial element which is well exploited in the context of networks and which can easily be translated into a mapping of the connections and relationships involved (Zook 2001). In addition, while the centre/periphery imagery has no necessary locational essentiality, the approach is driven by an underlying and lingering 'class' conception which resists an easy attachment to a 'nation-state to nation-state' set of linkages. The networks of connections, as a result, are rather more amorphously specified. The enduring patterns the approach uncovers are less 'nation-centered' than 'zone-centered', driven by the concentric ring analogy. These zones are either ones inhabited by antagonistically poised class interests or by political and economic elites able to exploit their favourable structural positions at the centre to control the periphery. Furthermore, in some cases this geographical specificity has been taken over by 'global cities' rather than nation-states, so that the network relationships between cities—which can also secondarily be conceived as hierarchically ordered—becomes the spatial mode for mapping connections and linkages. Thus, we have a 'Global Cities' imagery (e.g. Sassen 1991), which constitutes the new defining moment of globalization. Powerful 'global cities' utilize their structural position within international network linkages both to establish their power and to consolidate it against the interests of the structurally weak and disadvantaged.[8]

---

[8] There is a longer history to the world/global cities literature discussed here, see in particular Friedmann (1986).

Before we go on to evaluate these network approaches to the contemporary international system it is worth mentioning another more historically grounded approach, which has assessed the long process of urbanization in network terms. The origin of this is to be found with Hohenberg and Hollen Lees (1985) analysis of the urbanization of Europe, where this is seen in terms of a structure involving a Central Place system and a Network system of towns and cities. The Central Place system is seen essentially as a hierarchical set of relationships between a principal centre and its subordinate towns, and between these regional central places and other higher level ones, so there is a 'Russian Doll' like system of central places within central places. The Network system then joins these various central places with the 'outside world' beyond the town, the city, or the region, on an increasingly worldwide scale. These networks involve trade, information and influence, encouraging specialization and comparative advantage for urban areas to emerge. This basic model was taken up by De Landa (1997) to provide a dynamic model of urban growth, involving a complex system of markets and hierarchies combined *in* a conception of networks (what he calls 'meshworks') which sees these as self-organizing, self-governing entities caught in non-linear cycles of growth and decay, sudden fracture and reconstitution, etc., where the international connections between cities are crucial to the overall process. (See also Chapters 1, 5, and 8.)

7.4. An Evaluation

What are we to make of this style of analysis? Taking the global cities aspect of it first, the earlier incarnations of this were rather 'speculative' in character, invoking the importance of various large cities, which had an obvious and enduring international importance and merely re-invoking this in a new terminology of networks and globalization (e.g. Sassen 1991, 1994). Thus, it would be difficult to argue against a thesis that New York, London, and Tokyo were in some way 'global cities'. Clearly, their significance is in the designation 'global', implying a relative disentanglement from the domestic territories in which these cities are located and then finding a new pattern to their importance as power centres with respect to their relationship to *other* global cities. This interlinked set of network type relationship between cities represents the new pattern of power, demarcating what is different about the present era, and this is designated the key feature of contemporary globalization. Global cities are the command and control centres of the new global capitalist economy. That network of relatively disengaged 'global cities' is now the new 'core' in the international system, while their hinterlands come to represent the new 'peripheries'.

This early analytical stance is characterized as 'speculative' since it was not strongly based on any new systematic evidence of network connections (it was comparative 'case study' based). But what has marked more recent research is an attempt to seriously map the nature of the interconnections between cities to establish which ones—if any—are genuinely 'global' and which ones are secondary centres. Thus, there is no presupposition that any particular city that happens to be large and seemingly well connected internationally, is necessarily in the first rank of the global cities. The attempt has been to establish the 'globality' of cities in terms of a range of potential dimensions of connectivity and to subject these to a rigorous statistical analysis, deploying the techniques of SNA, principle component analysis, and other 'spatialized' tests (e.g. Beaverstock *et al.* 2000; Smith and Timberlake 2001; Taylor 2001; Taylor *et al.* 2001*a,b*; Townsend 2001). Smith and Timberlake use air passenger travel statistics between cities to calculate a hierarchy of city types over a twenty-year period (1977–97). They find a set of core cities, 'surprising continuities' in the hierarchy, but with some changes as Latin American cities fell in the connectivity hierarchy and East Asian ones rose. Townsend looks at Internet connections between cities to establish the dominant position of the US cities in 'Internet backbone networks'; with a number of secondary 'clusters' arrayed alongside this. But the work of Peter Taylor and his research group at Loughbrough University is particularly incisive in this respect. Not content just to invoke big cities as global cities, this research establishes a three level 'interlocking network' of intercity relations: nodal level (cities), internodal level (networks), and subnodal level (firms) by examining the connectivity of business service firms through their head-office and subsidiaries or branch-office relations.[9] This is used to draw a distinction between 'global cities' and 'world cities': the former comprising just London and New York while the latter includes many more cities that are variably configured with respect to the range of types of business service activity concerned (accounting, law, consultancy, banking and finance, advertising, etc.). Thus a complex and enduring 'structure' of city types and networks can be established, derived directly from the data on connectivity.[10]

7.5. Economic Connectivity as Globalization?

Set within the same intellectual space as these analyses of global cities, network interconnectivity and centre/periphery relations is another investigative framework that has had a somewhat longer pedigree. The 'world systems' approach to economic relationships has given rise to a set of detailed empirical investigations concerning the nature of the new global capitalist system and its networking type structures. These are designed to be more systematic about the location of *nations* in the world system and the dynamics of its evolution. In addition there is some attempt through these mechanisms to identify the system of control and dependency that operate between nations (Snyder and Kick 1979; Breiger 1981; Nemeth and

---

[9] From this perspective cities are 'nodes' but not 'actors'. However, this SNA approach could be supplemented by adding an ANT aspect to it. This would dissolve the local/global dichotomy (and presumably, the centre/periphery one as well) in favour of longer and more intensely connected, always 'localized', networks. Such that the idea of nodes is deployed in ANT it implies a topology with as many dimensions as connections rather than as a fixed point (the 'city') with certain definable characteristics (see Dicken *et al.* 2001). Cities would, as a result, be just another actor-network, caught in the same conceptual space as analysed with respect to discussion of ANT in Chapter 3. See also Chapter 8, where the dominant post-ANT position is reviewed.

[10] Taylor's strong underlying relationship to the 'worlds system' approach can be found in Taylor 1996. His position is an interesting one, however, in that—unlike a lot of those developing the global cities framework—he does not see the new 'world cities' as necessarily opposed to nation-states, and thereby undermining the significance and authority of nation states. Rather they are co-evolving in that new configuration designated as 'globalization' (Taylor 2000).

Applications and Empirical Comparisons

Smith 1985; Smith and Nemeth 1988). All these authors use an SNA blockmodel approach to establish exchange networks that determine positions in a hierarchy of market transactions operating from the periphery to the core. Refinements to the basic model have identified different patterns for different types of trade or capital flows (though these also tend to be 'interlocked' so that an overarching structure is preserved), and multiple and competing centres and peripheries have also been identified, so that there may be networks rather than a single network (Breiger 1981). This has provoked the suggestion that there might be a multi-strata world economy with several semi-peripheries and cores.

But essentially, what these approaches emphasize is that the *exogenous* structural position of nations in world trade-flow networks in large part determines their economic development prospects. This is done by correlating position in the periphery/semi-periphery/core hierarchy with historic economic growth records. Association is thereby taken as determination (at least in large part), so that low income and growth is correlated with peripheral or semi-peripheral status. However much these approaches try to shake off a conception that relies upon an *external* determining structure to limit the *internal* possibilities of growth and development, this is undermined by the emphasis on the network of the global system as the key structural constraint.

But these are essentially static takes on dependency and the world system. What has been happening over time? Several analyses from within this perspective addressed this issue (Smith and White 1992; Su 1995; Chase-Dunn *et al.* 2000; Kick and Davis 2001). These longitudinal studies, while uncovering a more complex structure, have nevertheless stressed the continuity of the core-periphery variable, indicating that there still exist stratum boundaries between concentric zones of some significance. These studies also note the high level of structural stability seen in the data even in periods of seemingly significant and rapid underlying economic change. In particular the 'core' has increased in size and density, as mobility of nations tends to be upwards rather than downwards. But there may also have been a real segmentation in world markets that set-in in the 1990s, where competition is essentially between clustered blocs rather than between a centre and various peripheries. In some ways the 1990s marked a return to the 1930s, with the re-emergence of spheres of influence (Su 1995), though the overall level of trade integration is higher, it is suggested (Chase-Dunn *et al.* 2000). Indeed, there were some signs even in the 1970s of the emergence of several competing cores, as mentioned above, and this pattern of the regionalization of trade relationship, rather than their total globalization, has become even more evident from within this perspective (Kleinknecht and Wengel 1998; Pelagidis and Chortareas 2002).

7.6. Commodity/Value Chains as Networks?

Another slightly different take on this world systems imagery is provided by the notion of value-chains or commodity-chains that operate internationally. While value chains and commodity chains are somewhat different conceptions they are often run together (e.g. Johnston and Lawrence 1988; IDS 2001). Value (or value-adding) chains are most closely associated with Michael Porter's investigations into competitive advantage (Porter 1985, 1990). His framework concentrates upon the role of the complete firm in the chain of firms that produce goods and services. Formally it stresses the key value-added element in any chain of international production. How and where is the value-added generated and which firm (or country) appropriates it? On the other hand commodity chains, whilst not neglecting the value-added component, tend to stress the various activities as discrete stages in the chain and how they are coordinated or governed.[11] Thus, we can think of a move along, say, an agricultural chain: from the farmer, to the broker, to the basic food processor, to the package goods producer, to the wholesale distributor, to the retailer, and then, finally, to the consumer, where the key aspect is the control and coordination of these activities. But the commodity chain approach can also deal with incomplete firms, so

[11] The connection between the contemporary global commodity chain analysis and the world systems approach operates through Wallerstein. See Hopkins and Wallerstein (1986) where a commodity chain is defined as 'a network of labour and production processes whose end result is a finished commodity' (p. 159).

that parts of the chain may fall across firms or several parts fall within a single firm. In addition, there is another related take on these matters expressed by the French term *filière* (thread) (Raikes *et al.* 2000). This approach has been mainly confined to agricultural product chains and is very much in a tradition of empirically tracing the technical linkages between elements in the supply chain, emphasizing physical flows and commodity transformations. Finally, it should be noted that one of the latest moves in the ANT approach reviewed in Chapter 3—the 'economy of qualities'— adopts a similar chain approach to the way the qualities of goods, and particularly services, are transformed as they move through a 'network' of supply involving design, production, distribution, and consumption stages (see Chapter 3, footnote 5, and Barry and Slater 2002). However, despite these initial differences, as just suggested the term 'value chain' is now used to summarize these various forms of linkages (the exception being the ANT version, which is not so much concerned with any value-added of the chain as with the con-figuration and reconfiguration of the actor-networks associated with the quality characteristics at each of its various stages).

The key point about this conception is that the value chain is seen as a whole rather than as simply an aggregation of its individual parts. If each player has a stake in the other's success, the entire value chain is the competitive unit. This imparts a network like character to the chains, and when they are conceived as stretching across borders they fit neatly into a globalization framework. What are being dealt with here then are issues of the integration of production across borders.

But this poses a problem of securing the 'cooperation' between players; hence the emphasis on coordination *and* governance. Geriffi, a key analyst in the global commodity chain (GCC) approach, tackles this by asking who 'organizes' the chain? Two responses have been forthcoming (Gereffi and Korzeniewicz 1994). On the one hand we have producer-driven chains, where the key lead agent is situated at the production end of the chain (say, a man-ufacturer), while on the other hand we have buyer-driven chains, where the lead agent is nearer the consumption end (a retailer, say). The first suits an own equipment manufacturing (OEM) style of production process while the latter suits an own brand-name manufacturing (OBM) style (though these are not mutually exclusive). For each of these chains, particular and key agents are seen as taking the responsibility of 'organizing' the governance of the chain, sometimes cooperatively, sometimes through more coercive means. And here is a site of much controversy: (a) can these distinctions between producer-driven and buyer-driven chains be maintained?[12]; (b) what is the precise role of power and authority within the chain, and how does it operate?; (c) who, as a consequence, appropriates the 'value-added' rents or surpluses and where are these located? This also raises a set of policy issues (Kaplinski and Morris 2001). How can new chains be established, successful ones fostered, adaptation and upgrading encouraged, key value-added stages be relocated, etc.

7.7. An Assessment of 'World-systems' and 'Value/Commodity Chain' Approaches

There are a number of issues that arise in connection to these value chain and core–periphery models.

In the first place, the original world systems approach, with its 'periphery/semi-periphery/core' structure was always predicated on an exploitative economic mechanism. And this lingers for all those subsequent variations that have tried to elaborate or update the approach. But the key issue is the actual mechanism by which the exploitation is organized. How are the surpluses (or in modern parlance 'rents') systematically moved from the periphery into the centre? Originally, the theory of 'unequal exchange' was argued to perform this task, but that has largely been discredited and forgotten. It foundered on the impossibility of demonstrating its empirical existence as a general mechanism of exploitation. But the issue remains for these approaches if they are to sustain their theoretical credentials. The fact that these approaches no longer address it head on undermines their credibility. What has tended to replace it is the

---

[12] These two basic forms of governance have recently been joined by another, emergent form, termed 'Internet-oriented chains' (Gereffi 2001*a,b*).

notion of 'fair trade', which is predicated on an ethical notion and has little to do with a strictly economic relation in the first instance.

In fact, of course, all this has been forgotten in the rush to re-interpret these matters in network terms. Networks, understood in a rather simple and conventional manner—as little more than systems of linkages—have come to stand in for a rigorous theoretical specification of the problem of surplus generation and appropriation, even as the formal architecture of the dependency/core-periphery imagery continues. Thus, there remain some incompatibilities here which cannot be glossed over if the larger theoretical and political claims made by these positions are to be sustained.

Second, with respect to value chain analysis, this clearly builds on a more nuanced conception of the global system than a cruder version of the core-periphery models. In as much that core–periphery models have stuck resolutely to their concentric ring analogy, they have missed the growing complexity of the international production system. But as we have seen, some of the empirical analyses from within this position have begun to recognize this. And a number of GCC analyses have uncovered relatively separate chains for a range of commodity types. However, here a further criticism of the GCC approach arises. Until very recently it has been thin on empirical analysis and even as it has tried to expand the range of production branches investigated these still remain confined to a relatively few case studies.[13] The classic GCC is to be found in the agricultural, clothing or foot-ware sectors (e.g. Gereffi 1999). It suits these basic and simple types of commodity production systems, where there is a clear and fairly unambiguous linear chain to be uncovered, and where innovation is minimal. The approach thrives on such linear (vertical—i.e. between firms, or horizontal—i.e. within firms) systems, which raise an issue as to whether it is a genuine 'network' that is uncovered. Indeed, it may be that 'production networks' are quite different to 'commodity chains' (Sturgeon 2001). Attempts to extend the GCC approach to more complex manufacturing

---

[13] See Raikes *et al.* (2000); IDS (2001); Kaplinski and Morris (2001); and Henderson *et al.* (2001) for reviews of a range of empirical studies undertaken within a value chain/GCC framework.

processes, and into the service sector more generally, have been far less successful (e.g. Geriffi 2001*b*). Indeed, where complex mechanical or electrical engineering are involved, with rapid technological progress, an alternative network imagery has been suggested; that of 'aerial displays' (e.g. Bernard and Ravenhill 1995 in the case of East Asian electronic sectors). This is explicitly designed to avoid a unidimensional, over-linear, and 'mechanical' approach that characterizes the notion of chains.

Third, GCC/value networks tend to encompass a range of coordinating and governance forms, including market and hierarchy without distinguishing properly between these and 'genuine' networks (if there are such things). It would seem in principle that chains could be either 'coordinated' by the dispersed arm's-length method of the price system and the market, or via a strict hierarchical 'governance' from a centre located at some definite point (Humphrey and Schmitz 2001, p. 22; Wood 2001, p. 43). GCC analysis tends to preserve the term 'governance' for all non-market forms of chain organization and 'coordination' for market forms of chain organization. Thus, 'networks' would presumably be placed more towards the governance end of the spectrum and away from the coordination end. However, there is a problem in that a strict market system made up of arm's-length exchanges across borders sounds more like traditional 'international trade' than a commodity/value chain, unless one wants to expand the notion of a commodity/value chain to encompass *any form* of linked product exchange. And if this is the case, then once again, this framework of analysis begins to look as though it includes too much. But whatever one makes of this issue there remains a genuine problem of demarcating where commodity/value chains end and where other forms of economic relationships/organization begin. What are the 'limits' of GCC/value chain analysis, and what is the 'beyond' of its particular analytical formulations? Is there anything that cannot be included as a commodity/value chain that can claim to be called economic production? So this question applies even for that activity confined within the broad realm defined as 'economic production'.

Fourth, we must ask whether the commodity or product is the appropriate level at which to pitch an analysis of global production networks. The trouble is that by resolutely pitching itself at the commodity chain level it does not easily lend itself to encompassing the fuller context in which internationalized production operates. This is not just an issue of it downplaying the wider 'institutional context' in which production must be set—though Richard Whitley's argument is well taken about the continued pertinence of national systems of business, something more or less completely ignored by GCC analysis (Whitely 1996—see also below). Of course, the GCC approach always involves more than just its commodity focus, but it rather strains at the edges to include other aspects and is not comfortable in embracing even what would normally be thought as a central aspect to contemporary 'globalization', that of its financial dimension.

And here we enter a final point of criticism. These approaches are resolutely 'productionist' in orientation. They fail to embrace the 'financialization' of the modern production system, and they hardly embrace the service sector economy either. Thus, whilst they are heavily concerned with the role of transnational corporations in the value chains, they fail to appreciate that these are as much, if not more so, *financial institutions* in the modern international system as they are manufacturing or service providing ones. 'Financial engineering' has become as important, if not more important, than 'production engineering' for many TNCs. In addition, this has important direct effects on the way they organize the production chain itself, so this is not something confined to an autonomous domain that can be ignored by a strict focus on the production chain (though see below for a way of thinking about the relative autonomy of the production and the financial levels). And what is said here about the commodity/value chain approach applies with extra force for its world-system precursor.

What is needed in the case of international economic network analysis is a more pragmatic approach. Networks need to be disengaged from any strong connection to an overarching and grand theoretical narrative and treated as rather more contingent, specific mechanisms. One way of doing this for international trade is shown in Fig. 7.1, which divides trade into three categories.

The first category includes those goods that are traded on organized exchanges, like primary products such as minerals and agricultural

1 **Those goods exchanged on 'organized markets'**
(e.g. minerals, raw materials, primary agricultural products)

2 **Those goods exchanged according to 'reference prices'**
(e.g. processed raw materials, chemicals, basic standardized components)

3 **Those differentiated goods and services exchanged on
the basis of 'networks'**
(e.g. complex manufactured goods and services)

Fig. 7.1. Types of trade
Note: This schema is based upon Rauch (1999).

products, where price is established according to classic market mechanisms. Here one might think of markets like the Chicago grain markets, the London metal exchanges, and the Rotterdam spot market for oil. The second category is intermediate goods that are traded according to 'reference prices' quoted in specialist publications and the like (such as chemicals, processed raw materials, etc.). For the prices of these goods one would consult a reference manual or trade price book. These are readily available in an openly published form. And the third type of trade is differentiated manufactured goods and services where there is no organized market or quoted reference prices. Here we do not find a uniform standard price but rather more of 'one-off' pricing, differentiated according to complex networks of supply.

Unlocking the determinants of trade with respect to each of these categories is not easy (see Rauch 1999). Although the first, and to a lesser extent the second, of these categories display a high international trade to production ratio so that a high proportion of their output is exported, these are declining in importance as components of total international trade. These categories of trade are closely (if negatively) correlated with the growth of wealth and income. But what has expanded rapidly is the third category, particularly complex manufactured goods. And this has a relatively low production to trade ratio, when a range of other variables that might determine this type of trade has been accounted for. The key here is other institutional, cultural and geographical influences, which act at the expense of income growth as such. There is a large amount of production and trade but relatively lower levels of it are exported abroad as a pure consequence of income growth, rather than as a consequence of other variables like distance, migration, and legal differences.[14]

Thus we have a situation where those categories of trade with high income elasticity related production propensity to export are declining in significance, while that category with a lower income elasticity related production propensity for export is increasing in importance. And the reasons for these different propensities are interesting and significant. Where there is an organized market for exchange, as in the case of the first category, the establishment of the exchange is relatively easy and cheap. Transaction costs are low. However, with sophisticated manufactured goods there are no organized markets to facilitate exchanges. Rather they are traded in the context of often one off, lengthy and complex networks of supply and distribution. Manufacturers have to set up webs of distribution systems, which are often singular and unique for each category of good. They require the seeking out of trading partners and the securing of a network of participants. But above all these systems are costly to set-up and maintain—transaction costs are high.[15] And this is one of the reasons why migration has been found to be such a stimulant to international trade. Migration establishes well-organized networks that can be capitalized on by those who seek to engage in international trade.

Furthermore, Rauch (1999) speculates that portfolio-type 'merger and acquisition' FDI and 'green field' FDI share many of the characteristics of the first and last trade categories as mentioned in the context of Fig. 7.1. M & A FDI is organized through well established and

---

[14] See Thompson (2002) for the full argument along these lines, and an analysis of its consequences for the idea of 'globalization'. See Shy (2001), ch. 11 for the network effects of 'cultural' variables like languages and religions.

[15] Note that here the idea of transaction costs is used to conduct the analysis, while in Chapter 3 the concept is heavily criticized. But there is a difference in emphasis between the two cases. What was criticized in Chapter 3 was TCA as a broad theoretical claim to say how *all* organizational relationship can be characterized. This does not mean that the term has no validity for distinct and particular areas of theoretically informed description, which is how it is being used here.

low transaction-cost Stock Markets, whereas green field FDI requires all the costly establishment of new sites, networks of suppliers and distribution systems, etc. In the late 1990s and early 2000s, of course, it was the high overseas orientation of M & A FDI that was dominant and eclipsed the less elastic and more networked 'green field' FDI form, but these trends and emphases could change in the future (indeed, as of 2002 international M & A activity was rapidly falling).

But there is a further reason to take this idea of trade networks seriously. TNCs are now estimated to conduct up to a third of all international trade as intra-firm trade. In addition, financial investments of various kinds, internal labour deployment, and inter-firm partnerships and agreements can also be considered in terms of cross-country networks operating within or between TNCs (Ietto-Gillies 2002). According to Ietto-Gillies all this is creating new 'fuzzy boundaries' around firms, as organizational, locational, and ownership relationships fragment and cross-fertilize between firms (see Chapter 5). The outcome is the creation of 'business networks' (not just production networks or interorganizational networks) incorporating the three dimensions of organization, location, and ownership into a strategically aligned but flexible whole. It may be that the ability to establish and manage complex international networks of this kind operating *within* TNCs confers real competitive advantages to those firms that are successful at this.

As far as the empirical basis for these networks is concerned data limitations prevent any clear confirmation that there are robust business networks in operation, though there are signs that large TNCs are spreading their affiliation relationships globally—so there is some locational diversification. But there seems still to be high single ownership advantages, and diversified organizational advantages are difficult to discern. Overall Ietto-Gillies sees a process of international fragmentation amidst integration developing, led by TNCs[16]—though a lot of this must remain speculative given the data limitations. What is more, once again in this analysis there is an

---

[16] This way of characterizing things is far from novel, however: see Doz (1987), Mytelka (1995).

excited and exaggerated embrace of the role of ICTs as a force for transforming the whole nature of TNC operations and leading the new business networks (see especially Ietto-Gillies 2002, ch. 1). In addition, this approach remains disappointingly 'productionist'. There is little serious consideration of TNCs as financial institutions with semi-autonomous financial objectives driving their overall strategy (Morgan 2001). Surely, any genuine 'business network' would have to include this aspect as a central feature of its analysis?

7.8. 'National Systems' and the Advent of Globalization

An area where we also see the network analogy deployed heavily in the international arena is in the case of technological systems (e.g. Leoncini and Montresor 2000) that are a subset of innovation systems. And innovation systems are just one of a range of economic activities that have traditionally been considered in terms of *national systems* of various kinds: national business systems, national production systems, national innovation systems, national financial systems, etc.

As discussed in Chapter 5, during the 1980s there was a flurry of new analytical work identifying the importance of industrial districts and regional economies as key elements in the competitiveness of different national economies. These 'industrial districts' were argued to embody a new 'local economy' that was robustly organized in networked terms, reliant upon flexible-specialization process technologies and lean-production techniques, and very much dependent upon the innovativeness of small- and medium-sized enterprises. This is not the time or place to review the discussions about this new model of development and economic organization, which produced fierce and determined supporters and opponents alike. While the model was argued to be well established in certain countries like Italy, Southern Germany, Denmark, and France, and in the United States in California and Massachusetts, it was thought to be notable by its absence in certain others, particularly the United Kingdom (Crouch and Farrell 2001).

However, during the 1990s there was a definite reaction against this model. The argument developed that these local networked economies (Chapter 5) were almost uniquely vulnerable to the new forces of globalization (Amin and Robins 1990; Amin and Thrift 1992; Harrison 1994). Rather than offering a different trajectory for economic development and remaining robust in the face of oligopolistically organized corporate giants, local industrial districts were likely to be internationally integrated into global networks very much dominated by TNCs, shaking out small firms dependent upon tasks no longer performed locally. This was part of a general process of the 'local' being overrun by the 'global', re-configuring and down-grading the former as just a pale outline lurking in the shadow of the latter. Local networks were being overrun by global networks.

However, more recent evidence has demonstrated that this pessimistic prognosis is far from the actual outcome. Industrial districts are alive and well, having quite effectively bounced back from the threat of obscurity announced by the globalization enthusiasts (Crouch *et al.* 2001; Whitford 2001). In so far as TNCs have had an effect on local industrial districts, they may have actually reinforced their competitive advantage rather than undermined it (Hirst and Thompson 1999, ch. 3). Italian industrial districts in particular—which amounted to something of the paradigm case for the original flexible-specialization and networked industrial district thesis—whilst having to re-invent themselves around 'diversification' rather than 'specialization', have nevertheless proved robust enough to compete with whatever the forces of globalization might have thrown at them (Locke 1995; Whitford 2001; Burroni and Tragalia 2001; Chapter 5 of this book). And, in different ways, this is true for the other areas and countries mentioned above (Crouch *et al.* 2001).

What is more, this is part of a general re-assessment of the impact of globalization on a variety of 'national systems', which were all argued to be under terminal threat from the forces of the international market place and its giant corporate players. Once again, national systems have proved to be more robust in the face of globalization than was at first thought possible (Whitely 1999; Hall and Soskice 2001*a*). It is very difficult to unpick such national systems where there are strong institutional complementarities between the different parts of its overall structure: typical production system, welfare system, labour market, financial system, innovation and technological system, legal system, quality control system, etc. Hall and Soskice (2001*b*) argue that, whilst change and adaptation are endemic in national systems, not everything about these surrender to a single 'neo-liberal' policy programme or surrender to the dictates of the giant transnational corporations. Distinctive national institutional arrangements remain. And even if one of these areas is subject to an 'incursion' from the forces of internationalization there tends to be compensatory reactions from the others. For instance, as the German corporate sector has increasingly embraced the pressures for shareholder value and the international norms of financial returns, its distinctive consensual labour relations regime has tended to strengthen rather than weaken (Beyer and Hassel 2002). German management found that the best way to meet the requirements demanded by the norms of international finance was to enlist the support of its labour force and protect this from any erosion in its position. Similarly, as international norms of quality control have been established by the ISO 9000 process, these have been absorbed into national systems of quality control without this much affecting the existing domestic institutional arrangements—indeed, the architecture of national standards are reinforced (Casper and Hancké 1999). Finally, as the law is being 'internationalized'—for example, within Europe for the case of contract law via the 1994 Consumer Protection Directive and the Principles of European Law—the notions of 'good faith' and 'fair dealings' are entering into otherwise quite hostile national legal environments. The Anglo-American legal systems have been based on adversarial principles that do not react very favourably to the more 'consensual' approach to disputation and the 'high principles' embodied in the notions of *bona fides*. However, the UK Anglo-American system has had to absorb this in the context of EU integration. But far from this producing a 'convergence' on one or other of the systems or an outright rejection, Teubner (2001) suggests it acts as an irritant to the system, producing new perturbations, cleavages, and divergences, very much moulded by the existing national institutionalized legal system into which the incursion is pushed (see Chapter 5 for the reasons advanced to account for this by this 'social systems' approach). It acts less as a transplant, more of an adaptation.

A final area where networking is thought to be an important ingredient in national systems concerns the *construction* of a national system focusing on the Eastern European (EE) countries of transition. Working in the tradition of SNA discussed in Chapter 3 and examples of the importance of corporate networking found in Japan (e.g. Gerlach 1992; Lincoln *et al.* 1996), David Stark has produced a series of analyses that highlight the post-socialist character of ownership networks amongst emergent private property in EE, particularly Hungary (Grabher and Stark 1997*a,b*; Stark *et al.* 1998; Stark and Vedres 2001).

Far from confronting the relatively well established *Keiretsu* network found in Japan, however, in EE there is a fluid and dynamic emergent system which Stark has characterized as 'recombinant property' (Stark 1996)—a mixture of public and private ownership forms, which blur enterprise boundaries in networks of interorganizational ownership.[17] The business groups (cliques) uncovered by this analysis are engaged in a strategic exercise of portfolio management of different kinds of property: state property, individual private ownership, employee shareholding property, firm ownership, interorganizational ownership, in a competitive game aimed at taking advantage of state subsidies, preferential trading conditions, state largesse in forgiving inherited debts, and benefiting from privileged access to new sources of capital, new markets, and technology transfers. Turbulence and uncertainty pervade this unstable economic and institutional environment, so the attempt here is to map a very dynamic macro network system (via 'sequence mapping' and 'periodicity graphing' in a 'network position state-space' matrix).

Clearly, none of this is as consolidated as those found in Japanese *keiretsu*, Korean *chaebol*, or Taiwanese 'related enterprise' business networks. And, without wishing to exaggerate, there is a problem that much of the EE emergent recombinant network groups could be quite quickly swept away as foreign capital enters these countries

---

[17] See Guthrie 1997 for a somewhat similar approach in the case of post-reform China.

with a vengeance. Foreign owned banks are particularly important in EE in consolidating ownership types and these seem intent upon a more conventional definition of property rights than that offered by the recombinant form identified so far (Czaban 2001). Of course, all corporate networks of this type are vulnerable at one level, and there seems no reason to expect that the new EE ones will be either more especially sheltered from, or susceptible to, external pressures than these others have been. But, as already indicated with the discussion of national systems above, these pressures exist, and analyses of well consolidated German and French macro-network corporate systems of this type point to the undoing of much of these in recent years (Morin 2000, figure 1, p. 40; Jurgens 2000, figure 1, p. 61 see also the discussion around Figure 3.2 in Chapter 3). Clearly, Stark provides a highly suggestive analytical approach. The question is whether his results can survive the kinds of pressures just discussed.

7.9. The Role of Networks in 'Governing' the International System

In this section we look briefly at the way networks have been enrolled as governing aspects of the international system. This has already been broached in the discussion of GCCs above but in this section we concentrate upon the more overtly political aspects to this involvement.

An original formulation of the network approach to international governance concerned the role of 'epistemic communities' (Krasner 1983; International Organization 1992). These are basically conceived as networks of expertise—knowledge workers who operate as agenda setters, researchers, analysts, policy advisers, sherpers, and the like for international organizations and the political elites who inhabit and circulate around the main decision-making fora of international governance. They are unelected and formally unaccountable but they exercise considerable informal power and influence. In the contemporary period they would probably be considered the main proponents and supporters of the 'Washington consensus'— committed to a neo-liberal policy programme of international macro-economic stability, liberalization, privatization, de-regulation, and fiscal rectitude. Some have argued that there now exists a 'global knowledge regime' made up of these types of expertise combined with a wider embrace of educational, scientific, and technological institutions (Schott 2001), heavily dominated by the United States. Again, the Internet is seen as a prime instrument for encouraging and fostering the development of this transnational regime, and establishing it as a 'global' phenomenon, but one nevertheless concentrated in advanced industrial countries (Koku *et al.* 2001).

A somewhat different deployment of the idea of networks in this field involves the role of NGOs in international governance mentioned in Chapter 6. And this operates as something of a counter-weight to the epistemic communities just described. Non-governmental organization networks provide the 'other' of the elite and establishment influence on international governance (e.g. Reinicke and Deng 2001). Their informality is welcomed and encouraged, but this has presented them with a problem of their legitimacy. On whose behalf do they speak and how can they be made accountable? (Hudson 2001). In analysing the networked nature of these NGOs, all the aspects discussed in Chapter 2's elaboration of the 'network model' come strongly into play. Given the vast literature on NGOs and this prior elaboration of how they might work, there is no reason to comment further on this aspect, other than to recognize the international nature of these organizations. The key problem facing INGOs is whether they are effective and make any difference to the issue areas in which they concentrate their activities. Are networks effective? In addition, how do they secure their legitimacy?

But this does enable us to raise a substantive issue that pervades a number of the areas covered in this chapter. Clearly, the general role of networks as part of any overall governance mechanism for the international system is posed by the analysis outlined here. What perhaps needs to be emphasized is that networks cannot be afforded a too important role in this overall governance schema. Networks need to be considered as just *one* of a number of mechanisms of governance, and probably not the most important one. There is a tendency to give networks an exulted status in the hierarchy of governance and coordinative mechanisms in the international arena. And this is encouraged by all the exaggerated discussion of the advent of a 'network society' occupying the space of international relations (Castells 1996; Messner 1997). If there is no 'network society' then networks must be considered as *just one governance mechanism* existing in a varied system of multilateral and multidimensional governance (Hooghe and Marks 2001). First of all there is the relationship between networks and markets and hierarchy, and various hybrids of these, existing at a kind of horizontal and intermediate level in overall governance and coordination (considered at length in Chapter 6). This would be bolstered and supported by what might be termed forms of 'self-governance' (and 'governing of the self'), very much conceived at the individual level. Here the advent of various new forms of 'private authority' is also relevant (Cutler *et al.* 1999). But, none of these 'levels' should ignore the crucial third level occupied by forms of authoritative governance provided by states, associations, and neo-corporate political structures (e.g. Crouch and Trigilia 2001). With respect to the debate about 'globalization' this complex of governance mechanisms can tend to get lost in the celebration of a new found significance for networks of all kinds, where networks are very loosely defined to encompass more or less everything organizational.

This is a mistake. In particular, the burden of the discussion conducted in this chapter is to re-emphasize the role of the nation-state as still the key institutional player in international governance, largely because there just has not been the shift towards transnationalized network activity to the extent that is often claimed. Thus, networks—any networks—cannot operate effectively without the support of a framework in which the state and the other authoritative or hierarchical governance institutions mentioned above, continues to play the leading role. That, at least, was something argued in Chapter 6 and which will be further emphasized in the next chapter.

7.10. Conclusions

Thus when considering the role of networks in the international system it is important to remember the constitutive role for the nation-state in the development of the world trading system. This started when state societies were created. It was not until the creation of state sovereignty and state control of society that world trade, as we understand it today, started to exist. Without sovereign states and some degree of control over long distance trade through their navies, it was too perilous to trade. It took several decades for the emergent states in eighteenth-century Europe, for instance, to finally eliminate piracy from the high seas, but this was an essential condition for the development of world trade. So territorially exclusive government and world trade grew together.

What is more, this basic link between nation-states and world trade continues today and is likely to continue into the foreseeable future. To think of international trade means thinking about governance *between* the national and the international level. What is happening contemporarily is essentially a new configuration of the system that was first established in the seventeenth century. The fact that this is contemporarily governed in the context of 'multilateralism' in its various forms should not divert us from the fact that what we see is the further development of international connectivity set within the basic institutional continuity of nation-state to nation-state interactions. When things go wrong at the international level, citizens still appeal to their national governments for help and assistance. This remains so whether the problems are with GM agricultural crop trade or with ICT and Internet service trade. People continue to lobby their own governments to do something first and expect them to 'represent' their grievance in the international forum on their behalf. There is some limited appeal over the heads of national governments directly to international governing bodies but these are few and far between, tend to require government involvement and support, and are expensive and time consuming to access for individuals or even corporate bodies.

This is not to argue that things have remained unchanged. But it is to argue that there are certain fundamental foundations that remain. Of course, today supranational processes are stronger than they were before. But it is a mistake to over-emphasize this. Since the establishment of the international telegraph system in the 1880s and 1890s we have also had a global media. The real speed reduction in global communications happened then. Within a period of twenty years what had taken over six weeks to get messages from deep within the United States to Europe, say (via horse drawn vehicles to the coast and then by sailing ship across the Atlantic) was reduced to just twenty minutes or less. And similar time reductions were experienced throughout the world between all of the main commercial centres and colonial outposts. Today's media technology makes possible different volumes of activity, and has speeded things up. But whether this is to say that we have passed into a 'new global network order' is another matter altogether, and probably just a move too far.

In addition, when networks are considered in an international environment they must be placed in their rightful context. Networks are just one of a number of governance and coordinative mechanisms. Just as was concluded in Chapter 6, the 'shadow of hierarchy' also hangs heavily over networks as they operate in the international domain. In particular, state formations continue to predominate in the international system. They provide both the legitimacy and the regulatory oversight for network operation. Networks do not of themselves constitute centres of coercive policing powers nor of military intervention. These still fundamentally remain the prerogative of national states, which in the last resort will have their way with respect to both markets and networks as they see fit.

Chapter 8

Conclusions

The main objective of this book has been to investigate the contemporary forms of network organization as these have arisen in the conceptual literature and in terms of their appearance in concrete empirical settings. Is it possible to theoretically ground the kinds of conceptions emerging in this dual framework and build them into an acceptable analytical claim on how network forms of organizational activity work? Clearly, as has been emphasized throughout, if the network model is to be found everywhere then it operates nowhere. If it does not allow for a demarcation between it and the market or hierarchy, say, then it is undermined as an analytical technique in its own right. The analysis in the previous chapters has offered evidence and arguments to suggest that it is possible to construct a network model that does provide a genuine, useful, and different analytical approach to social, political, and economic organization. The key features of the network model discussed in earlier chapters are summarized in a moment. It is these categories that describe how a certain range of social relations operate that specify a network model of coordination and governance. These practices just do not operate in the same manner for either hierarchy or the market. But given that networks are increasingly argued to be found everywhere responding to the question about the specific nature of networks becomes doubly important, and doubly difficult. In this final chapter, we return to some of the main issues tackled in the earlier discussion to provide an overall judgement on how successful the enterprise has been. As will become clear a rather tentative overall response is offered. There are as many outstanding questions left unanswered by what has been discussed so far as there are issues that it has resolved.

Since actor-network theory (ANT) and post-ANT conceptions of organizational operation help raise many of the general issues associated with the arguments presented in this book, I begin with a further critical engagement with this approach. It presents the most consistent alternative conception to the one argued for in the book and thus, it needs to be confronted head on.

8.1. ANT, Post-ANT, and the Dynamics of Networks

One of the original criticisms of ANT identified in Chapter 3 was that it could not stabilize firmly enough the extent of the systems of actor-networks it deals with to allow for robust or predictable analytical outcomes to emerge. From within the mainstream ANT approach there have been two responses to this criticism. On the one hand there is a notion that the 'construction of reality' being dealt with there is a *process* in which reality is in fact becoming increasingly stabilized. A self-organized transformation of looser into more permanent couplings is the modality of this process, orientated towards an operational closure, robustness, and theoretical consistency, founded on the reliability of experimentation. But this does not necessarily imply a fixed arrangement between both sides of an argument or experiment. In the case of Latour, for instance, the non-human artefacts in actor-networks are in danger of appearing as thoroughly socialized and anthropomorphized—possibly too thoroughly socialized and anthropomorphized one might add—as they are incorporated into pan-social enmeshments of heterogeneous actor-networks and alliances (Nowotny 1990). However, the retort from ANT to this criticism is that 'humans' and 'artefacts' are not the same but are 'equivalents' in the actor-networks. At best these artefacts are endowed with a kind of consciousness via their attachment to human representatives. The network is turned inside out again; techniques are not always the tools of people—people can also be the tools of techniques, they are caused to act by technical circumstances. So when people become the instruments of artefacts, those artefacts acquire, as it were, a 'vicarious consciousness' of their own.

The second retort from ANT about the stability of its actor-network structures is that these are in fact stable vessels in which the range of artefacts and agents are assembled together as immutable mobiles. They display both the characteristics of limitations to their extent, scope and function as at the same time they are flexible enough to cope with new attachments and new spaces for operation. These arguments were thoroughly rehearsed in Chapter 3.

But there remains a serious problem with the ability of these formulations to adequately deal with the kinds of criticisms of the approach raised in Chapter 3, and which are returned to in a moment in the case of boundaries around the idea and operation of networks. But first we need to confront a new turn in the ANT associated literature; what has been termed a post-ANT development in the previous chapters.

In relation to the issue of the ubiquity of networks one of the distinctive features of the contemporary discussions of their nature and existence is claims about the dynamic properties of networks. They are thought to offer an almost unique methodological opportunity to dispense with static forms of analysis and to embark on a genuine journey of self-organization and self-generation (even 'self-realization', it might be added) in their forms of operational existence. In this context, it is argued, there is no need for a clearly articulated 'alternative' simple model of their form and operational specificity. And what is true for networks is equally so for the case of hierarchy and market. The time for the kinds of models of these outlined in Chapter 2 is over. We now live in a complex world, a kind of open system where the future is unpredictable and unknowable and this undermines the possibility of constructing such models let alone the desirability of doing so.

A good deal of the intellectual background to this trend can be found in the discussion of complexity, evolutionary ecology, and related concepts discussed in Chapter 5. The key to understanding the present is to recognize that *the process* of change is the central issue. There can be no recognizable 'end-points' or models to aim for, or aim at (Thrift 1999; Thrift and Dewsbury 2000; Smith 2002). The 'becoming' has an epistemological precedence over the 'being' from this perspective, where the dynamics of performance displace the statics of representation.

There are a number of variants to this trend. But all see the ANT approach (and the analysis of networks more generally) as now just too static, rather than not static enough. Instead of immutable mobiles we need mutable ones (Law and Moi 2001, p. 613). What is needed is a fluid space for the conception of networks and for their operation, one that continually changes shape, celebrating the reverie of fire that invokes a flicker or an oscillation rather than as something that holds its position or shape. Alternatively, this can be seen as a 'performance' (Thrift 2000; Hinchliffe 2000). This celebrates the process of creative exorbitance, dancing 'bodies', talk as action not communication (or representation/signification), an endless process of direct practices, with no 'foreshadowing' in terms of a discernible outcome that might be constructed in advance.[1]

As against this kind of open systems methodology (of which there are many variants not mentioned here) the point of this book has been to mount a defence for a relatively closed system of both thought and existence. Whilst the ideas associated with this open-systems approach are attractive in one sense, they are also difficult to handle and to sustain in the longer run. They are attractive because they seem to prevent the ossification of thought and practice and an unimaginative, non-innovative analytical approach. But the problem with such open-systems methodology in general is that they inevitably display a high degree of redundancy (see also

---

[1] There is a variant of this 'pragmatic philosophy' where communication and language are more modestly mobilized into a methodology for understanding organizational life, and therefore networks as part of this. It works against the dominant 'variables paradigm' in social and economic analysis to re-emphasize a 'contextualist paradigm' of enchainment, categorizing types and modalities of action as instances of narrative data. The analytical issue for this alternative approach becomes one of the effectiveness of the stories that can be wrought from such narrative data. See Abbott (1992, 1997).

Chapter 5). As they are expansive and always threatening to collapse (because of the continual threat of leakages, overflowings, and undoings built into their dynamic) it becomes difficult to stabilize the networks they embody. Where and when do the fluid performances of the actors stop and relatively fixed representations emerge? Yet another opening could always be potentially attachable to the existing configuration, so that there is a never ending cascading of opportunities to disrupt and to reconfigure. This sets up high levels of redundancy as the 'system' must overcompensate for the inevitable experimental 'failures' that are written into its evolutionary dynamic (Chapter 3).

But high redundancy comes at a cost. Such 'systems' are expensive to run (intellectually and practically) and therefore relatively inefficient. Continual intellectual or social experimentation implies substantial waste, as failure has to be paid for. The advantage of a differentiated and more limited intellectual and organizational horizon offered by model building is that this presents the opportunity to compartmentalize the 'organization of the social' and, to some degree at least, to stabilize it. It means actors can find out where they are and what they are doing. An intellectual and organizational constancy and consistency is installed—at least for a reasonable period of time. This is useful in that it means experiences and reflections can be assessed, knowledges consolidated and reproduced, and successful models copied and compared. Not everything is under a continual scrutiny and in a continual state of flux.

Take the long, rich, and enormously complex history of industrialization for instance. This can be conveniently divided into several different phases that capture the essential characteristics of different 'little models' of the productive process: 'craft production', 'the American system of manufactures', 'mass (or Fordist)-production', 'flexible (or lean)-production'. With each of these models there is broad agreement on what they entail and the characteristics of the production and distribution systems they involve, their typical firm type, labour relations regime, accumulative and regulatory form and capabilities, etc. These models can be used to draw contrasts between their different aspects, to stabilize knowledge about them, help place particular developments in a context, and aid in the general business of suggesting what can be done to improve things or change things. Thus, there are real benefits to be gained from being able to produce the kinds of guidelines that are embodied in models of this type, and there is therefore good reason to continue this activity in the case of the network processes considered in this book.

From this point of view the analysis of social processes require the following operational procedures to render them into useful analytical devices and to make them manageable. First, they need to be periodized to divide them up into meaningful phases for contrasts, comparisons, etc., as summarized by the discussion of 'little models' just undertaken. Second, they need to be given some 'structure' (elements and levels involved, relationships between these, etc.) so as to generate the periodization just mentioned. Third, there is a need for some theory about how change occurs (rapid discontinuities, disjunctures, smooth passages, slow evolution, the agency involved, etc.). Fourth, there needs to be some idea as to 'where' the process is going, not in the sense of an 'end to history' or teleological 'final destination', but in terms of a meaningful objective or aim. Thus, in the case of a 'peace process', for instance, there must be at least some idea of what peace means. And similarly, in the case of the 'globalization process' there needs to be some idea of what globalization means as the concrete manifestation of a societal form. Without this it is difficult to see how sensibly analytical work can be done. Finally, there is a need to continually ask the question 'where are we in this process?' (which itself requires the notion of an 'end' in the sense just indicated). It is in the spirit of this approach to processes that the discussion of the network evolution is undertaken here, and this adds to the strictures about the need for simple and well understood 'analytical models' for an understanding of this dynamic.

What this ultimately amounts to is a methodological imperative to 'interrupt time'; to 'stop' the flow of history so as to generate some analytical stability. Of course actual time does not stop. The evolutionary imperative continues. But this just means that there must be a difference between evolutionary time proper and analytical time. For analytical purposes it is necessary to stop time so as to appreciate what the consequences of the actual flow of time really are. And, of course, this means that such an approach can hardly exist without a notion of 'representation'. The purpose of interrupting time is to provide the space for a representation of it. To understand the continual flow of 'performance' requires the analytical representation of that practice. This is not to deny the significance of the 'practices of performance', merely to register the dual necessity of the relational embrace between performative practices and representations.[2]

8.2. Boundaries

The open systems approach towards networks just criticized sees these as consisting of a number of activities and resources which can be related to one another in various ways. However, there remains a certain order to how they are related. Given a system of 'weak ties', for instance, each of them is not related to all the others. Instead there is a certain limitation. Actors form a limited number of dyads. But as these are not designed by any single actor according to a plan or strategic decision, this level of 'uncontrollability' of networks reinforces the opaqueness of networks from the point of view of the actors in it. Boundaries seen by one can be different to the boundaries seen by another. In a sense any boundary is arbitrary from this perspective—from a perspective *within* the network. Even different actors in the same firm may well have different perceptions of relationships within the firm, and similarly with networks proper. Every actor has the possibility of extending the network by building links to previously unrelated networks. So any one actor can only 'know' a limited part of the network, only exercise control over a limited network section.

[2] This is not the occasion to enter into a long debate about the proper relationship between any conception of representation and that of signification. For some time I have defended the epistemological primacy of signification over that of representation (Thompson 1980, 1985, 1991), but for the purposes of the exposition here I leave this (important) distinction aside. The point is to drive home the dual nature of practices/performances and representations. I do not see how one can analytically live without both of these, however problematic the actual relationship between them remains. The significance of a significatory conception of money was raised in Chapter 4 in the context of the discussion about the difficulty of valuing intangible assets.

Thus, boundaries are both complementary and contradictory to existing boundaries from this 'internalist perspective'; they will be recast as the parts are brought together in a different way or new actors added. And forming a new totality often imparts the existing players with new qualities. They might have to be redefined and reformulated. Given networks build on exploiting interdependencies, such an integration brings certain activities and resources together. As a consequence a certain 'distance' and 'boundary' is created towards other resources and activities. However, at the same time, relationships and networks can also be ways to bridge over boundaries, to bring activities and resources closer together. This is the paradox of networks. A network is a way of reducing the effects of certain boundaries by creating other ones. So in this approach boundaries in networks should never be conceived as given—neither in terms of the existence of actors or the boundaries they create. As the result of adaptive adjustment, actors orient themselves in a mutually consistent direction so as to increase cohesion and performance. Interdependence between actors grows stronger. But as this happens other relationships and alignments are adjusted to grow weaker, loosening the network. The network is both structured and restructured at the same time. Thus, the network here is conceived as a dynamic multidimensional bounded structure.

But an early problem identified with this way networks have traditionally been analysed appeared in the context of these ideas about boundaries around networks from the 'outside'. The overarching approaches to networks considered in Chapter 3, for instance, all seem to claim too much for their respective analytical enterprises. Social network analysis (SNA), as a mathematically precise analytical technique for identifying networks, needs a method for limiting the extent of networks that is not arbitrary or dependent upon individual whim (i.e. proclaimed from the 'inside'). But this has proved difficult if not impossible to consistently establish in practice (Alba 1982; Aldrich 1999).

In part, of course, this is simply a technical matter associated with the nature of SNA's particular empirically driven approach. But it also relates to another issue, the failure of SNA to adequately differentiate other forms of organizational structure than 'just' networks of various kinds. And this is a matter that the transaction cost approach is designed to address. From a transaction-cost analysis (TCA) perspective, networks (like hierarchies) are designed to economize on transaction costs, without 'overburdening' the organizational arrangement with excessive administrative costs, the down-side of a strictly hierarchical form of organization. The advantage of TCA is that it does introduce alternative forms of organizational structure into the analysis of networks. But it suffers from a similar problem to that of SNA in that it wants to reduce all the analytical work on organizational structure to a single technique, TCA. Thus, whilst SNA operates with a single organizational mode, TCA operates with a single conceptual tool. These illustrate the dual aspects to the concept of network with which we opened the methodological discussion in Chapter 1.

Whilst in many ways ANT responds imaginatively to both these problems in that its 'ultra social constructivist' approach tries to dissolve the distinction between an 'inside' and an 'outside' of networks—between the concept and its object—ultimately this also claims too much, it has been suggested. Again, there is a problem with the lack of a clear boundary between actor-networks and anything else that can claim to be organizational (or social?). And there is all the emphasis on the continual fragmentation and reconstruction of network boundaries as just described above. The advantage of an approach adopted in this book—where the stress has been on the specific logic to a limited form of network organization—is that this offers a ready made boundary condition, both conceptually and operationally, between something called a network and other coordination and governance arrangements. Of course, the analysis offered in the earlier chapters around these issues has only served to establish the *principles* associated with such a distinction. It has not conducted a thoroughgoing empirical investigation of the boundaries around any particular network conceived in this way, though it has hinted at how this could be done in the chapters on industrial organization, political networks, and in the case of international ICT and production networks.

The distinctive logic to networks tentatively announced in Chapter 4 involved an 'assemblage' of several features: the idea of non-reciprocal gift giving, the non-exchange involved in an 'excessive' energy dissipating set of relationships, and a non-instrumental or non-calculative notion of trust that arises from this context. These features give networks a theoretical rationale that is distinctive from other coordinating and governance devices. In addition, in recognizing the limited nature of networks, at the organizational level this led to several suggestions as to how networks relate to other coordinating and governance devices. In relation to industrial networks of the interorganizational type considered in Chapter 5 for instance, the classic market and hierarchical alternatives are made clearly visible. In the case of political networks considered in Chapter 6 the idea of the market and of hierarchy, conceived in related terms as other governance procedures that cast an organizational 'shadow' over the operation of policy networks, served to circumscribe the activity of political networks in various ways. Often this acts to the benefit of the overall social mechanism. And in the case of the international networks discussed in Chapter 7, again there were a range of alternative forms of hierarchical (state based) and market inspired governance arrangements that were brought into play to drive home a point about the still limited range of network operations in this field.

8.3. Networks as Relational Organizations

The emphasis in the analysis of this book has been to see networks as very much relational in operation. Thus, it has played down the positional aspects to both SNA type approach and the over-emphasis on the spatialities of networks that typifies the appropriation of ANT into 'economic geography' in particular, but which pervades most of the general ANT literature as well.

Social network analysis has operated with two main analytical formulations: the relational and the positional (Alba 1982). The relational approach focuses on the pathways in networks, and it lends itself to conceptualizing networks in terms of communications between participants and the distribution of resources amongst them. The positional approach, by contrast, concentrates more upon the patterns of similarity and difference in relational configurations, looking for hierarchical structures in particular (the 'bloc model' technique mentioned in Chapters 3 and 7 being classic examples of this). Of course, these are complementary within SNA. Neither approach necessarily excludes the other.

To a large extent this excessive spatialization of networks within ANT has to do with the iconic status of Foucault's position on space (Foucault 1986). For Foucault, where previously space had operated hierarchically, in the modern era it now tends to operate horizontally, connecting points and intersections. This lends itself nicely to a network type conception of space with the idea of 'extension' as relations of proximity between points and elements. Trees, matrices, grids, and series occupy this space. Although Foucault sees this as a move away from localization and emplacement, it still centrally invokes spatial positionality and place as the coordinates for network like structures.

An overtly relational approach would emphasize time over space, as suggested above in the context of the discussion of processes. And time here is also heavily periodized, but this is not to adopt a simple differentiation between these two. Again, they are intimately associated together. It is just to register a difference of emphasis, which provides the analysis of networks with a different feel and specificity.

And this relates to another issue that has increasingly crept into the analysis of networks as the chapters have unfolded. This sometimes goes under the name of the 'asymmetry' of networks; the fact that relationships within them are not necessarily equivalent for all parties, the fact that some can take better advantage of their position in networks than can others, the fact that there are differences of power and authority in networks, etc. This is the site of considerable controversy and some criticism of the whole network enterprise, relating as it does to the normative element in the analysis of networks.

On the surface it would seem that position has a precedence over relation in the cases of the way these 'powers' work in networks. But again, one might want to de-emphasize the role of power (and therefore position) in these contexts. Clearly, networks do actually function with these inequalities of power, so this is not to ignore their existence. If power inequalities grow too large, of course, at a meta-level the network would presumably collapse. So by and large networks cope with the differential access to power and authority, as normally understood, that no doubt occurs in all networks, and indeed all other aspects of social life. There is nothing unique about networks in this respect. Nor is there much to be gained from continually drawing attention to this aspect of their operation, since it adds little to an understanding about how these particular organizations coordinate or govern above what can be offered by the considerations discussed in all the chapters so far.[3]

8.4. Limits and Failures

One of the interesting aspects of the ubiquity of network argument is that it would turn the usual concerns about networks on their heads. Is the network approach just an interesting descriptive device or idea with little analytical content? Is it not possible (and tempting) to go around finding networks without these being of great intellectual significance? Clearly, if we look hard enough we will find networks all over the place. Indeed, given a simple definition of networks, more or less all forms of coordination could fall under its embrace, including hierarchy and market as we have seen. Clearly, if this were the case the 'swollen middle' (Hennart 1993) would be in danger of eclipsing both hierarchy and market, and the problem would be to explain how these continue to exist rather than the nature of networks.

In part this has to do with the limits or failure of networks, something one might add that has not received the attention it deserves

---

[3] For instance, an example of this might arise in the context of the analysis of gift giving considered in Chapter 4. Could gift giving almost unintentionally lead to 'hierarchy'? Take the case of 'antagonistic gift giving'—a feature of the conspicuous display/destruction of wealth associated with the potlatch—this amounts to the display of power and so in some ways might be thought to set up a hierarchy between those 'giving' in this manner and those 'receiving'. It is a mechanism for differentiating status positions. And no doubt this is true at one level. But what has been emphasized is not so much the gifts themselves—their form and status—but the nature of the inner relation(ship) they embody. What social arrangement does not give rise to a differentiated field of social statuses, authorities, and powers? The point is that in the case of networks considered here it is the other considerations as to how and why networks continue to function despite these inequities that are of prime interest.

in the literature (but see Miles and Snow 1992; Podolny and Page 1998). In as much that networks have become a mundane aspect of daily and organizational life they have become so familiar that we may not see either their downside or their limitations. They do not work smoothly, they snarl-up and they break-down (Barry 2000). However, we have been at pains to demonstrate the analytical take on this process; first to provide good reasons why networks might be more efficient and performatively effective than other coordinating or governance devices in various organizational contexts, and second to recognize the possibility of 'failure' but at the same time to register a certain distance from this particular formulation (Chapter 1, footnote 5). Furthermore, we have emphasized the relationship between networks and other mechanisms, something that the approach adopted here enables us to more easily do since it does not roll up all organizational matters into a single overarching conceptual terrain or operational one.

8.5. Final Comments

As far as is possible the discussion in the chapters above has not adopted a strong normative position on networks. Of course, given the book represents an attempt to provide a rationale and a case for networks, it has played to their strengths and positive characteristics. In those chapters where the positive case has been focused on most forcefully, there has been an inevitable imbalance in that presentation, but the argument has not adopted an overtly celebratory tone. Indeed, the chapters have also been concerned to present the limitations of networks and their downside aspects (e.g. in Chapter 6). What is more, the overall message of this book is that networks have to be seen in their proper place relative to the other coordinative and governance devices also analysed. And this place has often been considered as a subordinate one to the other mechanisms.

Finally however, is there a case to be made against networks? Should they be resisted? In particular, is there a case to resist, and not to be drawn into, 'networking' in particular? There seems to be a compulsion to become 'superbly networked' in the contemporary era.

Applications and Empirical Comparisons

'Networking' has become one of those activities that every self-respecting individual seems to need to do to 'get along' socially and politically. *Who* you know is as important as *what* you know for social success, and 'networking' to establish and reinforce contacts becomes a ubiquitous task for any ambitious person looking to secure success in their social life or career path. But networking in this sense seems to sum up a rather shallow view of how to get on. It can be associated with opportunism and careerism—looking for the main chance rather than caring about the real issues or participating in real debate. It is a substitute for serious political engagement, for instance, as a superficial sincerity sweeps across the political spectrum in the wake of the 'spin' and 'deceit' perpetrated by the official political machine.

If nothing else, however, the hope is that the analysis of this book has demonstrated that there is clearly a much more serious side to networks and networking than just this!

References

Abbott, A. (1992), 'From causes to events: Notes on narrative positivism', *Sociological Methods and Research* 20(4), 428–55.

—— (1997), 'Of time and space: The contemporary relevance of the Chicago School', *Social Forces* 75(4), 1149–82.

Adams, J. (1997), 'The family and management of the firm: an institutional theory', paper given at the *EAEPE Conference* (Conference Papers A–K), Athens, Panteion University, 6–9 November.

Adler, P. S. (2001), 'Market, hierarchy, and trust: The knowledge economy and the future of capitalism', *Organizational Science* 12(2), 215–34.

Akerlof, G. (1982), 'Labour contracts as partial gift exchanges', *The Quarterly Journal of Economics* 97, 543–69.

Alba, R. D. (1982), 'Taking stock of network analysis: A decades results', *Research in the Sociology of Organizations* 1, 39–74.

—— and T. Cerwinski (1997), *Complexity, Global Politics and National Security*, Washington, DC: National Defense University Press.

Alberts, D. S., J. J. Gartska and F. P. Stein (1999), *Network Centric Warfare: The Face of Battle in the 21st Century*, Washington, DC: National Defense University Press.

Aldrich, H. E. (1999), *Organizations Evolving*, Thousand Oaks, CA: Sage.

Aldridge, S., D. Halpern, and S. Fitzpatrick (2002), *Social Capital: A Discussion Paper*, Performance and Innovation Unit, Cabinet Office, April.

Allen, J. (2002), 'Living on thin abstractions: more power/economic knowledge', *Environment and Planning A* 34, 451–66.

Alliez, R. (1996), 'Capital times: tales from the conquest of time', *Theory Out of Bounds*, Vol. 6, Minneapolis and London: University of Minnesota Press (Preface by Giles Deleuze).

Amin, A. and K. Robins (1990), 'The re-emergence of regional economies: The mythical geography of flexible accumulation', *Environment and Planning D: Society and Space*, 8, 7–34.

References

Amin, A. and N. Thrift (1992), 'Neo-Marshallian nodes in global networks', *International Journal of Urban and Regional Research* 16(4), 571–87.

Amin, S. (1974), *Accumulation on a World Scale* (2 vols.), New York: Monthly Review Press.

Anderson, P. (1999), 'Complexity theory and organization science', *Organization Science* 10(3), May–June, 216–32.

Anderson, P. W., K. J. Arrow, and D. Pines (eds) (1998), *The Economy as an Evolving Complex System*, Redwood City, CA: Addison-Wesley Publishing Company.

Ancori, B., A. Bureth, and P. Cohendet (2000), 'The economics of knowledge: The debate about codification and tacit knowledge', *Industrial and Corporate Change* 9(2), 255–87.

Arrighi, G. (1978), *The Geometry of Imperialism*, London: New Left Books.

Arrow, K. J. (1971), 'Gifts and exchanges', *Philosophy and Public Affairs* 1(4), 354–62.

Atkinson, M. M. and W. D. Coleman (1992), 'Policy networks, policy communities and the problem of governance', *Governance* 5(2), 154–80.

Axelrod, R., (1981), 'The emergence of cooperation among egoists', *The American Political Science Review* 75, 306–18.

—— (1984), *The Evolution of Cooperation*, New York: Basic Books.

Bachmann, R. (2001), 'Trust, power and control in trans-organizational relations', *Organization Studies* 22(2), 337–65.

—— D. Knights, and J. Sydow (eds) (2001), 'Special issues: trust and control in organizational relations', *Organization Studies*, 22(2).

Baily, M. N. and R. Z. Lawrence (2001), 'Do we have a new E-economy?', *American Economic Review Papers and Proceedings*, May, 308–12.

Baldwin, R. E. and P. Martin (1999), 'Two waves of globalization: Superficial similarity and fundamental differences', in H. Siebert (ed.), *Globalization and Labour*, Tubingen: Mohr Siebeck.

Barnard, C. (1962), *The Functions of the Executive*, Cambridge, MA: Harvard University Press (first published in 1938).

Barry, A. (2000), 'Networks', in S. Pile and N. Thrift (eds), *City A–Z*, London: Routledge.

—— (2001), *Political Machines: Governing a Technological Society*, London: The Athlone Press.

—— and D. Slater (2002), 'Introduction: the technological economy', *Economy and Society*, 31(2), 175–83.

Bataille, G. (1984), 'The notion of expenditure' in *Visions of Excess: Selected Writings, 1927–1939*, Minneapolis: University of Minnesota Press.

—— (1997), 'Part III general economy', in F. Botting and S. Wilson (eds), *The Bataille Reader*, Oxford: Blackwell Publishers.

Bateson, G. (1987), *Steps to an Ecology of Mind*, Northvale, NJ: Jason Aronson.

Beaverstock, J. V., R. G. Smith, and P. J. Taylor (2000), 'World-city network: A new metageography?', *Annals of the Association of American Geographers* 90, 123–34.

Bender, B. (1998), 'Buying into networkcentric warfare', *Janes's Defence Weekly*, May 13.

Berkowitz, S. D. (1988), 'Markets and market-areas; some preliminary formulations', in B. Wellman and S. D. Berkowitz (eds), *Social Structures: A Network Approach*, Cambridge: Cambridge University Press, pp. 261–303.

Bernard, M. and J. Ravenhill (1995), 'Beyond product cycles and flying geese: Rationalization, hierarchy and the industrialization of East Asia', *World Politics* 47(2), 171–209.

Beyer, J. and A. Hassel (2002), 'The effects of convergence: Internationalization and the changing distribution of net value added in large German firms', *Economy and Society* 31(3), 309–32.

Blair, M. M. and S. M. H. Wallman (2001), *Unseen Wealth: Report on the Brookings Task Force on Intangibles*, Washington, DC: The Brookings Institution.

Boix, C. and D. Posner (1998), 'The origins and political consequences of social capital', *British Journal of Political Science* 28(4), 686–93.

Boulding, K. (1955), *A Reconstruction of Economics*, New York: Wiley.

Bourdieu, P. (1977), *Outline of a Theory of Practice*, Cambridge: Cambridge University Press.

Braithwaite, V. and M. Levi (1999), 'A state of trust' in V. Braithwaite and M. Levi (eds), *Trust and Governance*, New York: Russell Sage Foundation.

Breiger, R. (1981), 'Structures of economic interdependence among nations', in P. Blau and R. Merton (eds), *Continuities in Structural Inquiry*, Beverley Hills: Sage.

Bromiley, P. and L. L. Cummings (1989), 'Transaction costs in organizations with trust', Strategic Management Research Centre Working Paper, University of Minnesota, Minneapolis.

Brynjolfsson, E., L. M. Hitt, and S. Yang (2001), 'Intangible assets: how the interaction of computers and organizational structure affects stock market valuations', MIT, http://ebusiness.mit.edu/erik/.

References

Burroni, L. and C. Trigilia (2001), 'Italy: economic development through local economies', in C. Crouch *et al.* (eds), *Local Production Systems in Europe: Rise or Demise?* Oxford: Oxford University Press.

Burt, R. S. (1988), 'The stability of American markets', *American Journal of Sociology*, 94, 356–95.

—— (1992), *Structural Holes: The Social Structure of Competition*, Boston, MA: Harvard University Press.

Callon, M. (1986), 'Some elements of a sociology of translation: domestication of the scollops and the fishermen of St Brieuc Bay', in J. Law (ed.), *Power, Action and Belief: A New Sociology of Knowledge?* London: Routledge and Kegan Paul.

—— (1993), 'Variety and irreversibility in networks of technique, conception and adoption', in D. Foray and C. Freeman (eds), *Technology and the Wealth of Nations: The Dynamics of Constructed Advantage*, London: Pinter Publishers.

—— (ed.), (1998), *The Laws of the Markets*, Oxford: Basil Blackwell.

—— and Law, J. (1989), 'On the construction of sociotechnical networks: Content and context revisited', *Knowledge and Society: Studies in the Sociology of Science Past and Present* 8, 57–83.

—— C. Méadel, and V. Rabeharisoa (2002), 'The economy of qualities', *Economy and Society* 31(2), 194–217.

Cambridge Journal of Economics (1997), 'Special issue on contracts and competition', *Cambridge Journal of Economics* 21(2).

Casper, S., and B. Hancké (1999), 'Global quality norms within national production regimes: ISO 9000 standards in the French and German car industries', *Organization Studies* 20(6), 961–85.

Castells, M. (1996), *The Rise of the Network Society*, Oxford: Basil Blackwell.

—— (2001), *The Internet Galaxy*, Oxford: Oxford University Press.

Castilla, E., H. Hwang, E. Granovetter, and M. Granovetter (2000), 'Social networks in Silicon Valley', in C. -M. Lee, W. F. Miller, M. G. Hancock, and H. S. Rower (eds), *The Silicon Valley Edge*, Stanford: Stanford University Press.

Cebrowski, A. K. and J. J. Gratska (1998), 'Network centric warfare: its origins and future', *United States Naval Institute Proceedings* 124(1).

Cerwinski, T. (1998), *Coping With Bounds: Speculation on Nonlinearity in Military Affairs*, Washington, DC: National Defense University Press.

Chase-Dunn, C. (1989), *Global Formation: Structures of the World-Economy*, Oxford: Basil Blackwell.

—— Y. Kawano, and B. C. Brewer (2000), 'Trade globalization since 1795: waves of integration in the world-system', *American Sociological Review* 65(1), 77–95.

Cheal, D. (1988), *The Gift Economy*, London: Routledge.

Cohen, D. (2002), 'All the world's a net', *New Scientist*, 13 April, 25–9.

Coleman, J. S. (1982), 'Systems of trust', *Angewandte Sozialforschung* 10, 277–300.

—— (1990), *Foundations of Social Theory*, Cambridge: MA, Harvard University Press.

—— (1998), 'Social capital in the creation of human capital', *American Journal of Sociology* 94, S95–S119.

Cooke, P. and K. Morgan (1998), *The Associational Economy*, Oxford: Oxford University Press.

Council of Economic Advisors (2002), *Economic Report to the President 2002*, US Government Printing Office, Washington (February).

Council on Competitiveness (2001), *US Competitiveness 2001: Strengths, Vulnerabilities and Long Term Priorities* (M. E. Porter and D. van Opstal), Washington, DC: Council on Competitiveness.

Cowan, R., P. A. David, and D. Foray (2000), 'The explicit economics of knowledge codification and tacitness', *Industrial and Corporate Change* 9(2), 211–53.

Crouch, C. and H. Farrell (2001), 'Great Britain: falling through the holes in the network concept', in C. Crouch *et al.* (eds), *Local Production Systems in Europe: Rise or Demise?* Oxford: Oxford University Press.

—— and C. Triglia (2001), 'Conclusions: Still local economies in global capitalism?', in C. Crouch *et al.* (eds), *Local Production Systems in Europe: Rise or Demise?* Oxford: Oxford University Press.

—— P. Le Galès, C. Trigilia, and H. Voelzkow (eds) (2001), *Local Production Systems in Europe: Rise or Demise?* Oxford: Oxford University Press.

Cutler, A. C., V. Haufler, and T. Porter (eds), *Private Authority and International Affairs*, Albany: State University of New York Press.

Czaban, L. (2001), 'Foreign direct investment in Eastern Europe: the main force of economic restructuring'. Paper presented at ESRC Transnational Communities Programme Conference Multinational Enterprises: Embedded organisations, transnational federations or global learning communities? University of Warwick, September 6–8, 2001, Manchester Business School.

Danby, C. (2002), 'The curse of the modern: a post Keynesian critique of the gift/exchange dichotomy', *Research in Economic Anthropology* 21, 13–42.

Das, T. K. and T. Bing-Sheng (2001), 'Trust, control, and risk in strategic alliances: An integrated framework', *Organization Studies* 22(2), 251–83.

References

Daveri, F. (2000), 'Is growth an information technology story in Europe too?', Universita di Parma, and IGIER, September.

Davis, J. (2001), 'Gifts and trade', in J. Amariglio, S. Cullenberg, and D. F. Ruccio (eds), *Postmodernism, Economics and Knowledge*, London: Routledge.

De Landa, M. (1997), *A Thousand Years of Nonlinear History*, New York: Zone Books.

De Sanerclens, P. (1993), 'Regime theory and the study of international relations', *International Social Science Journal* 150, 453–62.

Derrida, J. (1992), *Given Time:1. Counterfeit Money*, Chicago and London: The University of Chicago Press.

—— (1995), *The Gift of Death*, Chicago: The University of Chicago Press.

Dicken, P., P. F. Kelly, K. Olds, and H. Wai-Chung Yeung (2001), 'Chains and networks, territories and scales: Towards a relational framework for analysing the global economy', *Global Networks* 1(2), 98–112.

Dixit, A. (1995), *The Making of Economic Policy: A Transaction Cost Perspective*, New York: Oxford University Press.

Doz, Y. (1987), 'International industries: fragmentation *versus* globalization', in H. Brooks and B. R. Guile (eds), *Technology and Global Industry*, Washington, DC: National Academy Press.

Durkheim, E. (1933), *The Division of Labour in Society*, New York: The Free Press (first published in 1893).

Ethridge, H. L. and R. S. Sriram (1993), 'Chaos theory and nonlinear dynamics: an emerging theory with implications for accounting research', *Journal of Accounting Literature* 12, 67–100.

Fehr, E. and S. Gächter (2000), 'Fairness and retaliation: the economics of reciprocity', *Journal of Economic Perspectives* 14(3), 159–81.

Foster, J. (1997), 'The analytical foundations of evolutionary economics: From biological analogy to economic self-organization', *Structural Change and Economic Dynamics* 8, 427–51.

—— (2000), 'Competitive selection, self-organisation and Joseph A. Schumpeter', *Evolutionary Economics*, 311–28.

Foucault, M. (1970), *The Order of Things*, London: Tavistock Publications.

—— (1986), 'Of other spaces', *Diacritics*, Spring, 22–7.

Frank, A.-G. (1979), *Dependent Accumulation and Development*, New York: Monthly Review Press.

Fraumeni, B. M. (2001), 'E-Commerce: measurement and measurement issues', *American Economic Review Papers and Proceedings*, May, pp. 318–22.

Friedmann, J. (1986), 'The world city hypothesis', *Development and Change* 17, 69–73.

—— (2000), 'Reading Castells: *Zeitdiagnose* and social theory', *Environment and Planning D: Society and Space* 18, 111–20.

Fukuyama, F. (1992), *The End of History and the Last Man*, London: Penguin Books.

—— (1995), *Trust: The Social Virtues and the Creation of Prosperity*, London: Penguin Books.

Gambetta, D. (ed.) (1988*a*), *Trust: Making and Breaking Cooperative Relations*, Oxford: Blackwell.

—— (1998*b*), 'Mafia: the price of trust', in D. Gambetta (ed.), *Trust: Making and Breaking Cooperative Relations*, Oxford: Basil Blackwell.

Garson, G. D. (1998), *Neural Networks: An Introductory Guide for Social Scientists*, London: Sage.

Gereffi, G. (1999), 'International trade and industrial upgrading in the apparel commodity chain', *Journal of International Economics* 48, 37–70.

—— (2001*a*), 'Beyond the produce-driven/buyer-driven dichotomy: The evolution of global value chains in the Internet era', *IDS Bulletin* 32(3), 30–40.

—— (2001*b*), 'Shifting governance in global commodity chains, with special reference to the Internet', *American Behavioural Scientist* 44(10), 1616–37.

—— and M. Korzeniewicz (eds) (1994), *Commodity Chains and Global Capitalism*, Westport: Praeger Publishers.

Gerlach, M. L. (1992), 'The Japanese corporate network: A blockmodel analysis', *Administrative Science Quarterly* 37, 105–39.

Giddens, A. (1990), *The Consequences of Modernity*, Cambridge: Polity Press.

Goodman, N. (1951), *The Structure of Appearances*, D. Reidel Publishing Co.

—— (1978), *Ways of World Making*, Hackett Publishing.

Ghoshal, S. and P. Moran (1996), 'Bad for practice: a critique of the transaction cost theory', *Academy of Management Review* 21, 13–47.

Grabher, G. (2001), 'Ecologies of creativity: The village, the group, and the heterarchic organization of the British advertising industry', *Environment and Planning A* 33, 351–74.

Grabher, G. (ed.) (1993), *The Embedded Firm: On the Socioeconomics of Industrial Networks*, London: Routledge.

—— and D. Stark (1997*b*), 'Organizing diversity: Evolutionary theory, network analysis and postsocialism', *Regional Studies* 31(5), 533–44.

—— and D. Stark (eds) (1997*a*), *Restructuring Networks in Post-Socialism: Legacies, Linkages, and Localities*, Oxford: Oxford University Press.

Graham, A. (2001), 'The internet: an assessment', *Oxford Review of Economic Policy*, 17(2), 145–58.

References

Granovetter, M. (1973), 'The strength of weak ties', *American Journal of Sociology* 78, 1360–80.

—— (1982), 'The strength of weak ties: a network theory revisited', in P. Marsden and N. Lin (eds), *Social Structure and Network Analysis*, Beverly Hills, CA: Sage.

—— (1985), 'Economic action and social structure: The problem of embeddedness', *American Journal of Sociology* 91, 481–510.

—— (1992), 'Problems and explanations in economic sociology', in N. Nohria and R. G. Eccles (eds), *Network and Organizations: Structure, Form, Action*, Cambridge, MA: Harvard University Press.

Gregory, C. A. (1981), 'A conceptual analysis of a non-capitalist gift economy with particular reference to Papua New Guinea', *Cambridge Journal of Economics* 5, 119–35.

—— (1982), *Gifts and Commodities*, London: Academic Press.

Grieco, J. M. (1990), *Cooperation Among Nations*, Ithaca: Cornell University Press.

Gudeman, S. (2001), 'Postmodern gifts' in J. Amariglio, S. Cullenberg, and D. F. Ruccio (eds), *Postmodernism, Economics and Knowledge*, London: Routledge.

Gust, C. and J. Marquez (2000), 'Productivity developments abroad', *Federal Reserve Bulletin*, October, 665–81.

Guthrie, D. (1997), 'Between Markets and Politics: Organizational responses to reform in China', *American Journal of Sociology* 102(5), 1258–304.

Hacking, I. (1999), *The Social Construction of What?* Cambridge, MA: Harvard University Press.

Hagedoorn, J. (1990), 'Organizational modes in inter-firm cooperation and technological transfer', *Technovation* 10(1), 17–30.

—— and J. Schakenraad (1990), 'Strategic partnering and technological cooperation', in B. Dankbaar, J. Groenewegen, and H. Schnek (eds), *Perspectives in Industrial Economics*, Dordrecht, Kluwer.

Hall, P. A. and D. Soskice (eds) (2001a), *Varieties of Capitalism: The Institutional Foundations of Comparative Advantage*, Oxford: Oxford University Press.

—— and D. Soskice (2001b), 'An introduction to varieties of capitalism', in P. A. Hall and D. Soskice (eds), *Varieties of Capitalism: The Institutional Foundations of Comparative Advantage*, Oxford: Oxford University Press.

Hall, R. E. (2000), 'E-Capital: The link between the stock market and labour market in the 1990s', *Brookings Papers on Economic Activity* 2, 73–118.

Hansen, A. and J. Mouritsen (1999), 'Managerial technology and netted networks. "Competitiveness" in action: The work of translating performance in a high-tech firm', *Organization* 6(3), 451–71.

Hargittai, E. and M. A. Centeno (2001), 'Defining a global geography', *American Behavioral Scientist* 44(10), 1545–60.

Harrison, B. (1994), *Lean and Mean*, New York: Basic Books.

Hassard, J., J. Law, and N. Lee (1999), 'Preface: Actor network theory', *Organization* 6, 387–90.

Helper, S., J. P. MacDuffie, and C. Sabel (1997), *The Boundaries of the Firm as a Design Problem*, Columbia Law School, November. Available on Sabel's web site: http://www.columbia.edu/~cfs11/.

—— J. P. MacDuffie, and C. Sabel (2000), 'Pragmatic collaborations: Advancing knowledge while controlling opportunism', *Industrial and Corporate Change* 9(3), 443–87.

Henderson, J., P. Dicken, M. Hess, N. Coe, and H. Wai-Chung Yeung (2001), 'Global production networks and the analysis of economic development', University of Manchester, mimeographed.

Hennart, J. -F. (1993), 'Explaining the swollen middle: Why most transactions are a mix of "market" and "hierarchy" ', *Organization Science* 4(4), 529–47.

Herrnstein Smith, B. (1988), *Contingencies of Value*, Cambridge, MA: Harvard University Press.

Hetherington, K. and J. Law (2000), 'After networks', *Environment and Planning D: Society and Space* 18(2), Introduction.

Hinchliffe, S. (2000), 'Performance and experimental knowledge: Outdoor management training and the end of epistemology', *Environment and Planning D: Society and Space*, 18, 575–95.

Hirshman, A. O. (1970), *Exit, Voice and Loyalty*, Cambridge, MA: Harvard University Press.

Hirst, P. Q. (1994), *Associative Democracy: New Forms of Economic and Social Governance*, Cambridge: Polity Press.

—— (1997), *From Statism to Pluralism*, London: UCL Press.

—— and G. F. Thompson (1999), *Globalization in Question* (second edition), Cambridge: Polity Press.

—— and J. Zeitlin (1991), 'Flexible specialization versus post-Fordism: theory, evidence and policy', *Economy and Society* 20(1), 1–56.

—— and J. Zeitlin (eds) (1989), *Reversing Industrial Decline?* Oxford: Berg.

Hohenberg, P. M. and L. Hollen Lees (1985), *The Marking of Urban Europe: 1000–1994*, Cambridge: Harvard University Press.

References

Hollingsworth, J. R., P. C. Schmitter, and W. Streeck (eds) (1994), *Governing Capitalist Economies: Performance and Control of Economic Sectors*, New York, Oxford: University Press.

Hollis, M. (1998), *Trust Within Reason*, Cambridge: Cambridge University Press.

Hooghe, L. and G. Marks (2001), *Multi-level Governance and European Integration*, Boulder: Rowman and Littlefield.

Hoogvelt, A. (1997), *Globalization and the Post Colonial World: The New Political Economy of Development*, Basingstoke: Macmillan.

Hopkins, T. K. and I. Wallerstein (1986), 'Commodity chains in the world economy prior to 1800', *Review* 10(1), 157–70.

Howard, P. E. N., L. L. Rainie, and S. Jones (2001), 'Days and nights on the internet: the impact of a diffusing technology', *American Behavioral Scientist* 45(3), 383–404.

Hudson, A. (2001), 'NGOs' transnational advocacy networks: From "legitimacy" to "political responsibility"?', *Global Networks* 1(4), 331–52.

Hull, R. (1999), 'Actor network and conduct: The discipline and practices of knowledge management', *Organization* 6(3), 405–28.

Hummels, D. (2000), 'Time as a trade barrier', Purdue University, October.

Humphrey, J. and H. Schmitz (2001), 'Governance in global value chains', *IDS Bulletin*, 32(3), 19–29.

Hyde, L. (1979), *The Gift: Imagination and the Erotic Life of Property*, New York: Random House.

IDS (Institute for Development Studies) (2001), 'The value of value chains: Spreading the gains from globalization', *IDS Bulletin Special Issue* 32(3), July.

Ietto-Gillies, G. (2002), *Transnational Corporations: Fragmentation Amidst Integration*, London: Routledge.

International Organisation (1992), Special issue on 'Epistemic communities' 64(1).

Johanson, J. and L.-G. Mattsson (1987), 'Interorganizational relations in industrial systems: a network approach compared with the transactions-cost approach', *International Studies of Management and Organisation*, 17(1), 34–48.

Johnson, J. and P. Picton, (1996), 'How to train a neural network', *Complexity* 2(1), 13–28.

Johnston, R. and P. R. Lawrence (1988), 'Beyond vertical integration—The rise of the value-adding partnership', *Harvard Business Review*, July–August, 94–101.

Jones, C., W. S. Hesterly, and S. P. Borgatti, (1997), 'A general theory of network governance: Exchange conditions and social mechanisms', *Academy of Management Review* 22(4), 911–45.

Jordan, G. and K. Schubert (1992), 'A preliminary ordering of policy network labels', *European Journal of Political Research* 21(1–2), 7–28.

Jurgens, U., K. Naumann, and J. Rupp (2000), 'Shareholder value in an adverse environment: The case of Germany', *Economy and Society* 29(1), 54–79.

Kaplinski, R. and M. Morris (2001), *A Handbook for Value Chain Analysis*, IDS, University of Sussex.

Kaufman, F., G. Majone, and B. Ostrom (eds) (1986), *Guidance, Control and Evaluation in the Public Sector*, Berlin: de Gruyter.

Kavanaugh, A. L. and S. J. Patterson (2001), The impact of community computer networks on social capital and community involvement', *American Behavioural Scientist*, 45(3), 496–509.

Kay, N. M. (1992), 'Markets, false hierarchies and the evolution of the modern corporation', *Journal of Economic Behaviour and Organization* 17, 315–33.

Keohane, R. O. (1984), *After Hegemony: Cooperation and Discord in the World Political Economy*, Princeton: Princeton University Press.

—— (2001), 'Governance in a partially globalized world', *American Political Science Review* 95(1), 1–13.

Kick, E. L. and B. L. Davis (2001), 'World systems structure and change', *American Behavioural Scientist* 44(10), 1561–78.

Kickert, W. J., E.-H. Klijn, and J. F. M. Koppenjan (eds) (1997), *Managing Complex Networks: Strategies for the Public Sector*, London: Sage.

Kittler, F. A. (1990), *Discourse Networks, 1800/1900*, Stanford, CA: Stanford University Press.

—— (1999), *Gramophone, Film, Typewriter*, Stanford. CA: Stanford University Press.

Klaes, M. (2000*a*), 'The history of the concept of transaction costs: Neglected aspects', *Journal of the History Economic Thought* 22(2), 191–216.

Klaes, M. (2000*b*), 'The birth of the concept of transactions costs: Issues and controversies', *Industrial and Corporate Change* 9(4), 567–93.

Kleinknecht, A. and J. T. Wengel (1998), 'The Myth of economic globalization' *Cambridge Journal of Economics* 22(4), 637–47.

Klier, T. H. (1999), 'Agglomeration in the US auto supply industry', *Economic Perspectives*, Federal Reserve Bank of Chicago.

Knoke, D. (2001), *Changing Organizations: Business Networks in the New Political Economy*, Boulder, CO: Westview Press.

—— and J. H. Kuklinski, (1982), *Network Analysis*, Beverly Hills: Sage.

References

Kogut, B. (1998), 'The network as knowledge', www.wharton.edu.

—— (2003), *The Global Internet Economy*, Cambridge MR, MTT Press.

Koku, E., N. Nazer, and B. Wellman (2001), 'Netting scholars: Online and offline', *American Behavioural Scientist*, 44(10), 1752–74.

Kramer, R. M. and T. R. Tyler (eds) (1996), *Trust in Organizations*, Thousand Oaks: Sage.

Krasner, S. (1983), *International Regimes*, Ithaca: Cornell University Press.

Krohn, W., G. Kuppers, and H. Nowotny (eds) (1990), *Selforganization: Portrait of a Scientific Revolution*, Dordrecht: Kluwer Academic Publishers.

La Porta, R., F. Lopez-de-Silanes, A. Shleifer, and R. W. Vishny (1997), 'Trust in large organizations', *American Economic Review Papers and Proceedings*, May, pp. 333–37.

Lane, C. and R. Bachmann (eds) (1998), *Trust Within and Between Organizations*, Oxford: Oxford University Press.

Latour, B. (1987), *Science in Action. How to Follow Scientists and Engineers through Society*, Cambridge, MA: Harvard University Press.

—— (1990), 'Drawing things together', in M. Lynch and S. Woolgar (eds), *Representation in Scientific Practice*, Cambridge, MA: MIT Press.

—— (1993), *We Have Never Been Modern*, Hemel Hempstead: Harvester Wheatsheaf.

—— (1999), 'On recalling ANT', in J. Law and J. Hassard (eds), *Actor Network Theory and After*, Oxford: Basil Blackwell Publishers.

Law, J. (1992), 'Notes on the theory of the actor-network: Ordering, strategy, and heterogeneity', *Systems Practice* 5(4), 379–93.

—— (1994), *Organizing Modernity*, Oxford: Basil Blackwell.

—— and J. Hassard (eds) (1999), *Actor Network Theory and After*, Oxford: Basil Blackwell Publishers.

—— and A. Moi (2001), 'Situating technoscience: An enquiry into spatialities', *Environment and Planning D. Society and Space* 19, 609–21.

Lazaric, N. (2000), 'The role of routines, rules and habits in collective learning: Some epistemological and ontological considerations', *European Journal of Economic and Social Systems* 14(2), 157–71.

—— and E. Lorenz (eds) (1998), *Trust and Economic Learning*, Cheltenham: Edward Elgar.

Leamer, E. and M. Storper (2001), 'The economic geography of the Internet age', *Journal of International Business Studios*, 32(4), 641–65.

Lee, N. and S. Brown (1994), 'Otherness and the actor network: The undiscovered continent', *American Behavioural Scientist* 37(6), 772–90.

—— and J. Hassard (1999), 'Organization unbound: Actor network theory, research strategy and institutional flexibility', *Organization* 6(3), 391–404.

—— and P. Stenner (1999), 'Who pays? Can we pay back?', in J. Law and J. Hassard (eds), *Actor Network Theory and After*, Oxford: Blackwell.

Leifer, E. M. and H. C. White (1997), 'A structural approach to markets', in M. S. Mizruchi and M. Schwartz (eds), *Intercorporate Relations*, Cambridge: Cambridge University Press, pp. 85–108.

Leoncini, R. and S. Montresor (2000), 'Network analysis of eight technological systems', *International Review of Applied Economics* 14(2), 315–34.

Lewis, J. D. and A. Weigert (1985), 'Trust as a social reality', *Social Forces* 63(4), 476–985.

Lincoln, J. R., M. L. Gerlach, and C. L. Ahmadjian (1996), 'Keiretsu networks and corporate performance in Japan', *American Sociological Review* 61(February), 67–88.

Locke, R. M. (1995), *Remaking the Italian Economy*, Ithaca: Cornell University Press.

Lorenz, E. H. (1988), 'Neither friends nor strangers: informal networks of subcontracting in French industry', in D. Gambetta (ed.), *Trust: Making and Breaking Cooperative Relations*, Oxford: Basil Blackwell.

Lucking-Reiley, D. and D. F. Spulber (2001), 'Business-to-business electronic commerce', *Journal of Economic Perspectives* 15(1), 55–68.

Luhmann, N. (1979), *Trust and Power*, Chichester: Wiley.

—— (1997), 'Limits of steering', *Theory, Culture and Society* 14(1), 41–57.

Lyons, B. and J. Mehta (1997), 'Contracts, opportunism and trust: self interest and social orientation', *Cambridge Journal of Economics* 21, 239–57.

Malpas, J. and G. Wickham (1995), 'Governance and failure: on the limits of sociology', *Australian and New Zealand Journal of Sociology* 31(3), 37–50.

Mason, C. M. and R. T. Harrison (1995), 'Closing the regional equity capital gap: The role of informal venture capital', *Small Business Economics* 7, 153–72.

Mauss, M. (1990)[1923], *The Gift*, London: Routledge and Keegan Paul.

McGuckin, R. H. and B. van Ark (2002), *Performance 2001: Productivity, Employment, and Income in the World's Economies*, The Conference Board, Report No.13, January.

McKinsey and Company (2001), *US Productivity Growth: 1995–2000*, New York, McKinsey and Co, October 17.

McMorrow, K. and W. Roeger (2001), 'Potential output: Measurement methods, "new" economy influences and scenarios for 2001–2010—a

References

comparison of the EU15 and the US', EU, Brussels, *Economic Papers No.150* DG Economic and Financial Affairs, April.

Messner, D. (1997), *The Network Society: Economic Development and International Competitiveness as Problems of Social Governance*, London: Frank Cass.

Miles, R. E. and C. C. Snow (1992), 'Causes of failure in network organizations', *California Management Review* 34(4), 53–72.

Miller, P. (1998), 'The margins of accounting', in M. Callon (ed.), *The Laws of the Markets*, Oxford: Basil Blackwell.

—— (2001), 'Governing by numbers: why calculative practices matter', *Social Research* 68(2), 379–95.

Mirowski, P. (2001), 'Refusing the gift', in J. Amariglio, S. Cullenberg, and D. F. Ruccio (eds), *Postmodernism, Economics and Knowledge*, London: Routledge.

Moran, P. and S. Ghoshal (1996), 'Theories of economic organization: The case for realism and balance', *Academy of Management Review* 21(1), 58–72.

Morgan, G. (2001), 'Transnational communities and business systems', *Global Networks*, 1(2), 113–30.

Morin, F. (2000), 'A Transformation in the French Model of Shareholding and Management', *Economy and Society* 29(1), 36–53.

Munro, R. (1999), 'Power and discretion: Membership work in the time of technology', *Organization* 6(3), 429–50.

Murdoch, J. (1995), 'Actor-networks and the evolution of economic forms: Combining description and explanation in theories of regulation, flexible specialization, and networks', *Environment and Planning A* 27(5), 731–57.

—— (1997), 'Inhuman/nonhuman/human: actor-network theory and the prospects for a nondualistic and symmetrical perspective on nature and society', *Environment and Planning D. Society and Space* 15, 731–56.

Mytelka, L. K. (1995), 'Dancing with wolves: Global oligopolies and strategic alliances', in J. Hagedoon (ed.), *Technical Change and the World Economy*, Cheltenham: Edward Elgar Press.

Naas, M. (1997), 'The time of a detour: Jacques Derrida and the question of the gift', *Oxford Literary Review* 18, 67–86.

Nemeth, R. J. and D. A. Smith (1985), 'International trade and world-system structure', *Review* viii(Spring) 517–60.

Nowotny, H. (1990), 'Actor-networks vs. science as a self-organizing system: a comparative view of two constructivist approaches', in

W. Krohn, G. Kuppers, and H. Nowotny (eds), *Selforganization: Portrait of a Scientific Revolution*, Dordrecht: Kluwer Academic Publishers.

OECD (2001), *The Well Being of Nations: The Role of Human and Social Capital*, Paris: OECD.

—— (2002), 'The latest official statistics on electronic commerce: a focus on consumers' internet transactions', (www.oecd.org), Paris: OECD.

Organization (1999), Special Issue on *Actor Network Theory* 6(3).

Ostrom, E. (1990), *Governing the Commons: The Evolution of Institutions for Collective Action*, Cambridge: Cambridge University Press.

—— (2000), 'Collective action and the evolution of social norms', *Journal of Economic Perspectives* 14(3), 137–58.

—— and R. Gardner (1993), 'Coping with asymmetries in the commons: Self-governing irrigation systems can work', *Journal of Economic Perspectives* 7(4), 93–112.

Oulton, N. (2001), *ICT and Productivity Growth in the United Kingdom*. Bank of England, Working Paper No. 140, Bank of England, London.

Pappi, F. U. and C. H. C. A. Henning (1998), Policy networks: More than a metaphor?', *Journal of Theoretical Politics* 10(4), 553–76.

Paterson, J. and G. Teubner (1998), 'Changing maps: empirical legal autopoiesis', *Social and Legal Studies* 7(4), 451–86.

Pawlett, W. (1997), 'Utility and excess: the radical sociology of Bataille and Baudrillard', *Economy and Society* 26(1), 92–125.

Pearce, F. (ed) (2002), Special issues 'College de Sociologie', *Economy and Society* 31(4), November.

Pecora, V. (1997), *Households of the Soul*, Baltimore and London: The John Hopkins University Press.

Pelagidis, T. and G. E. Chortareas (2002), 'Trade flows: A facet of regionalism or globalization?', *Cambridge Journal of Economics* (forthcoming).

Piore, M. and C. Sabel (1984), *The Second Industrial Divide*, New York: Basic Books.

Podolny, J. M. (1993), 'A status-based model of market competition', *American Journal of Sociology* 98(4), 8229–72.

—— and K. L. Page (1998), 'Network forms of organization', *Annual Review of Sociology* 24, 57–76.

Polanyi, M. (1957), *Personal Knowledge: Towards a Post-Critical Philosophy*, London: Routledge and Kegan Paul.

—— (1967), *The Tacit Dimension*, London: Routledge and Kegan Paul.

Porter, M. (1985), *Competitive Advantage: Creating and Sustaining Superior Advantage*, Basingstoke, Macmillan.

References

Porter, M. (1990), *The Competitive Advantage of Nations*, Basingstoke: Macmillan.

Powell, W. W. (1990), 'Neither markets nor hierarchy: Network forms of organization', *Research in Organizational Behaviour* 12, 295–336.

Putnam, R. D. (1993*a*), 'The prosperous community', *The American Prospect* 4(13), 1–5.

—— (1993*b*), *Making Democracy Work: Civic Traditions in Modern Italy*, Princeton: Princeton University Press.

—— (1995), 'Bowling alone: America's declining social capital', *Journal of Democracy* 6(1), 65–78.

—— (2000), *Bowling Alone: The Collapse and Revival of American Community*, New York: Simon and Schuster.

Raikes, P., M. Friis Jensen, and S. Ponte (2000), 'Global commodity chain analysis and the French *filière* approach: comparison and critique', *Economy and Society* 29(3), 390–417.

Rauch, J. E. (1999), 'Networks versus markets in international trade', *Journal of International Economics* 48, 7–35.

Reinicke, W. H. and F. Deng (2000), *Critical Choices: The United Nations, Networks, and the Future of Global Governance*, Ottawa: International Development Research Centre.

Reve, T. (1990), 'The firm as a nexus of internal and external contracts', in M. Aoki, B. Gustfasson, and O.E. Williamson (eds), *The Firm as a Nexus of Treaties*, London: Sage.

Rhodes, R. A. W. and D. Marsh (1992), 'New directions in the study of policy networks', *European Journal of Political Research* 21(1–2), 181–205.

Riles, A. (2001), *The Network Inside Out*, Ann Arbor: The University of Michigan Press.

Roeger, W. (2001), 'The contribution of information and communication technologies to growth in Europe and the US: A macroeconomic analysis', *Economic Papers No. 147*, EU, Brussels, DG Economic and Financial Affairs, January.

Rose, N. (1996), 'The death of the social? Reconfiguring the territory of government', *Economy and Society* 24(3), 327–56.

Sabel, C. (1989), 'Flexible specialization and the re-emergence of industrial districts', in P. Q. Hirst and J. Zeitlin (eds), *Reversing Industrial Decline? Industrial Structure and Policy in Britain and her Competitors*, Oxford: Berg.

—— (1990), *Studied Trust: Building New Forms of Cooperation in a Volatile Economy*, Geneva: International Institute for Labor Studies.

References

—— (1991), 'Moebius strip organizations and open labour markets', in P. Bourdieu and J. S. Coleman (eds), *Social Theory for a Changing Society*, Boulder, CO: Westview Press.

—— (1993), 'Constitutional ordering in historical context', in F. Scharpf (ed.), *Games in Hierarchies and Networks*, Frankfurt am Main: Campus Verlag.

—— (2001), 'Diversity, not specialization: The ties that bind the (new) industrial districts', Conference paper *Complexity and Industrial Clusters: Dynamics and Models in Theory and Practice*, Milan, June 19–20.

—— G. Herrigel, and H. Kern (1990), 'Collaborative manufacturing', in H. G. Mendius and U. Wendeling-Schröder (eds), *Zulieferer im Netz-Zwischen Abhängigkeit und Pärlnerschaft*, Köln, Bund Verlag.

Sabel, C. F. and J. Cohen (2001), 'Sovereignty and solidarity in the EU: A working paper where we face some facts', paper prepared for the conference on *Reconfiguring Work and Welfare in the New Economy: A Transatlantic Dialogue*, University of Wisconsin-Madison, May.

—— and J. Zeitlin (1985), 'Historical alternatives to mass production: Politics, markets and technology in nineteenth-century industrialization', *Past and Present*, 108, 133–76.

—— and J. Zeitlin (eds) (1997), *World of Possibilities: Flexible and Mass Production in Western Industrialization*, Cambridge: Cambridge University Press.

Sassen, S. (1991), *The Global City: New York, London, Tokyo*, Princeton, NJ: Princeton University Press.

—— (1994), *Cities in the World Economy*, Thousand Oaks: Pine Forge Press.

Scharpf, F. (1997), *Games Real Actors Play: Actor-Centric Institutionalism in Policy Research*, Boulder, CO: Westview Press.

—— (ed.) (1993), *Games in Hierarchies and Networks*, Frankfurt am Main: Campus Verlag.

Scholte, J.-A., (2000), *Globalization: A Critical Introduction*, Basingstoke: Macmillan.

Schott, T. (2001), 'Global webs of knowledge: Education, Science, and Technology', *American Behavioural Scientist* 44(10), 1740–51.

Schumpeter, J. (1950), *Capitalism, Socialism, Democracy*, New York: Harper & Brothers.

Scott, J. and C. Griff (1984), *Directors of Industry*, Cambridge: Polity Press.

Shachar, J. and E. Zuscovitch (1990), 'Learning patterns within a technological network: The case of the European space program', in B. Dankbaar, J. Groenewegen, and H. Schenk (eds), *Perspectives in Industrial Organization*, Dordrecht: Kluwer Academic Publishers.

References

Shy, O. (2001), *The Economics of Network Industries*, Cambridge: Cambridge University Press.

Simon, H. A. (1996), *The Sciences of the Artificial* (Third edition), Cambridge MA: MIT Press.

Skelcher, M. (1998), *The Appointed State: Quasi-Governmental Organizations and Democracy*, Milton Keynes: The Open University Press.

Smith, A. (1979), *An Inquiry into the Nature and Causes of the Wealth of Nations*, Oxford: Clarendon Press.

Smith, D. A. and R. J. Nemeth (1998), 'An empirical analysis of commodity exchange in the international economy: 1965–80', *International Studies Quarterly* 32, 227–40.

—— and M. F. Timberlake (2001), 'World city networks and hierarchies, 1977–97: An empirical analysis of global air travel links', *American Behavioural Scientist* 44(10), 1656–78.

—— and D. R. White (1992), 'Structure and dynamics of the global economy: Network analysis of international trade 1965–1980', *Social Forces* 70(4), 857–93.

Smith, R. G. (2002), 'World city actor-networks', *Research Bulletin 71*, GaWC Research Group, Loughborough University.

Snyder, D. and E. Kick (1979), 'Structural position in the world system and economic growth, 1955–1970: A multiple-network analysis of transnational interactions', *American Journal of Sociology* 84, 1096–126.

Solow, R. M. (1987), 'We'd better watch out', *New York Times Book Review* (July 12, p. 36).

Stark, D. (1996), 'Recombinant property in Eastern European capitalism', *American Journal of Sociology* 101, 722–84.

—— and B. Vedres (2001), 'Pathways of property transformation: Enterprise network careers in Hungary, 1989–2000', New York: Columbia University, August.

—— S. Kemeny, and R. Breiger (1998), 'Postsocialist portfolios: Network strategies in the shadow of the state', *American Sociological Association Conference*, San Francisco, August.

Steier, L. and R. Greenwood (2000), 'Entrepreneurship and the evolution of angel financial networks', *Organization Studies* 21(1), 163–92.

Stinchcome, A. L. (1985), 'Contracts as hierarchical documents', in A. L. Stinchcombe and C. Heimer (eds), *Organization Theory and Project Management*, Bergen, Norwegian University Press.

Stockman, F. N., R. Ziegler, and J. Scott (1985), *Networks of Corporate Power*, Cambridge: Polity Press.

Stoker, G. (1998), 'Governance as theory: five propositions', *International Social Science Journal* 155, March, 17–28.

Strathern, M. (1995), *The Relation*, Cambridge: Prickly Pear Press.

Streeck, W. and P. C. Schmitter (1985), 'Community, market, state and associations? The prospective contribution of interest governance to social order', in W. Streeck and P. C. Schmitter (eds), *Private Interest Government: Beyond Market and State*, London: Sage.

Sturgeon, T. J. (2001), 'How do we define value chains and production networks?', *IDS Bulletin* 32(3), 9–18.

Su, T. (1995), 'Changes in world trade networks: 1938, 1960, 1990', *Review* xviii(3), 431–57.

Sugden, R. (1984), 'Reciprocity: The supply of public goods through voluntary contributions', *The Economic Journal* 94, 772–87.

Taylor, P. J. (1996), *The Way the Modern World Works: World Hegemony to World Impasse*, Chichester: John Wiley.

—— (2000), 'World cities and territorial states under conditions of contemporary globalization', *Political Geography* 19(1), 5–32.

—— (2001), 'Specification of the world city network', *Geographical Analysis* 33, 181–94.

—— G. Catalano, and D. R. F. Walker (2001*a*), 'Measurement of the world city network', GaWC Research Bulletin No. 43. Loughborough University.

—— G. Catalano, and D. R. F. Walker (2001*b*), 'Exploratory analysis of the world city network', GaWC Research Bulletin No.50, Loughborough University.

Teubner, G. (1993), *Law as an Autopoietic System*, Oxford: Basil Blackwell.

—— (1996), 'De Collisione Discursum: Communicative rationalities in law, morality, and politics', *Cardozo Law Review* 17(4–5), 901–18.

—— (1997), 'The kings many bodies: the self-destruction of law's hierarchy', *Law and Society Review*, 31(4), 763–87.

—— (2001*a*), 'Economies of gift—positivity of justice: The mutual paranoia of Jaques Derrida and Niklas Luhmann', *Theory, Culture and Society* 18(1), 29–47.

Teubner, G. (2001*b*), 'Legal irritants: How unifying law ends up in new divergences', in P. A. Hall and D. Soskice (eds), *Varieties of Capitalism: The Institutional Foundations of Comparative Advantage*, Oxford: Oxford University Press.

Thatcher, M. (1998), 'The development of policy network analyses: From modest origins to overarching frameworks', *Journal of Theoretical Politics* 10(4), 389–416.

References

The Council on Competitiveness (2001), *U.S. Competitiveness 2001: Strengths, Vulnerabilities and Long-Term Priorities*, Washington, DC, The Council on Competitiveness.

The World Bank (2002), www.worldbank.org/scapital (home page for World Bank's Social Capital web-site).

Thompson, G. F. (1980), 'Economic calculation as "Sign" ', *Economy and Society* 9(1), 75–89.

—— (1985), 'Approaches to "Performance" ', *Screen* 26(5), 78–90, September–October.

—— (1991), 'Is accounting rhetorical? Methodology, Luca Pacioli and Writting' *Accounting, Organizations and Society* 16(4/6), 572–99.

—— (1993*a*), 'Network coordination', in R. Maidment and G. F. Thompson (eds), *Managing the United Kingdom: An Introduction to its Political Economy and Public Policy*, London: Sage.

—— (1993*b*), *The Economic Emergence of a New Europe? The Political Economy of Cooperation and Competition in the 1990s*, Cheltenham: Edward Elgar.

—— (1996), 'The market system', in M. Mackintosh, V. Brown, N. Costello, G. Dawson, G. Thompson, and A. Trigg (eds), *Economics and Changing Economies*, London: Thompson Business Press.

—— (1997*a*), 'Accounting and calculation for trust based networks: optimizing time or gifting time?', paper given at the *Accounting, Organization and Society Conference*, Copenhagen, September 4–6.

—— (1998), 'Globalisation versus regionalism?', *Journal of North African Studies* 3(2), 59–74.

—— (2002), 'Are there any limits to globalization: international trade flows and capital movements' mimeographed, The Open University (forthcoming in *Review of International Political Economy*).

—— (2003), 'The American economy: From the "new paradigm" to downturn and recession?', in J. Perraton and B. Clift (eds), *Where are National Capitalisms Now?*, London: Macmillan.

—— J. Frances, R. Levacic, and J. Mitchell (eds) (1991), *Markets, Hierarchies and Networks: The Coordination of Social Life*, London: Sage.

Thrift, N. (1999), 'The place of complexity', *Theory, Culture and Society* 13(3), 31–69.

—— (2000), 'Afterwords' *Environment and Planning D: Society and Space* 18(2), 213–55.

Titmuss, R. (1971), *The Gift Relationship: From Human Blood to Social Policy*, London: RKP.

Townsend, A. M. (2001), 'Network cities and the global structure of the Internet', *American Behavioural Scientist* 44, 1697–716.

References

Tsai, W. and S. Ghoshal (1998), 'Social capital and value creation: the role of intrafirm networks', *Academy of Management Journal* 41(4), 464–76.

United Nations Conference on Trade and Development (UNCTAD)(2001), *E-Commerce and Development Report 2001*, UN, New York.

Uslaner, E. M. (2000), 'Trust, civic engagement, and the Internet', mimeographed, University of Maryland, College Park.

Uzzi, B. (1996), 'The sources and consequences of embeddedness for the economic performance of organizations; The network effect', *American Sociological Review* 61, August, 674–98.

—— (1997), 'Social structure and competition in interfirm networks: The paradox of embeddedness', *Administrative Sciences Quarterly* 42, 35–57.

—— (1999), 'Embeddedness in the making of financial capital: How social relations and networks benefit firms seeking financing', *American Journal of Sociology* 64(4), 481–505.

Venables, A. J. (2001), 'Geography and international inequalities: The impact of new technologies', Background Paper for *Globalization, Growth and Poverty*, World Bank, Washington, 2002.

Waarden, F. van. (1992), 'Dimensions and types of policy networks', *European Journal of Political Research* 21(1–2), 29–52.

Wadhwani, S. B. (2001), 'Do we have a new economy?', *Bank of England Quarterly Bulletin*, Winter, 485–510.

Waldfogel, J. (1993), 'The deadweight loss of Christmas', *American Economic Review*, 83, 1328–36.

Wallerstein, I. (1974), *The Modern World System 1*, New York: Academic Press.

Wasserman, S. and K. Faust (1994), *Social Network Analysis: Methods and Applications*, Cambridge: Cambridge University Press.

Weiner, A. B. (1992), *Inalienable Possessions: The Paradox of Keeping-While-Giving*, Berkley, CA: University of California Press.

Wellman, B. (1979), 'The community question', *American Journal of Sociology* 84, 1201–31.

—— (ed.) (1999), *Networks in the Global Village*, Boulder, CO: Westview Press.

—— A. Quan Haase, J. Witte, and Hampton, K. (2001), 'Does the internet increase, decrease, or supplement social capital?', *American Behavioural Scientist*, 45(3), 436–55.

White, H. C. (1981), 'Where do markets come from?', *American Journal of Sociology*, 87, 517–47.

White, H. C. (1988), 'Varieties of markets', in B. Wellman and S. D. Berkowitz (eds), *Social Structures: A Network Approach*, Cambridge: Cambridge University Press, 226–60.

References

Whiteley, P. F. (1997), 'Economic Growth and Social Capital', ECPR Workshop on *Social Capital and Politico-economic Performance*, University of Bern, April.

Whiteley, R. (1996), 'Business systems and global commodity chains: Competing or complementary forms of economic organization?', *Competition and Change* 1(4), 441–25.

—— (1999), *Divergent Capitalisms*, Oxford: Oxford University Press.

Whitford, J. (2001), 'The decline of a model? Challenge and response in Italian industrial districts', *Economy and Society* 30(1), 38–65.

Wilkinson, J. (1997), 'A new paradigm for economic analysis?', *Economy and Society* 26(3), 305–39.

Williamson, O. E. (1975), *Markets and Hierarchies: Analysis and Antitrust Implications*, New York: Free Press.

—— (1992), 'Markets, hierarchies, and the modern corporation: An unfolding perspective', *Journal of Economic Behaviour and Organization* 17, 335–52.

—— (1993), 'Calculativeness, trust, and economic organization', *Journal of Law and Economics* xxxvi(April), 453–86.

—— (1993), 'Opportunism and its critics', *Managerial and Decision Economics* 14, 97–107.

—— (1994), 'Transaction cost economics and organization theory', in N. J. Smelser and R. Swedberg (eds), *The Handbook of Economic Sociology*, Princeton: Princeton University Press.

—— (1996a), *The Mechanisms of Governance*, New York: Oxford University Press.

Williamson, O. E. (1997b), 'Economic organization: the case for candor', *Academy of Management Review* 21(1), 48–57.

Wise, R. and D. Morrison (2000), 'Beyond the exchange: The future of B2B', *Harvard Business Review*, November–December, 88–96.

Wolf, M. (2002), 'Countries still rule the World', *The Financial Times*, 6 February.

Wood, A. (2001), 'Value chains: An Economist's perspective', *IDS Bulletin* 32(3), 41–5.

World Bank (2002), *World Development Report 2002*, Washington: World Bank.

Wortham, S. (1997), 'Bringing criticism to account: Economy, exchange and cultural theory', *Economy and Society* 26:(3), August, 400–18.

WTO (2001), *Annual Report and Accounts, Vol.2, Statistical Tables*, World Trade Organization, Geneva.

Yang, S. and E. Brynjolfsson (2001), 'Intangible assets and growth accounting: Evidence from computer investments', MIT, http://ebusiness.mit.edu/erik/.

Zider, B. (1998), 'How venture capital works', *Harvard Business Review*, November–December, 131–9.

Zook, M. A. (2001), 'The internet: Old hierarchies or new networks of centrality? The global geography of internet content market', *American Behavioural Scientist* 44, 1679–96.

Index

Index

Index

Index

Index

Index

United Kingdom (UK) 57, 151, 170, 172,
    175, 178, 185–7, 216
  advertising industry 199
  Conservative government 175
  government 168
  National Health Service 22, 186
  Performance and Innovation Unit 168
  political economy, characteristics vii
  venture capital funds in 143
United Nations Conference of Trade and
    Development 195
United States 187, 216
  advertising industry 199
  cities 204
  civic traditions 171
  Conference Board 194
  Council of Economic Advisors 194
  domestic vulnerabilities 63
  General Social Survey 170
  output 198
unproductive gift 100
unstructured *n*-person games 165
urbanization 203
Uzzi, B. 147

value-adding chain 69
value adding partnerships 116
'value chain' approach 190
  assessment of 209–16
  as networks 207–9
value:
  of network connection 145
  networks 211
van Ark, B. 194
venture capital and networking 141–3
venture capitalist firms 142
vertical integration 117
vertical policy coordination 159
vicious cycle of decline and mistrust 172

virtuous cycle of economic prosperity and
    trust 172
visual metaphor 137
voice, concept of 43, 44
Volkswagen 117
voluntary compliance 138
von Hayek, F. 27
von Mises, L. 27
vulnerabilities 63

Wadhwani, S. B. 194
Wallerstein, I. 201, 207
Washington consensus 220
Wasserman, S. 55, 65
Weber, M. 91
weightless economy 195
Weiner, A. B. 101
Wellman, B. 66
'Westminster model' of political
    governance 185
White, H. C. 63
Whiteley, R. 171
Whitley, R. 212
Wickham, G. x
Williamson, O. E. 31, 54, 67–70, 72, 81,
    94, 96–8, 117, 172
World Bank 128, 167
world cities 64, 205
2002 World Development Report 128
world GDP 195
world systems approach 64, 207
  assessment of 209–16
  to economic relationships 205
World Values Survey (WVS) 171
World Wide Web (WWW) 191–200
www.internetindicators.com 195
www.net-profit.co.uk 195

Zeitlin, J. 116

DATE DUE

DISCARD